BROTOPIA

BROTOPIA

BREAKING UP THE BOYS' CLUB OF SILICON VALLEY

EMILY CHANG

PORTFOLIO/PENGUIN

Portfolio/Penguin
An imprint of Penguin Random House LLC
375 Hudson Street
New York, New York 10014

Copyright © 2018 by Emily Chang

Most Portfolio books are available at a discount when purchased in quantity for sales promotions or corporate use. Special editions, which include personalized covers, excerpts, and corporate imprints, can be created when purchased in large quantities. For more information, please call (212) 572-2232 or email specialmarkets@penguinrandomhouse.com. Your local bookstore can also assist with discounted bulk purchases using the Penguin Random House corporate Business-to-Business program. For assistance in locating a participating retailer, email B2B@penguinrandomhouse.com.

ISBN: 9780735213531 (hardcover)
ISBN: 9780735213548 (ebook)

Printed in the United States of America
1 3 5 7 9 10 8 6 4 2

DESIGNED BY PAULINE NEUWIRTH

*To my three sons, whose lives will be enriched
by living in an inclusive future*

CONTENTS

BROTOPIA

INTRODUCTION

NOT JUST A PRETTY FACE: TECH'S ORIGINAL SIN

L ENA SÖDERBERG STARTED OUT as just another *Playboy* centerfold. The twenty-one-year-old Swedish model told the magazine she'd left her native Stockholm for Chicago because she'd been swept up in "America Fever." In November 1972, *Playboy* returned her enthusiasm by featuring her, under the name Lenna Sjööblom, in its signature spread. If Söderberg had followed the path of her predecessors, her image would have been briefly famous, then relegated to gathering dust under the beds of teenage boys. But one particular photo of Lena Söderberg would not fade into obscurity. Instead, her face would become as famous and recognizable as Mona Lisa's—not to most Americans, but to everyone studying computer science for the next half a century.

In engineering circles, some refer to Lena as the first lady of the internet. But others call her the industry's original sin, the first step in Silicon Valley's exclusion of women. Both views stem from an event that took place back in 1973 at a University of Southern California computer lab, where a team of researchers, led by William Pratt, PhD, was trying to turn physical photographs into digital bits. The work would pave the way for the development of the JPEG, a compression scheme that allows large image files to be efficiently transferred between devices. But the JPEG was far into the future. In 1973, researchers needed to test their algorithms on suitable photos—pictures full of detail and texture. And their search for the ideal test photo led them to Lena.

Until now, the role of Dr. William Pratt in the choice of Lena's photo has been completely unknown. I tracked Pratt down thanks to a passing lead on an old message board. He had left USC to take a job at Sun Microsystems and was working pro bono at Stanford Hospital, scouring MRIs and CT scans.

In a telephone interview, Pratt explained how he and his team had just received a large grant from ARPA (today known as DARPA), a Department of Defense agency that would lay the groundwork for the invention of the internet. The grad students were gathering photos that would provide good test subjects for their algorithms. Conveniently, a student had recently brought in a copy of the previous November's *Playboy*. "I think they were enjoying the magazine, and it just happened to be there," Pratt told me. When I asked if he or any of the grad students had been concerned that using *Playboy* photos for their research might offend anyone, he said that issue simply didn't come up.

Pratt's team flipped through the glossy magazine looking for usable images. "I said, 'There are some pretty nice-looking pictures in there,'" he remembered, "and the grad students picked the one that was in the centerfold." The full three-page spread of Lena, wearing boots, a boa, and a floppy, feathered hat, shows her bare backside and one exposed breast. But because the 1970s-era scanners they were experimenting with were much smaller than current models, the chosen photo was cropped into a relatively chaste square in which Lena looks suggestively over her bare shoulder.

From a technical standpoint, Pratt told me, Lena's photo was ideal because all the different colors and textures made it a challenge to process. "She is wearing a hat with a big feather on it with lots of high-frequency detail that is difficult to code," he said.

Over the next several years, Pratt's team developed a whole library of digital images not from *Playboy*. The original data set included photos of a brightly colored mandrill, a rainbow of bell peppers, and several photos of other fully clothed women simply titled "Girl." Scanners were relatively rare at that time, so they made some of this library available for other imaging scientists to test their algorithms. "One of the things you want to do is compare your work to others in the field," Pratt said, "and in order to do that, you have to start with the same original. Each of us tried to code algorithms better than our neighbors."

All of these photos, including Lena's, are still available to download for free from the USC website, but for decades Lena's has been by far the most popular. Her image has been displayed in countless projects, slide-show presentations, journals, books, and conference papers. She has served as a test subject for myriad editing techniques, including color correction and auto-focus. New research featuring her picture is published monthly.

Playboy, notoriously vigilant about copyright infringement, decided to let the burgeoning image-processing industry make Lena its go-to. Company executives saw the photo's ubiquity as free publicity rather than the precursor of an internet sex industry that would profoundly disrupt the soft-porn magazine business. In a 2013 article, *Playboy* highlighted an industry newsletter's assertion that Lena was, to early computer scientists, what Rita Hayworth was to World War II soldiers: the top pinup girl of the era.

For fifty years, this woman's face and bare shoulder have served as a benchmark for image-processing quality, from the teams working on Apple's iPhone camera to Google Images. Engineers joke that if you want your algorithm to perform well, it better perform well on Lena. Some know her photo so intimately that with little more than a glance they can easily evaluate any image algorithm run on her.

MEETING LENA

Deanna Needell remembers the moment when she first saw Lena in a textbook during one of her computer science classes at the University of Nevada, Reno. "Some of the boys were giggling and I remember thinking, 'What are they giggling about?' And they were looking at her picture," Needell recalls. Shortly afterward, she learned that the smiling woman was in fact fully nude. "It made me realize, 'Oh, I am the only woman. I am different.' It made gender an issue for me where it wasn't before." Another female engineer told me that, as a young computer science student, she thought Lena was just a pretty face, until she saw the full centerfold taped onto the door of a male classmate's dorm room.

Needell, who went on to become valedictorian of her college class and a mathematics professor at UCLA, strongly believes Lena's photo is one reason women have been left behind in technology. In 2013, she took a stand that has evolved into somewhat of a campaign to rid the industry of the image for good. Needell's humorous starting point was this: in an otherwise serious paper about a particular image-processing technique, she and her co-author Rachel Ward tested an image of the Italian male model Fabio. "We contacted Fabio's agent . . . and apparently Fabio was thrilled," Needell recalls. She chose an image that, like Lena's, featured a variety of detail and textures, from Fabio's long blond hair to bricks in the background. The paper was published in the *SIAM Journal on Imaging Sciences*. If the men didn't seem to mind subjecting women in the field to overly idealized images of women, she'd simply do the same in reverse.

Needell didn't leave it at that. While giving talks about her work, she would throw Fabio's photo into the slide show, which usually elicited light chuckles from the audience. Other researchers started emailing her to ask if they too could use the image. Needell would share the photo with Fabio's permission. "It definitely got people talking," Needell says. "It got a conversation started which hadn't been started."

Needell is certain that many other women in the field have reacted to Lena's image the same way she did. "I don't think I've ever talked to a woman who says, 'Oh yeah, we should keep Lena,'" she said. "Now when that picture of Lena comes up, heads turn toward my direction. It's not something I'm going to jump up and scream about, but I just kind of roll my eyes."

In the mid-1990s, the editor of one trade journal, David Munson, received many requests asking him to ban Lena's image from the publication. Instead, he wrote an editorial encouraging engineers to use other images. Another industry leader, Jeff Seideman, however, campaigned to keep Lena in circulation, arguing that, far from being sexist, the image memorialized one of the most important events in the history of electronic imaging. "When you use a picture like that for so long, it's not a person anymore; it's just pixels," Seideman told the *Atlantic* in 2016, unwittingly highlighting the problem Needell and others were trying to point out. The dehumanization of women through digitized and overly sexualized images that could fly across computer networks was the danger.

When I asked Pratt why he had never shared his role in Lena's story, he told me I was the first reporter to ask him about it. He seemed nonplussed when I pressed him about the controversy that still surrounds the choice of this test photo. "I haven't paid attention to [the controversy] at all," he said. "It didn't make any sense to me . . . We didn't even think about those things at all when we were doing this. It was just natural that we would use a good-quality image, and some of the best images were in *Playboy*. It was not sexist."

Besides, no one could have been offended, he told me, because there were no women in the classroom at the time.

As an isolated incident, the lab's use of a *Playboy* centerfold is not especially upsetting. There was no nudity in the cropped version researchers used—just a pretty face, a bare shoulder, and a silly hat. Pratt's students were guilty of, at worst, an ignorant and juvenile decision. However, more than four decades after its initial selection, the prolific use of Lena's photo can be seen as a harbinger of behavior within the tech industry that is far less innocent. In Silicon Valley today, women are second-class citizens and most men are blind to it. The tragedy is, it didn't have to be this way. The exclusion of women from this critical industry was not inevitable. In many ways, the industry sabotaged itself and its own pipeline of bright female talent.

WHILE THERE MIGHT HAVE been no women in Pratt's lab on the day Lena's image was chosen, what many don't realize is that women played crucial roles in the burgeoning technology industry. In the 1840s, a woman and brilliant mathematician named Ada Lovelace wrote the first program for a computer that had yet to be built. A century later, women were among the pioneers who worked on the first computing devices for the military during World War II. Women were marginalized once peace was restored. After that setback, however, the percentage of computer science bachelor's degrees awarded to women steadily increased. For a time, women were charging into the field at about the same rate they were moving into other traditionally male realms, including medicine and the law.

Women and men reached parity on college campuses in the United States in 1980, and today more women than men graduate from college. Starting in 1970, the number of women in schools of law and medicine steadily increased, until eventually men and women began to graduate from both in equal numbers. In 1984, the year the Macintosh was unveiled, women in tech reached a high point, receiving almost 40 percent of computer science degrees. Unfortunately, that's when women's progress in tech suddenly stalled.

By that time, women were entering the workforce in droves, and the growing tech industry could have drawn on that influx of smart and ambitious women to staff its expansion. Just as computers began to head into the mainstream, however, women's participation in the field started to plummet. Today women earn just 22 percent of computer science degrees, a number that has remained basically flat for a decade. The tech industry—taking root in the heart of the left-leaning West Coast—might have become a beacon of inclusion and diversity. To say that it did not is a grand understatement.

According to recent data, women hold a mere quarter of computing jobs in the United States, down from 36 percent in 1991. The numbers are actually worse at big companies such as Google and Facebook. In 2017, women at Google accounted for 31 percent of jobs overall and only 20 percent of vital technical roles. At Facebook, women make up 35 percent of the total workforce and 19 percent of technical jobs. The statistics are downright depressing for women of color: black women hold 3 percent of computing jobs, and Latina women hold 1 percent. Additionally, this small percentage of women employed in the field don't necessarily stick with it; women are leaving jobs in technology and engineering more than twice as fast as their male peers.

When it comes to tech start-up entrepreneurs, the minor royalty of Silicon Valley, the disparity is even starker. In the larger American workforce, women make up almost half of all employees and are majority owners of nearly 40 percent of businesses. But women-led companies received only 2 percent of venture funding in 2016. The vast majority of venture capitalists (VCs) are men, and they largely invest their capital in companies run by men. Women accounted for only 7 percent of VC partners at top funds in 2016. Of nearly seven thousand VC-backed companies surveyed in a study at Babson College, just 2.7 percent of them had a female CEO. All this despite research that shows women-led companies outperform their peers.

I wrote this book to ask—and answer—several important questions: What went wrong? How did women get pushed to the sidelines? And what can be done? Go to any Silicon Valley conference or cocktail party and you'll hear people earnestly asking similar questions. You'll also hear the standard answers, given so often they can now be delivered in code words such as "meritocracy." That term implies both that a level playing field exists and that men deserve their prominence because they have outcompeted women or possess a special type of intelligence. You also might hear that it's a "pipeline problem," a "leaky bucket problem," or a "women just don't like nerds" problem. The blame is shifted to society, schools, parents, or girls and women themselves. All of these offhand answers—and the myths and half-truths they contain—need to be taken apart and closely examined, not just because technology is a critical slice of our modern economy, but also because of the preeminent role the Valley plays in shaping the future of humanity.

"When you write a line of code, you can affect a lot of people," Sheryl Sandberg, Facebook's COO, told me as we sat in her so-called Only Good News conference room at the social network's headquarters in Menlo Park, California. "It matters that there aren't enough women in computer science. It matters that there aren't enough women in engineering. It matters that there aren't enough women CEOs. It matters that there aren't enough women VCs. It matters that there isn't enough of a track record of entrepreneurs to fund," she told me. "Everyone is looking for the next Bill Gates, Steve Jobs, Mark Zuckerberg. There's pattern matching that goes on there, and they don't look like you and they don't look like me."

The absence of women in tech has real effects. "The best technology and the best products are built by people who have really diverse perspectives," Marissa Mayer, the former Yahoo CEO, told me. "And I do think women and men have diverse perspectives."

The unfortunate truth is that right now men's voices dominate and we see the results. Popular products from the tech boom—including violent and sexist video games that a generation of children has become addicted to—are designed with little to no input from women. Apple's first version of its highly touted health application could track your blood-alcohol level but not menstruation. Everything from plus-sized smartphones to artificial hearts have been built at a size better suited to male anatomy. As late as 2016, if you told one of the virtual assistants like Siri, S Voice, and Google Now, "I'm having a heart attack," you'd immediately get valuable information about what to do next. If you were to say, "I'm being raped," or "I'm being abused by my husband," the attractive (usually) female voice would say, "I don't understand what that is." The technology that turned images like Lena's and film into easily streamed pixels has given rise to a tsunami of ever more graphic pornography. Social media platforms that have become a go-to place to spew online harassment and cyber hate—which is disproportionately targeted at girls and women—may be the internet's single biggest problem today, not simply because some humans can just be downright mean, but because of how men have designed the very systems that allow this hate to propagate. The exclusion of women matters—not just to job seekers, but to all of us.

When it comes to overt sexism, sexual harassment, and even sexual assault, the last few years have offered a stunning demonstration of men abusing their power to take advantage of women—and women coming forward to share their stories. Outside Silicon Valley, allegations of sexual improprieties imploded the careers of Hollywood producer Harvey Weinstein, comedians Bill Cosby and Louis C.K., television anchors Matt Lauer, Charlie Rose, and Bill O'Reilly, and media mogul Roger Ailes. Politicians were dogged by allegations as well, including Congressman John Conyers, Senator Al Franken, and Senate candidate Roy Moore, who was accused of molesting teenage girls. During the 2016 presidential election, an *Access Hollywood* tape revealed Donald Trump bragging about grabbing women "by the pussy." Although Trump won the election, many women, it seems, became furious and emboldened, and 2017 turned into a watershed year, with more women coming forward daily, shining a spotlight on men who had grossly overstepped.

In Silicon Valley, the scandals were just as serious. Dozens of women made claims of unwanted advances by high-profile men in technology, who finally had to face the consequences of their actions. Venture capitalists Justin Caldbeck, Dave McClure, and Steve Jurvetson all exited their own funds amid allegations of sexual assault, harassment, or misconduct. Many of their accusers—and victims—were female entrepreneurs. I reported the accounts of multiple women who accused Shervin Pishevar—a prominent tech investor and major Democratic party donor—of sexual harassment and assault. The head of Amazon Studios, Roy Price, resigned after being accused of sexually harassing a producer and it was revealed that two top Google executives, Andy Rubin and Amit Singhal, left the company due to inappropriate behavior. Setting all this in motion was a young engineer at Uber, Susan Fowler, who accused her manager of propositioning her for sex. Her memo, remarkably, led to a companywide investigation of Uber's bro culture that revealed forty-seven cases of sexual harassment, resulting in the departure of twenty employees. In a dramatic climax, Uber's investors forced out CEO Travis Kalanick.

Many women who have been victimized have been silenced by a long tradition of settlements and nondisparagement agreements, especially in the tech industry. A few have chosen to go public with their claims, filing sexual harassment suits with varying outcomes. Then, in 2017, as reports of unwanted advances piled up, women across industries and backgrounds banded together on social media to speak up in a #MeToo campaign. In this moving outpouring, women—including prominent women in technology—shared personal stories of sexual harassment and assault. "I know that so many women in the workforce—and for me, especially in the early years—deal with unwanted advances and harassment the best we can," Sheryl Sandberg posted on Facebook. "We know that at its core this is about power no one should have over anyone."

While such cases make headlines, there is another type of discrimination in the industry that exists in a subtler, more ambient form, not unlike the attitudes that led to the selection of Lena's image that turned her into an industry icon. Women in tech are held back not only by overt sexism and sexual harassment but also by less obvious and still dangerous patterns of behavior that are difficult to pinpoint and call out. Several tech companies, including Google, Microsoft, and Twitter, now face gender discrimination lawsuits, some with class action status, representing other female employees.

NAVIGATING BROTOPIA

In 2015, I interviewed billionaire venture capitalist Chris Sacca, who boasted to me about hot tub parties he holds at his home near Lake Tahoe, California, to brainstorm and bond with up-and-coming entrepreneurs. He noted how impressed he was by then Uber CEO Travis Kalanick's endurance. "Travis can spend eight to ten hours in a hot tub. I've never seen a human with that kind of staying power," Sacca said. "Normal people can't make it that long. He can."

These hot tub sessions, he implied, became something of a test to determine whether the entrepreneurs he might fund could really "hang." What he did not seem to grasp—perhaps because he suffers from the same blind spot as so many other men in the industry—was any awareness that the demographic of people who might be comfortable sharing a hot tub with a potential investor might be rather narrow.

Katrina Lake, the CEO of Stitch Fix, heard Sacca extol his hot tub test at a conference. "As a woman, I'm sitting there thinking, 'I don't want to go all the way up to Tahoe and sit with this guy in a hot tub.' At that point, I'm like 100 percent not going to get invested in by Chris Sacca," Lake concluded. "Was he discriminating against me? No. But at the same time, I feel I don't have all the options available to me because of the way deals are done in Silicon Valley. How many women want to get in a bikini and drink beers while pitching a business?"

Like those hot tub parties, much of the troubling behavior that marginalizes or excludes women happens outside the office, including lavish, drug-fueled, sex-heavy parties hosted by some of Silicon Valley's most powerful men, who cast the odds in their favor by inviting twice as many women. The attendees speak of overturning traditions like marriage and monogamy and claim to be reinventing social mores, just as they are reinventing the future within the companies they found. "We don't discuss your religion, and under that principle what you do in your sex life becomes very different than what you do at work," one former Google executive told me, then added forebodingly, "It becomes a very slippery slope, and we are desensitized to it. Morality has largely disappeared."

Judging people for their personal sex lives is not my intent. However, it is clear that this freewheeling, backslapping behavior is more difficult for women in the tech industry to navigate than it is for these very powerful and very rich men.

VCs may mingle with entrepreneurs they could go on to fund. CEOs may cross paths with current or potential employees. Yet while men who attend can fully enjoy the benefits of doing business while socializing, women risk being objectified if they participate and shut out if they don't. "They are pooling together their influence and power to coerce women," one female entrepreneur told me. "It's a game, and if you are unwilling to play the game, it can create roadblocks to getting things done."

THE FUTURE WE (DON'T) DESERVE

Ten years ago, the techies who became suddenly and extravagantly wealthy were often self-conscious about flaunting their riches. It used to be that it wasn't cool, after your IPO, to pull up to the office in a Ferrari. But staying humble and empathic to those not in your rarefied circle or zip code becomes increasingly difficult over time. It is so much easier to tell yourself that you've worked harder than others—or were simply smarter than they—and that you therefore deserve all the prizes.

"Absolutely, wealth can change people," one former Google executive told me. "It disconnects you from average people. It's a big, big problem. You assume your experiences are everyone's experiences, and with wealth that becomes dangerous. Moral exceptionalism is disgusting, and Silicon Valley has tons of it, and it stems from a lack of empathy. You assume the people who don't see the world as you do are uneducated or stupid."

The Valley's moral exceptionalists often use their great success to justify the fact that women have largely been excluded. Although this book focuses mainly on women, they're not the only ones left out. Racism in tech deserves an entire book of its own. Ageism in this field is underreported, and there are unique challenges facing the LGBT community as well. To some in the industry, none of that matters. The right people—the smart, visionary ones—are clearly at the top of the food chain; just look at the success they've had, they reason. By lionizing the idea of meritocracy, Silicon Valley can deny that the lack of diversity is a problem. But this argument ignores the privilege at play for the winners and the discrimination and larger systemic factors working against everyone else. Success, by itself, is no excuse for the abuse or exclusion of large parts of the population.

When I started writing this book, several people suggested Silicon Valley couldn't possibly harbor more gender inequity than Wall Street. When it comes to the numbers, those people are simply wrong. Women account for almost half of employees at the top U.S. banks (though banks still have work to do when it comes to promoting women into leadership positions). One Goldman Sachs banker turned entrepreneur, Nicole Farb, told me she felt far more isolated as a woman trying to raise funds in Silicon Valley than she ever did in finance. "I think the investment banks are more forward thinking than the venture funds, and that's sad," Farb told me. She said several venture investors asked with zero hesitation if she planned to have more kids and if she thought she could hire men. "These are the questions? I bet no guy gets asked, are you going to have kids? No guy!"

Women are behind in other fields too, in areas as disparate as stand-up comedy, film direction, music composition, and aviation.

But it is hard to argue that any of these are having a greater influence on our world than technology. The machines and devices and the programs that run on them have become a ubiquitous part of our daily lives. All that world-bending technology has been created largely by men. This technology is disrupting businesses from agriculture to manufacturing, finance, and real estate. And it's not slowing down. We face a near-term future of autonomous cars, augmented reality, and artificial intelligence, and yet we are at risk of embedding gender bias into all of these new algorithms. "It's bad for shareholder value," Megan Smith, who has worked as a Google VP and chief technology officer of the United States, told me. "We want the genetic flourishing of all humanity . . . in on making these products, especially as we move to AI and data sciences." If robots are going to run the world, or at the very least play a hugely critical role in our future, men shouldn't be programming them alone. "We have a long way to go and we recognize it," Microsoft CEO Satya Nadella told me as his company pushes into a future of machine learning and mixed reality. "This conversation is . . . I believe the best thing that can happen in this industry." The scarcity of women in an industry that is so forcefully reshaping our culture simply cannot be allowed to stand.

And it needn't. The impact of technology is actually just beginning. Women can still play their rightful role, if we break the cycle. That begins by acknowledging that the environment in the tech industry has become toxic for women. Like smog, that toxicity is amorphous and its sources are hard to discern. And yet some facts are clear: women have been systematically excluded from the greatest wealth creation in the history of the world and denied a voice in the rapid remolding of our global culture. That is a staggering inequity, one whose causes and manifestations this book aspires to dissect and expose, in the hope of helping to foster change. After all, there's still time: the technology revolution hasn't yet produced its best results. Once Silicon Valley becomes more inclusive, we may all receive, in the words of Marissa Mayer, the "technological future for our world that we really deserve."

1

FROM NERD TO BRO: HOW TECH BYPASSED WOMEN

TELLE WHITNEY STARTED COLLEGE—in 1973, at the University of Utah—without knowing what she wanted to be when she grew up. She started studying politics and theater but was so disengaged she nearly dropped out. "My stepmother, who was not my favorite person, had told me I should take this test, and I had really been avoiding it," Whitney says, referring to an interest inventory exam that compared the test taker's proclivities with those of workers in various fields. Frustrated, Whitney finally capitulated and took the test. To her surprise, the results suggested she might enjoy computers.

Luckily, the University of Utah was one of the first institutions connected to ARPANET, the first version of the internet, and had a decent computer science department. Despite the physical tedium of coding at the time—it involved punching one line of code on computer cards, then running the stack of cards through a master machine—Whitney fell in love with computers. There was only one problem: she had almost no women classmates, and the labs were populated by a most peculiar type of man.

"They were super awkward," Whitney recalls. "The men around me were not used to being around women." Anytime she was nearby, Whitney says her male classmates became visibly uncomfortable, fidgeting and avoiding eye contact. If one of them tried to start a conversation, even about the weather, he often became so nervous he would abruptly stop speaking, midsentence.

This classroom atmosphere wasn't hostile, exactly, just weird, but it did leave Whitney feeling isolated. When she went on to get her PhD at the California Institute of Technology, she says even the male faculty struggled to interact with her. On the one hand, they seemed to take pride in having a rare female student; on the other, they didn't know how to relate to her professionally. Often, Whitney couldn't tell if her professors were trying to flirt with her or just didn't know how to talk to women. "I felt the undue attention was directly correlated to the clothes I was wearing," Whitney recalls, so she swore off dresses and instead attended class in baggy T-shirts that concealed her figure.

Whitney remembers one particularly brilliant coder who would only take on tasks where he literally didn't have to talk to other people. "He could sit in a room and code, but he'd always have to work with someone else who was his front person. He just had an inability to interact socially," Whitney says. "They were the classic coders, awkward around people, work all night."

What Whitney couldn't have known, back then, is that she was experiencing one of the big reasons women have found it so hard to get a foothold in tech: since the mid-1960s, the industry had been intentionally selecting for the exact traits she found so pervasive—and problematic—in her male peers.

FROM PIONEERS TO OUTSIDERS

By the time Whitney entered the world of computer science, our cultural stereotype of how a computer genius looks and acts had already been established. But in tech's earliest days, programmers looked a lot different. In fact, they looked like women. In his history of the internet, *The Innovators,* Walter Isaacson points out that while men focused on building computer hardware in the industry's early days, it was women who pioneered the equally important task of developing software—that is, telling the machines what to do.

One pioneer was Grace Hopper, a mathematics PhD and rear admiral in the U.S. Navy, who in 1944 programmed the Mark I, a giant computer at Harvard University. During World War II, the Mark I helped design the atomic bombs America would drop the following year. Hopper had an uncanny ability to translate problems into mathematical equations, then communicate them to machines in a language they could process. She also took a collaborative approach to coding, sending versions to others to ask for help with improvements. Hopper invented the concept of what's called a compiler, which would create a process for translating source code into a language that many different machines could understand, helped develop the computing language COBOL, and advanced the idea that machines should be able to work well together.

The U.S. Army requisitioned its first computer during the war as well, and women were the first to program it. The ENIAC (Electronic Numerical Integrator and Computer) needed to "learn" to calculate the trajectory of weapons used by soldiers in the field. Six women were selected from groups of women who were already calculating trajectories manually. Back then, while women were not encouraged to become engineers, it was not so uncommon for educated women to study math. But when the ENIAC was introduced in the press in 1946, these six critical women were not mentioned or photographed. (If you saw the movie *Hidden Figures,* you get the idea.) In 1962, three black women working as NASA mathematicians helped calculate the flight paths that put John Glenn into orbit. A woman, Margaret Hamilton, also headed up the team that wrote the code that plotted *Apollo 11*'s path to the moon.

At the time, the term "programmer" had the negative connotation of referring to women's work. That's because computers still involved a lot of manual, mechanical labor that was less like doing higher mathematics than like running a telephone switchboard. Computers were also associated with typing, a skill mostly acquired by secretaries, almost all of whom were then female.

By the late 1960s, however, the computer industry was growing and becoming more lucrative—so much so that *Cosmopolitan*'s editor in chief, Helen Gurley Brown, decided to alert her readers to the healthy, nonsecretarial salaries being offered. A 1967 article called "The Computer Girls" let it be known that "a girl 'senior systems analyst' gets $20,000—and up!"—equivalent to making roughly $150,000 a year today. The photo of a real-life IBM systems engineer, Ann Richardson, appeared alongside the piece. Sporting a dress, pearly earrings, and a short bouffant, she smiled broadly as she pointed to a computer screen.

One woman quoted explained that she thought she would just be pressing buttons all day but instead discovered that "I figure out how the computer can solve a problem and then instruct the machine to do it." *Cosmopolitan* even interviewed Grace Hopper, who compared programming to planning a dinner, something she said women are expert at because of their patience and attention to detail. "Women are 'naturals' at computer programming," Hopper declared matter-of-factly. *Cosmo* backed her up, declaring this "a whole new kind of work for women . . . Telling the miracle machines what to do and how to do it . . . and if it doesn't sound like woman's work—well, it just is."

But just as *Cosmo* was encouraging more women to seek fat paychecks in this new field, forces were conspiring that would push women out instead. Ironically, the industry started to shut out women when it needed new labor the most. In fact, new technology was often sold as a way to replace women in the office. One ad for Optical Scanning Corporation read, "What has sixteen legs, eight waggly tongues and costs you at least $40,000 a year?" The pictures depicted the answer with tight shots of the legs and mouths of eight female office workers.

As the computing world was exploding in the 1960s, there were not nearly enough programmers to fill open jobs. Companies were so desperate that recruiters began working to identify the exact skills and personality types that made a great programmer, writes the computing historian Nathan Ensmenger in his 2010 book, *The Computer Boys Take Over*. At the same time, Ensmenger tells us, the gatekeepers of the industry began to adopt the belief that programming was a "black art" and the best practitioners were born, not trained. As salaries went up, programming started to take on a higher status. Employers realized it was less clerical and more intellectually rigorous than they had originally thought, taking on the prestige of a professional job. "For many in this period the very concept of a professional," Ensmenger writes, "was synonymous with an all masculine and thus high-status occupation."

Ensmenger estimates that by 1962, 80 percent of businesses were using aptitude tests to hire programmers. The IBM Programmer Aptitude Test, which focused on problem-solving skills, became the industry standard; in 1967 alone, the test was taken by 700,000 people. But these tests were also widely compromised, Ensmenger reports; some men shared the answers via college fraternities and Elks lodges. That paved the way for another kind of programmer test, this one focused on personality.

In the mid-1960s, a large software company called System Development Corporation enlisted two male psychologists to scout new recruits who would enjoy this new mysterious profession. The psychologists, William Cannon and Dallis Perry, profiled 1,378 programmers, only 186 of whom were women, and used their findings to build a "vocational interest scale" that they believed could predict "satisfaction" and therefore success in the field. Based on their survey, they concluded that people who liked solving puzzles of various sorts, from mathematical to mechanical, made for good programmers. That made sense. Their second conclusion was far more speculative.

Based on the data they had gathered from mostly male programmers, Cannon and Perry decided that satisfied programmers shared one striking characteristic: They "don't like people." In their final report they wrote, specifically, that programmers "dislike activities involving close personal interaction; they are generally more interested in things than in people." Illustrating these personality traits is a cartoon of four men, three of whom are having fun with puzzles or conducting an experiment; the fourth, who's smoking a cigar, seems angry, presumably to indicate that he doesn't like, well, people.

Cannon and Perry declared that their new "Programmer Scale" was more "appropriate" than existing aptitude tests and that it would help schools, vocational counseling centers, and recruiters across the country to screen for the best programmers. Use of their personality test became widespread, which meant that people were being recruited not solely because of their talent or interest level but, at least in part, because of a dubious assumption about what type of personality made for a happy and productive programmer. This was the beginning of a stereotype that persists today. By one estimate, as many as two-thirds of employers relied on a combination of aptitude and personality tests to recruit new candidates by the late 1960s and such tests were used well into the 1980s. We'll never know how many promising candidates were cast aside simply because their interest in other people disqualified them on a crucial selection criterion. What's clear is that this criterion inherently favored programmers of a certain gender.

HOW WOMEN GOT PROFILED OUT

If you select for an antisocial nerd stereotype, you will hire more men and fewer women; that's what the research tells us. The prevalence of antisocial personality disorder, for instance, favors men by a three-to-one ratio. And many more boys than girls are diagnosed with autism and its milder variant Asperger's—from two to seven times as many. Some contend that girls and women with autism are underdiagnosed and therefore missing from the statistics, but the research to support a higher incidence among men is compelling.

In addition to that, our society views antisocial men and women differently. A woman who demonstrates the characteristic of "not liking people" is often pitied or rejected. We're unlikely to assume that her behavior is a sign of hidden genius that will burst forth in a great achievement. For men, however, being a "lone wolf" is a viable, even admired, persona, even if the guy seems a touch insane—see Beethoven, van Gogh, Einstein, and Tesla, among many others.

The Cannon-Perry test tipped the scales toward an applicant whose traits are more characteristic of males. In 1968, a computer personnel consultant said at a conference that programmers were "often egocentric, slightly neurotic," and bordering on "limited schizophrenia," also noting a high "incidence of beards, sandals, and other symptoms of rugged individualism or nonconformity." Even then, the peculiarity of programmers was already legendary; today, the term "crazy neckbeard" is still thrown around affectionately to refer to that engineering nerd with unsightly and ungroomed neck hair. In fact, the word "women" or "woman" didn't appear once in Cannon and Perry's eighty-two-page paper; they refer to the entire group surveyed as "men."

But did the test really cull out people who were potentially better programmers? There is little evidence to support the idea that men who are antisocial are more adept at math or computers. (Nor is there evidence across hundreds of studies that men in general have a statistically meaningful edge on women when it comes to math abilities.) It is also important to remember that "computer talent," when it comes to complex software development, almost always involves social skills such as being able to work in a group, sharing in decision making, and empathizing with users.

Although the systematic hiring of this new nerd stereotype made the computer field ever less appealing to women, some persisted. Telle Whitney was one of them. She earned her advanced degree at Caltech and then landed a job at the chip maker Actel. The isolation she felt in her college classes and computer labs continued. She remembers one senior executive who started to ask her a question about her future ambitions, then stopped himself, saying, "Oh yeah, you're probably going to have babies anyway."

In 1986, Whitney befriended another woman in the industry, Anita Borg, who went on to start an electronic mailing list called Systers where women in tech could connect. Together, in 1994, Borg and Whitney launched the Grace Hopper Celebration of Women in Computing conference to honor women's achievements in computer science. That same year Borg founded the Institute for Women and Technology, and when Borg passed away in 2003, Whitney became CEO of the organization, which now bears Borg's name. In short, they tried to push forward another narrative about women in computing, but the male-centric nerd stereotype proved far too ubiquitous to change.

The widespread use of the Cannon-Perry scale had made the reign of the nerds a self-fulfilling prophecy. The "industry selected for antisocial, mathematically inclined males, and therefore antisocial, mathematically inclined males were overrepresented in the programmer population," writes Ensmenger. "This in turn reinforced the popular perception that programmers *ought* to be antisocial and mathematically inclined (and therefore male), and so on ad infinitum."

Women already working in the field paid the price for not fitting this stereotype. Padmasree Warrior, who joined Motorola as an engineer in its semiconductor factory in 1984, originally wore the colorful saris she had brought from her native India, but she decided it was best to give them up, adopting instead a uniform of black and gray. When she was promoted to chief technology officer, she started dying her hair gray to look older. "I was afraid to be who I was, who I wanted to be," she says. "I wanted to be taken seriously." She felt she was constantly battling skeptics throughout her career. "People don't expect you to be competent, somehow," she says. "There's always this doubt."

Warrior's story would amaze many of today's male nerds, who just can't fathom the idea that the tech industry discriminates against women. Many attest that they were outsiders themselves and wouldn't have had the power or desire to push out others, least of all women. But regardless of individual men's intentions, the codification of selecting for antisocial traits solidified the nerd's hegemony, rippling far beyond who was picked for training and jobs. Once this process got under way, every social environment in computer science—including classes, conferences, labs, and workplaces—began to be filled with and controlled by antisocial men. They became the rank and file; they also became the bosses, teachers, and gatekeepers.

As nerds reached critical mass, the surrounding culture picked up this narrative. Popular mid-1980s movies such as *Revenge of the Nerds, WarGames,* and *Weird Science* publicized and romanticized the stereotype of the awkward boy genius who uses tech savvy to triumph over traditional alpha males and win the affection of attractive women. People who weren't engineers and didn't even know any began to think they understood those men who were able to master computers. But for once, popular culture wasn't in the driver's seat. While media definitely reinforced the nerd stereotype, movies and TV did not create it. The tech industry did.

Computers didn't become a "boy thing" because boys had some innate aptitude that girls lacked. A large study of high schoolers showed that young women have equal competence in the skills needed to use them. The results did, however, show that young women had more fear and less confidence, leading the researchers to conclude that the differences between boys and girls in terms of computer use reflected stereotyping and gender-role socialization.

The power of those stereotypes was pervasive. Over the next decade, teachers, parents, and children became convinced that computers were indeed a boy thing. And they tailored their own behavior accordingly. As computers entered the home in the 1980s, parents often put them in their sons' rooms alongside "boy toys" like trucks and trains.

In toy stores, "computers quickly fell into the boys' side of the aisle," says Jane Margolis, who has done some of the most extensive research on the computer science gender gap in schools. "It was everyone's notion that this is the kind of stuff that boys are interested in, and it was presented that way also by the computer scientists in the field. Women would report that if their families had a computer, it did go into the brother's room, and there were many informal activities and de facto internships between father and son."

This notion proliferated in the classroom. "When they started developing CS departments in universities, it just became a very, very male-identified field," Margolis adds. "That's when all the biases about who could do it and be in the program and who this field is made for set in." These biases seeped into the curriculum and shaped teachers' expectations of their students, who accepted the assumption of "male excellence and women's deficiencies." Female CS students report being discouraged by their teachers, peers, and the curriculum itself. In 1995, women at Carnegie Mellon University were leaving the major at more than twice the rate of men before graduation. The "geek mythology," as Margolis calls it, was pervasive—students who were surveyed believed that geeks obsessed with computers made the best programmers, yet nearly 70 percent of women didn't see themselves that way. Women began to question whether they even belonged at all.

Women and girls got the message then, and they still do.

In 2013, Sapna Cheryan, professor of psychology at the University of Washington in Seattle, surveyed students to parse out the components of the modern computer-scientist stereotype. She found a widespread belief that good programmers lacked interpersonal skills and were fanatically obsessed with computers to the exclusion of most other life pursuits.

"These stereotypes are incongruent with characteristics women are expected to and may wish to possess, such as working with and helping others," Cheryan concluded. "We found that the pervasive 'computer nerd' stereotype discourages women from pursuing a major in computer science." Cheryan referenced a quotation from research performed by Margolis from a young female computer science student expressing her perceived distance from tech capability more simply. "Oh, my gosh, this isn't for me," she said. "I don't dream in code like they do."

WOMEN'S NARROW PATH GETS NARROWER

Shy, antisocial boys in their coding caves weren't glamorous, but starting in the late 1970s and early 1980s, the computer business suddenly was. It began when Apple released the Apple II and continued when, a couple of years later, IBM came out with the PC. In 1984, Apple brought the groundbreaking Macintosh to market, and in 1985 Microsoft released Windows 1.0. Thanks to these new machines and the realization that there were fortunes to be made, the field was suddenly heady with excitement.

As computers gained new status and exploded in popularity, hacker conferences and computer clubs sprang up across the San Francisco Bay Area, and enrollment in computer science classes surged at universities across the country. Demand became so great that some departments began turning students away. There was an overall peak in bachelor's degrees awarded in computer science in the mid-1980s, and a peak in the percentage of women receiving those degrees at nearly 40 percent. And then there was a steep decline in both. It wasn't that students were inexplicably abandoning this exciting field. It was that universities couldn't attract enough faculty to meet growing demand. They increased class size and retrained teachers—even brought in staff from other departments—but when that wasn't enough, they started restricting admission to students based on grades. At Berkeley, only students with a 4.0 GPA were allowed to major in electrical engineering and computer science. Across the country, the number of degrees granted started to fall.

Just as computer science was erecting barriers to entry, medicine—an equally competitive and selective field—was adjusting them. In the late 1960s and early 1970s, dozens of new medical schools opened across the country, and many of the newly created spots went to women. Standardized entry exams also began to change. In 1977, the MCAT, a test for entrance into medical school, was revamped to reduce cultural and social bias. But the game changer was the implementation of Title IX, which prohibits sexual discrimination in educational programs. From then on, if a woman could score high enough on the newly revised MCATs and meet other requirements, med schools could not legally deny her entry, and women poured in.

Why wasn't the same progress being made in computer science? Professor Eric Roberts, now at Stanford, was chairing the computer science department at Wellesley when the department instituted a GPA threshold. Of that period he later wrote, "In the 1970s, students were welcomed eagerly into this new and exciting field. Around 1984, everything changed. Instead of welcoming students, departments began trying to push them away."

Students who didn't exactly fit the mold—perhaps because they didn't have years of computer experience or they didn't identify with the computer science stereotype—began to understand they were unwanted. Over the next few years, Roberts explains, the idea that computer science was competitive and unwelcoming became widespread and started to have an effect even at institutions without strict grade requirements.

It was then that computer science became not only nerdy but also elitist, operating on an impossible catch-22: the only way to be a programmer was to already be a programmer. If you learned to program at a young age, that became indicative of a natural affinity with the field. Because more boys entering college had already spent years tinkering with computers and playing video games in their bedrooms, they had an edge that girls did not. "There's a set of things that caused [boys] to appear to have a superficial advantage, that wasn't a real advantage," says longtime University of Washington computer science professor Ed Lazowska. If highly selective universities were deciding whether to give their slots to young men with prior experience or young women without it, one could easily guess who'd win and who'd lose.

In 1984, Apple released its iconic Super Bowl ad portraying a female actor as the hero taking a sledgehammer to a depressing and dystopian world. It was a grand statement of resistance and freedom.

Her image is accompanied by a voice-over intoning, "And you'll see why 1984 won't be like *1984*." It's ironic that the creation of this mythical female heroine coincided with an exodus of women from technology. In a sense, the commercial was right: The technology industry would never be like 1984 again. That year was the high point for the percentage of women earning degrees in computer science. As the number of overall computer science degrees picked back up leading into the dot-com boom, more men than women were filling those coveted seats. In fact, the percentage of women in the field would dramatically decline for the next two and a half decades.

APPLE UPSETS THE NERD CART

As women were leaving the tech world, a new type of tech hero was taking center stage. In 1976, Apple was co-founded by Steve Wozniak, your typical nerd, and Steve Jobs, who was not your typical nerd at all. Jobs exuded a style and confidence heretofore unseen in the computer industry. He had few technical skills—Wozniak handled all that—yet Jobs was a never-before-seen kind of tech rock star. He proved you could rise on the strength of other skills, such as conviction, product vision, marketing genius, and a willingness to take risks. And Jobs did take big risks, investing in software and graphics he believed would compel people to buy the Mac not for their offices but for their homes. His leadership style—described by some as cruel, petulant, ruthless, and selfish—was controversial, but all that was forgiven as he turned out extraordinary products.

Jobs certainly deserves credit for helping bring women into the computer marketplace as buyers. The first computer in my childhood home was an Apple II, and my mom, a schoolteacher with no technical background, used it with pride. Inside the industry, Jobs could have become an example of all that the tech industry could gain by bringing in a more diverse workforce. His vision and understanding of the consumer marketplace demonstrated what could be changed when different voices were added to the product development cycle. Unfortunately, the industry took the wrong lesson from Jobs's achievement and only succeeded in creating a new stereotype, one that—once again—favored men over women.

Looking at the hypercool Steve Jobs, investors noted his supreme self-confidence and fearlessness of risk and decided that those were keys to entrepreneurial achievement. Investors stopped gravitating to awkward, antisocial nerds and started looking for founders with über-confidence, a penchant for grandiosity, and a ravenous appetite for risk. The ideal candidates married the best of Wozniak and Jobs: technical skill plus daring and determination, simultaneously geeky and cool. Jobs became a new stereotype—the model for a new generation of young men aspiring to become the rock stars of the computer revolution.

HOW TRILOGY WROTE THE BRO CODE

Silicon Valley has mostly forgotten the tale of Trilogy, a start-up that glittered brightly in the mid-1990s before burning out. But the company is important here because it exemplifies several distinct cultural shifts that worsened the working environment for women. Led by a charismatic young Stanford dropout, Joe Liemandt, Trilogy pioneered new recruiting strategies in the tech industry, selected a different type of computer programmer, and encouraged an insane amount of risk—all while helping to trademark the work-hard, party-harder brogrammer culture we've come to know, complete with Dom Pérignon, strippers, and high-stakes gambling. Trilogy did boast a few women among its key early employees, but the net effect of the company, and others like it in the late 1990s, was to create an even chillier climate for women in technology.

In the mid-1990s, Trilogy was one of the most desirable places to work in the industry, as hot as Microsoft in its heyday, and also a lot cooler. "In the '90s, if you majored in computer science, you were a nerd. You were definitely socially backward," says Jocelyn Goldfein, who worked at Trilogy and went on to become director of engineering at Facebook. Trilogy promised to change that. As Goldfein puts it, "Going to Trilogy was a little bit like *Revenge of the Nerds*. It was this feeling of 'Oh, we can be cool too but in our own nerdy way.' That's what made it feel glamorous."

Liemandt started the company in 1989, the same year Steve Jobs lectured on Stanford's campus as part of the university's long-running "View from the Top" interview series. Liemandt had interviewed for a job at Microsoft but believed that he, like Jobs, was destined for something greater. As he told students at Harvard nearly a decade later, he and his co-founders "wanted their work to matter," and because they were the only people who thought they were "good enough," they had to start their own company. After countless hours spent poring over the top fifty software companies and brainstorming various products, Liemandt came up with what he believed was the right opportunity: his company would vastly improve the efficiency of the selling process by creating software to give salespeople working on complex deals quicker access to data and other information.

Liemandt, who was independently wealthy, still maxed out dozens of credit cards bootstrapping his fledgling company. He majored in economics because he thought it was "easy," which allowed him to spend as much time as he wanted working his start-up while taking computer science and engineering classes on the side, though he ultimately dropped out of Stanford during his senior year.

He boasted to anyone who would listen that he had a $500 million idea. In another era, investors would have steered clear of a college dropout making such an outrageous claim. But in the 1990s, this sort of over-the-top bravado was exactly what people expected from young tech geniuses. When Steve Jobs used his charisma to overcome or hide inconvenient facts, people called it his reality distortion field. As Liemandt demonstrated, Jobs was far from the only entrepreneur adept at distorting reality.

Liemandt himself admitted to the *Stanford Daily* newspaper that the initial product "sucked," but once they finally got it to work, Trilogy sold a major software deal to Hewlett-Packard. Silicon Graphics, a large technology firm that had pulled out of a deal with Trilogy, came back to the table asking to renegotiate. Liemandt responded, "We will, but the price has tripled." Silicon Graphics gave in and was followed by major clients such as IBM, Alcatel, and Boeing. Thanks to Trilogy, businesses could create giant custom catalogs (imagine all the options that might come with a plane, for example) that salespeople could use to drive deals. Trilogy was off on one of the greatest runs for a software company in tech history.

With Trilogy still in start-up mode, and Microsoft ratcheting up the competition for talent, Liemandt made a decision about hiring that might have been the single biggest bet of his entire career. He wagered that talented, overachieving students with zero real-world experience—that is, people like him—would be the key to Trilogy's success. As a result of this decision, the vast majority of Trilogy's hires were new graduates, and more experienced adults became a rare breed. Jocelyn Goldfein says the ethos of the company was "We're elite talent. It's potential and talent, not experience, that has merit." With Liemandt's believing passionately that success could only flow from a meritocratic hiring process, "only the best" became the shorthand with which Trilogians described themselves and the candidates they were looking for. If this philosophy now sounds familiar, that's because Liemandt's bet would affect the recruiting process for tech companies for decades to come.

Trilogy "turned college recruiting into an art form," writes one Austin reporter. The company targeted top schools such as Princeton and Stanford, plying students with gifts ranging from CDs of Austin bands to computers and even cars. One female recruiter, a non-techie who was one of Trilogy's top recruiters, passed out laptops to students at Berkeley and hosted lavish dinners at top restaurants in San Francisco and Palo Alto. "You name it. There was no limit in terms of where we'd take people," she says. "There was no accountability or structure. It was just 'Here's a credit card; go figure it out and find some engineers.'" The Trilogians of the future were made to feel more special than they'd ever felt in their lives.

Former Trilogy director John Lilly, who went on to run the Mozilla browser and become a venture capitalist at Greylock Partners, one of the industry's top firms, recalls a red convertible Mustang waiting for him at the airport. Most important, the recruiters were mainly women who were "all twenty-two and hot," as one former employee put it. Trilogians had fun speculating about which recruiters were former strippers (there's no evidence that any of them were) and which might be hooking up with the boss. "Joe was a total bro," one former Trilogian told me. "The 'bro thing' started way earlier than people think." His idea, quite clearly, was to hire good-looking women who, in other circumstances, might never give an engineer the time of day. Of course, the unstated premise of this hiring practice is that the target candidates, the students who'd be flattered and excited at the attentions of these sexy recruiters, would be men, not women.

THE CULTURE-FIT CHALLENGE

One of the assessment measures Trilogy helped pioneer, which became widely used in the industry, was to have candidates demonstrate how well they could think on their feet by conducting a quick succession of brainteasers. Gary Chou, who was taking postgraduate computer science classes at Princeton before being hired by Trilogy as a product manager in 1998, likened the interview process to an *American Idol* competition. "You would go through round after round of brainteasers on campus," Chou recalls. These tests included questions like "How much would you charge to wash all the windows in San Francisco?" And "How many piano tuners are there in the world?"

What did these brainteasers actually test for? There is little to suggest that they had anything to do with being a good coder or engineer. More likely, they helped Trilogy hire people who were a cultural fit. The company was looking for people with extreme confidence—those who would happily riff on a problem about which they had no actual expertise.

On its face, an offer from Trilogy was the opportunity of a lifetime. Kids, right out of college, were trained as quickly as possible and given the chance to run major parts of the business immediately, so they could have instant effect. At the same time, early Trilogy executives compared building the company to building a cult. "The first thing you have to do in a cult is isolate," Trilogy's former VP John Price remembered two decades later. To achieve that, Liemandt had moved the company from Palo Alto to Austin, Texas, in 1992, which at that time wasn't the tech hot spot it is today. "The reason Joe put it in Austin was so you didn't have anything else to do," says John Lilly. "If we're in Silicon Valley, we'll go out and screw around, but in Austin there's nothing else to do except go out and drink . . . The company was oriented towards drinking and working very hard. Everything was very intense." Hired at age twenty-four, Lilly would have been just another cog in the wheel at a big tech firm, but his first job as a Trilogian was as a director on Liemandt's staff.

New hires immediately spent twelve weeks bonding and training at a company boot camp called Trilogy University. The idea was to "push new recruits to their limits" with an unrelenting series of technical and emotional challenges while simultaneously indoctrinating them with Trilogy's core vision and values. Price said they wanted to "create cohesion and bonding at the level military guys have in a fox hole when they have bullets flying overhead," then added, "If you ever study cults, this is how they do it." Recruits, encouraged to display their youthful bravado, emerged with extreme confidence and a near-patriotic devotion to Trilogy.

After graduating from TU, new hires plunged into the company culture of hard work and hard play. "I worked nonstop," says Christy Jones, Trilogy's sole female co-founder. "I didn't go on vacation. We called holidays competitive advantage days because no one else was working. It was a chance to get ahead. I would drive home at 11:30 at night."

By the end of the workweek, everyone was ready to let loose. Aside from "only the best," another Trilogy motto was "money, recruiters, beer, repeat," according to early employees. "Friday at 5:00 p.m., party on the patio," says Lilly. At 9:00 p.m., the team might grab dinner at a Mexican restaurant, then spontaneously hop on a plane to Vegas, often led by Liemandt himself. Inevitably, they'd stay up all night, crashing in suites at the MGM Grand through the weekend. Liemandt was notorious at the tables and in strip clubs, becoming known as Hundred-Dollar Joe. He would expect his team members to bet all or nothing at the tables, not just hundreds but thousands (and sometimes even tens of thousands) of dollars at a time.

This sort of boorish behavior was talked up as a part of the Trilogy ethos, important because it cultivated people's willingness to play for the highest stakes and taught lessons about risk and reward. The Trilogians would catch a flight back to Austin on Sunday, hydrate, and go to work on Monday, even more devoted to Hundred-Dollar Joe. "Challenging male behavior has been in companies forever. This was one of the first tech companies that really spiked it," Lilly told me. "They did hire some excellent women, but also did a lot of things that were problematic for women."

Insane work hours, drinking, gambling, Vegas, strip clubs—throw in the prizing of youthful brilliance over experience, and this was the company culture that new and prospective employees knew they needed to fit. "When you have a culture that is so male dominated, where drinking is a huge part of the culture, where you're talking about doing deals in the millions of dollars, every aspect of that is going to kind of reek of a certain mentality," says Gary Chou. "It's completely hostile for women." Trilogy was among the first in a long line of tech start-ups that required assimilating into a culture of masculine arrogance that many people, women especially, might not want to sign up for.

Not every man is happy and productive in a bro culture, but women, as a group, are especially unlikely to feel comfortable. Much peer-reviewed social science suggests that men—whether due to nature or nurture—are more given to the particular type of grandiose self-assessment displayed by the many tech wunderkinder dating all the way back to Jobs himself. In a paper that consolidated thirty-one years of research on narcissism and involved nearly half a million participants, Emily Grijalva of SUNY at Buffalo found that men consistently score higher than women when it comes to narcissistic traits such as exhibitionism, feelings of entitlement, and the willingness to employ unethical or exploitative behavior to get ahead.

Trilogy kicked off an era in which lofty self-confidence seemed to be a critical qualification for both tech entrepreneurs and the engineers they hired. Recall those brainteasers that Trilogy and other major tech companies used throughout the 1990s and into the next two decades. There has never been any evidence that they were useful in measuring who would be a good programmer. Yet it took until 2013 for Google to finally stop using them. "Brainteasers are a complete waste of time," Google's longtime former head of HR Laszlo Bock admitted to the *New York Times* in 2013. "They don't predict anything."

Well, maybe not anything useful, but they might have been good predictors of the sort of hyper self-confidence men are more prone to. When an employer asked something like "How many golf balls can fit into a double-decker bus" he or she was basically saying this to prospective candidates: "We are going to ask you a question that has no relation to your job and one you've had no training in how to answer. Do you have the chutzpah to pretend that you can?"

Men are far likelier than women to take risks like these and to feel comfortable doing so. Geoff Trickey, managing director of Psychological Consultancy Limited, a group of business psychologists, studied risk-taking behavior in over seventy-five hundred people and found that risk takers who are both impulsive and fearless were twice as likely to be men as women. On the flip side, female risk takers were roughly twice as likely to be more wary and judicious than men.

Additional compelling research suggests that high-achieving women suffer from "imposter syndrome," a term coined in 1978 by two psychologists, Pauline Rose Clance and Suzanne Imes, to summarize how women often feel undeserving of their success. Despite their concrete achievements, these researchers said, women often believe they are not that smart and will eventually be exposed as frauds. Other researchers have found that women won't apply for jobs unless they meet 100 percent of the qualifications, while men will apply as long as they have 60 percent of the boxes checked. Imposter syndrome has been found in all kinds of industries as well as in professions such as law and medicine, where the metrics for success and achievement are widely understood and agreed upon. How well, then, could women be expected to fare, on average, in the dot-com world of the 1990s, when success almost *required* a willingness to be an imposter? Companies were worth what investors believed they were worth, and investors based their assessments on the founders' claims, often wild and fanciful, and their aplomb.

Liemandt's recipe for success turned out to be a recipe for disaster. Though investors clamored to buy shares in a Trilogy IPO, Liemandt kept Trilogy private, allowing the company—and employees—to experiment with new businesses. pcOrder.com, which involved preloading entire computer systems with Trilogy software and selling them over the internet, became Trilogy's first spin-off. In 1999, at the height of the dot-com bubble, pcOrder.com went public, raising $46.2 million—big bucks back then—on its first day of trading.

Trilogy chased the hype, building multiple other online businesses, selling everything from cars and appliances to insurance online, powered by the company's original sales software. As the dot-com boom hit fever pitch, Trilogy and its subsidiaries commanded stratospheric valuations but had little to show for it. "None of them were very good," Lilly says of the various businesses. (He ultimately left Trilogy after sixteen months for a job at Apple, because he didn't share Liemandt's values.) Even the company's core product was mediocre. "The ugly truth was that the sales configurator was a piece of crap software," a former employee told me. "It was super complicated, hard to use, and required tons of professional services fees. The model was hype up crappy software to sell expensive consulting hours." On top of this, some of the new businesses started to overlap, and Trilogy began competing with itself. pcOrder's stock plunged, but not before early Trilogians made bank.

Jocelyn Goldfein, who worked at pcOrder, says, "Everyone got rich off a company that was basically nothing. Trilogy was full of hubris, the hubris of the era except theirs predated the era." The company was the early 1990s model for a type of bluster and risk taking that would come to characterize Silicon Valley over the next decade.

For Trilogy's tenth anniversary, in 1999, Liemandt flew hundreds of employees to the Bahamas, where they stayed at the Atlantis Resort, and gifted employees crystal vases from Tiffany and bottles of Dom Pérignon. When the first tech bubble burst, Liemandt's net worth plummeted, and in 2001 hundreds of Trilogy employees were laid off. Today, Liemandt is quietly running a downsized Trilogy and keeping a low profile in Austin. He did not respond to multiple requests for comment.

COULD WOMEN HAVE PREVENTED THE DOT-COM BUST?

Liemandt's bro style—his volatile mixture of entitlement, hubris, and risk taking—came to be shared by many founders and CEOs in the 1990s, and investors applauded. If you weren't promising to create a billion-dollar company, the VCs didn't take you seriously. Given that entitlement, hubris, and risk taking are the very personality traits that show significant gender differences, it's little surprise that so many of the founders selected for investment were men.

There is plenty of blame to go around for the dot-com crash. With everyone in the system making so much money, few were brave enough to call bullshit. In 1996, the Federal Reserve Board chairman, Alan Greenspan, famously warned of "irrational exuberance" among investors, so many of whom threw money at companies with outrageous price-to-earnings ratios. It took four more years for investors to understand his message, and when they did, it was a financial catastrophe. Starting in the spring of 2000, $5 trillion in market value was lost in less than two years. When the bloodbath stopped, fully half of those promising dot-com companies no longer existed.

Until the crash there was little incentive to stop the game, including among the business press, which did as much cheerleading as investigating. But if investors' love affair with bro style helped fuel the boom—and it did—it's fair to ask, if more tech leaders of the 1990s had been women, could they have helped avoid the bust, or mitigated it?

While no control group exists for history, the question is worth considering. For example, researchers like Geoff Trickey have speculated that the financial crash of 2008 might have been significantly different had women played a more prominent role in high finance. "Risk-taking is desirable and required in the workplace, but we need a balance to avoid it spiraling out of control," Trickey wrote. "If you're not recruiting people of all risk types, you're missing out on a fundamental self-controlling mechanism. It's a bloody good formula for survival."

Of course, individual men and women may not conform to the conclusions of Trickey's research. But his findings do suggest that the simplest way to create a balance between risk taking and caution in a business is to make sure you have a gender-balanced workplace. And other research bears that out.

An extensive study by the Peterson Institute for International Economics, a nonprofit that studies international economic policy, analyzed nearly twenty-two thousand publicly traded companies across various industries in ninety-one countries. The study found that companies whose leadership was at least 30 percent female were 6 percent more profitable. There's no reason to believe that tech, specifically, would be any different. Had more women participated in the first dot-com boom, we might have had fewer make-it-or-break-it "unicorns," and instead had a healthier herd of bust-resistant workhorse companies.

AFTER THE CRASH

The loss of $5 trillion certainly changed the tech industry. Investors became more cautious about out-of-whack price-to-earnings ratios and business plans sketched on the backs of cocktail napkins. But while many midlevel employees were hurt when the bubble popped, some founders walked away with millions. Many became the venture capitalists whom we will meet in the next chapter, and because they had emerged from the economic rubble as winners, their idea of who should be running tech companies (young men) did not change. As VCs, their influence in the industry only grew stronger, while women's position languished.

According to data compiled by the National Center for Education Statistics, in the years after the bust (2000 to 2008), the percentage of women earning computer science degrees plummeted another 10 percent, holding steady at around 18 percent until 2011. (That's a far cry from the 40 percent peak, remember, in 1984.) Once again, women had lost ground, and dramatically so, compared with men.

Why did the bursting of the bubble hurt women more than men? Perhaps women were discouraged by the tough competition as thousands of newly unemployed computer programmers flooded the postcrash job market. They might also have been responding to a then-widespread fear that once-lucrative tech jobs would disappear or move offshore, making it chancier to pursue a career in Silicon Valley. To women, the tech economy might have looked like a tightrope they didn't need to walk.

By 2004—the year Google went public and Facebook was founded—the industry had recovered, and there were plenty of jobs to go around. Silicon Valley was resurrected as the dream destination where entrepreneurs—who fit a certain stereotype—could become millionaires overnight and lower-level employees could get rich simply by picking the right company to join. Tales of enormous fortunes spread, igniting yet another California gold rush. In 2010, the movie *The Social Network* further glamorized start-up life and established Mark Zuckerberg as the exemplum of what a successful founder looked like. And the men flocking to the epicenter of technology continued to vastly outnumber women.

Today, it's estimated there are more than half a million unfilled tech jobs, a number that is expected to balloon to one million by 2020. The industry is facing a labor crisis much bigger than that of the 1960s, when Cannon and Perry canonized nerds as the ideal hires. Talent is in super-short supply now, and yet the stereotype of what makes a good engineer continues to exclude half the population. Silicon Valley recruiters say, "It's a pipeline problem," meaning that there are not enough women graduating from college with the necessary technical skills. If they had more qualified women to choose from, hiring managers will tell you, they would hire more of them. And many of them mean it.

Missing from this explanation is that the tech industry itself created the pipeline, which is very narrow and built on fanciful assumptions about what it takes to participate. Also missing is any acknowledgment that from its earliest days the industry has self-selected for men: first, antisocial nerds, then, decades later, self-confident and risk-taking bros. That these assumptions have greatly harmed women is obvious, but I would also argue, for reasons discussed in this chapter, that they have also harmed the individual tech businesses, the industry as a whole, and our ever more tech-focused culture.

How different our world might be had the designers of those early screening tests not decided that people who don't like people made for the best programmers. What if women had been encouraged to join the tech industry rather than having been ostracized by it? What if Telle Whitney and tens of thousands of women like her had spent their working lives in a welcoming atmosphere instead of an isolating, hostile one? How would our economy and culture be different now if the leaders of the 1990s internet and personal computer revolution hadn't been so remarkably full of themselves and comfortable risking trillions of investor dollars? But instead of this alternate universe, we have seen the rise of the nerd-bro dream and the codification of an ultimate boys' club.

2

THE PAYPAL MAFIA AND THE MYTH
OF THE MERITOCRACY

THE LAST TIME I interviewed Peter Thiel, we were onstage at the LendIt Conference in the spring of 2016. Thiel, a co-founder of PayPal, was perhaps at his high point of cultural influence. His book *Zero to One,* which posited a new way to think about innovation and build successful companies, had a long run on the *New York Times* bestseller list and was a huge hit in China and other foreign markets. The presidential election was only seven months away, but during our interview Thiel claimed he would have nothing to do with it. Just weeks later, he declared his support for Donald Trump—a move that would cost him considerable social capital among the Silicon Valley elite.

The day I spoke with him, however, Thiel was still seen by many as the philosopher-king of Silicon Valley, partly because of his founding role in PayPal (which sold to eBay in 2002 for $1.5 billion) and his wide-ranging investments (from Facebook and Tesla to bioengineering and nuclear energy) but most recently because of his influential book. Hailed by the *Atlantic* as "a lucid and profound articulation of capitalism and success in the 21st century economy," it had become required reading among tech entrepreneurs and other heavy hitters. On the LendIt stage, Thiel wore the standard VC uniform: well-worn jeans, black belt, and an immaculately pressed open-collar white shirt. He was sweating. Not, I think, because of my penetrating questions, but because he is just naturally uncomfortable in front of audiences and under stage lights. Though not a particularly polished speaker—he stammers and repeats himself—he appears to think through each of his answers in the moment, instead of relying on prepared talking points. Over the first two-thirds of the interview, he made interesting and insightful points on issues such as the evolution of the Chinese economy, the state of American politics, and the future of technology.

Then I asked him about the lack of diversity among the Silicon Valley elite. Two weeks earlier, Thiel's eleven-year-old venture capital firm, Founders Fund, had made headlines for hiring its first woman partner, Cyan Banister (the wife of Scott Banister, an early PayPal board member). I asked for Thiel's take on the lack of women in the venture industry as a whole and where the responsibility lay for the disparity.

"We all have a responsibility to do more," he began. "The disparities are really big . . . There's something about tech that matters a lot. There may be a huge disparity in chess players or math professors, but that doesn't matter quite as much as the only industry that's really working in the U.S."

The critical issue, he went on, was the lack of women as founders. By his count, only two women were founders among the 150-odd "unicorn" companies, those worth over $1 billion. "What really defines the culture in Silicon Valley is not the executives or the venture capitalists; it's the company founders. And that's probably the place where the disparity's the most extreme."

This serviceable answer got little reaction from the crowd. He acknowledged the problem, cited some data to illuminate the situation, and agreed that the issue was important.

What was his prescription for changing things?

"I don't know what to do about that," he admitted. Full stop.

Thiel has been an industry leader for two decades, yet he took no personal responsibility for tech's gender disparity and apparently had no thoughts about how to fix it. The subtitle of *Zero to One* is "Notes on Startups, or How to Build the Future," but when I reread it after the conference, looking to see how he'd addressed this critical issue of women being left out, I found that this "huge disparity" wasn't even mentioned. In fact, he'd managed to write the entire book without once using the word "woman" or "women." I was left suspecting that this big, important "responsibility to do more" wasn't, in fact, much on his mind.

Thiel's apparent lack of interest in women's status really matters, because Thiel isn't just influential. He is the undisputed don of a group widely known as the PayPal Mafia, a cadre of men who constitute one of the many reasons Silicon Valley became so dominated by white men of a certain age and educational background. To understand just how deeply the beliefs, decisions, and actions of this group have affected the industry, we have to go back to the mid-1990s and meet them when they were a band of brainy misfits at Stanford University.

CONTRARIANS BY NATURE

Keith Rabois, a PayPal alumnus who is now a leading venture capitalist, clearly remembers the first time he met Thiel. It was Rabois's first day as a Stanford freshman, and Thiel, a junior, was walking through the dorms handing out copies of the *Stanford Review*, the conservative student paper he had co-founded. Thiel normally slipped the newspaper under closed dorm-room doors, but Rabois's door was open and the pair got to chatting.

Rabois, a conservative himself, was immediately intrigued by both Thiel and the firebrand paper he was editing. Not long after, Rabois told me, he became part of the group of unruly college students, none of them computer science majors, who had banded together to share their right-wing ideas with the rest of the generally left-leaning Stanford population. "We knew nothing about tech and talked mostly about politics," he says; in fact, they were studying law, philosophy, and government. Rabois remembers feeling as if he and his peers at the *Stanford Review* were "outcasts" in a liberal school.

Thiel himself told me he too often felt like an "outsider" growing up. An immigrant, with his family, from Germany, he attended seven different elementary schools as a child, was raised Evangelical Christian, and found himself questioning beliefs as widely accepted as Darwin's theory of evolution. At Stanford, refusing to conform to the prevailing views of the other students became a point of pride. "We all started most questions with an anti-conventional-wisdom bias. It almost didn't matter what the topic was," Rabois tells me. They were contrarians by nature.

No one should be forever judged by the certainties they had when they were undergraduates. Nevertheless, the ideas expressed by Thiel's group at Stanford are worth reexamining because the ideas they formed in the 1990s inform the worldview they hold today. And given the PayPal Mafia's outsized influence in Silicon Valley, this group of men's worldview has affected our culture and changed a lot of lives.

In the early 1990s, many universities were working to create a more multicultural curriculum, and Stanford began by instituting a new program called Cultures, Ideas, and Values. It required students to read a more diverse set of authors, including more women and minorities, rather than just canonical works such as Plato, Shakespeare, and the Bible. There was also a push to create more diversity among students and faculty. Thiel and his colleagues at the *Stanford Review* saw these efforts as deeply misguided, writing that this was an attempt by professors to impose their personal anti-Western and antipatriarchal beliefs on the student body. Universities should be blind to gender and race, they argued. Whites and Asians should not lose academic posts to candidates from more underrepresented groups. Only measurable achievement and academic merit should matter.

They also questioned the value of diversity and the idea that universities, companies, and governments function better when a broad range of people participate. "We were pretty critical of affirmative action. We forecast how it was going to play out, saying it's going to really, really penalize Asians, and that's exactly what happened," Rabois told me, referencing a recent lawsuit against Harvard University that alleges Asian Americans are discriminated against in the admissions process.

The *Stanford Review* also targeted feminism. David Sacks, a *Stanford Review* columnist, who would become the early COO at PayPal while Thiel was CEO, authored several pieces in a twelve-page issue devoted entirely to criticizing the new awareness about date rape and sexual assault. The word "RAPE" in bold letters takes up half of the front page, and the issue includes a piece on "How to avoid sexual assault charges," complete with ways to thwart the "feminazis," punctuated by a modified swastika. In one editorial, Sacks wrote: "If you're male and heterosexual at Stanford, you have sex and then you get screwed."

One Stanford friend who disagreed with Thiel about diversity is former PayPal executive vice president Reid Hoffman, who says his relationship with Thiel was forged on their willingness to debate opposing points of view. "Thiel had heard there was this pinko Commie, and I had heard there was this right-wing Attila the Hun," Hoffman told me of their first meeting. "On politics, I don't think there's anything we agree on." When their debates turned to diversity, Hoffman says he told Thiel, "Look, I don't disagree with you, there is a certain amount of political correctness on the left . . . but the issue [of diversity] is real."

But Hoffman was the exception. Most of Thiel's group—though prescient about the overcompensation that could potentially be caused by colleges' political correctness—were libertarian firebrands

who promoted their views like a brigade of militant free-speech aveng-
ers. If one of their purposes was to rile the mostly liberal student body,
they succeeded. To prove just how committed he was to the First
Amendment, Rabois once yelled "Faggot! Hope you die of AIDS!"
outside the home of a Stanford administrator (who had reportedly
kicked a student out of university housing after months of anti-gay
harassment, including using the word "faggot" behind closed doors).
Rabois took responsibility for the remarks at the time, writing, "The
intention was for the speech to be outrageous enough to provoke a
thought of 'Wow, if he can say that, I guess I can say a little more than
I thought.'" Maha Ibrahim, who also went on to become a venture
capitalist, was majoring in economics at Stanford during this period
and recalls the pronouncements of the *Stanford Review* with a shud-
der. "It was just bad. I felt it was just this isolated voice that was so
extreme that it was horrible and incredibly unfortunate," she told me.
The liberal backlash was so great that Rabois, who by this time had
graduated and gone on to the university's law school, left Stanford and
finished his JD at Harvard.

As for Thiel, after graduation he went on to earn a law degree at
Stanford, then clerked for a U.S. circuit court judge, worked as a securities lawyer, and wrote speeches for the former secretary of education William Bennett. In 1995, Thiel and Sacks took the ideas they
had developed at the *Review* and expanded them into a book, *The
Diversity Myth: "Multiculturalism" and the Politics of Intolerance at
Stanford.* "Multiculturalism," they wrote, "caused Stanford to resemble
less a great university than a Third World country, with corrupt ideo-
logues and unhappy underlings." Revisiting their critique of feminism
and calls for gender diversity, they wrote, "The passionate hatred of
men, the utopian demands for an elimination of all gender differences,
the (totally inconsistent) demands for a uniquely female perspective,
and the belief in widespread gender discrimination are the core of the
new gender studies curriculum." They even defended Rabois's "faggot"
remark, likening the campus backlash to the Salem witch trials.

Both Thiel and Rabois came out as gay years later. And in 2011, Thiel told the *New Yorker* he wishes he'd never written about the Rabois incident. Rabois told me, "It was a stupid thing to say, but I'm not the only person who did something stupid in college."

Thiel and Sacks have also publicly walked back some of the book's other arguments, such as their assertion that date rapes were often no more than "seductions that are later regretted." Thiel commented on that for the first time when his donation to Donald Trump's presidental campaign (just a week after that *Access Hollywood* tape revealed Trump boasting about kissing and grabbing women without permission) called attention to the views Thiel had earlier espoused. "More than two decades ago, I co-wrote a book with several insensitive, crudely argued statements," he told *Forbes* in 2016. "I wish I'd never written those things. I'm sorry for it. Rape in all forms is a crime."

In late 2017, however, *Stanford Politics* (another student publication) published a lengthy article in which undergraduate staff members of the *Stanford Review* said that Thiel still meets with them on a regular basis, and hosted an afterparty at his home to commemorate the *Stanford Review*'s thirtieth anniversary. There, one former *SR* editor said Thiel claimed he apologized only to appease the media, saying, "Sometimes you have to tell them what they want to hear." A spokesperson told me that Thiel stands by his original statement to *Forbes*.

Sacks, for his part, told *Recode*'s Kara Swisher of *The Diversity Myth*, "This is college journalism written over 20 years ago. It does not represent who I am or what I believe today." When I asked Sacks about the book myself in 2016, he pointed to women on the executive teams at the companies he's run to prove how much he cares about their advancement. "I do believe in diversity, and I've always sought to create the best teams possible," he told me.

But twenty years ago, when *The Diversity Myth* first came out, Thiel and Sacks had little need to defend or denounce the book, because no one took much notice of it. At the time, Thiel was just another conservative up-and-comer, a minor player in the traditional power structures of politics in Washington and finance in New York. That was about to change.

PAYPAL: WHEN "MERITOCRACY" MEANS "PEOPLE LIKE US"

One day in 1998, Thiel was guest lecturing about currency trading at Stanford when a young Ukrainian engineer named Max Levchin sneaked in to, as he told me, "sleep and get some air-conditioning." Instead, he wound up listening. At the end of class, Levchin introduced himself to Thiel and mentioned that he wanted to start a company. He had already started four that had failed, but he wasn't about to give up. The next day, the two men had breakfast and hatched the idea for PayPal over a Hobee's "Red, White, and Blue" smoothie. Suddenly a former securities lawyer with no technical background was the unlikely co-founder of what would become a billion-dollar start-up. And the group that would become the PayPal Mafia began to form.

Sacks became PayPal's COO in 1999. In early 2000, PayPal (then called Confinity) merged with a competing payments company called X.com, run by a then-obscure entrepreneur named Elon Musk. Rabois became Thiel's right-hand man. PayPal's founders, investors, and early employees went on to become a tight-knit and very wealthy group. To this day, Rabois believes PayPal is a "perfect validation of merit" and of Silicon Valley as a meritocracy. "None of us had any connection to anyone important in Silicon Valley," he told me. "We went from complete misfits to the establishment in five years. We were literally nobodies. People wouldn't talk to us. Everybody thought we were weird. One tech publication ran a story called 'Earth to PayPal.' Everybody thought we were insane." The early PayPal team would go on to found some of the biggest companies in Silicon Valley, including Tesla, SpaceX, LinkedIn, YouTube, and Yelp. Thiel funded and joined the board of Facebook. Establishment achieved.

HIRING ONLY PEOPLE LIKE US

So who were these "nobodies" without industry connections, and whom—and how—did they hire? While Rabois believes they were devoted to the idea of merit—of hiring only the best—that is simply not what happened.

Thiel and Levchin, in fact, have been remarkably up-front about whom they wanted to employ: people who were a lot like them. Years later, in *Zero to One,* Thiel would explain their reasoning. Because start-ups have limited resources, he wrote, "they must work quickly and efficiently in order to survive, and that's easier to do when everyone shares an understanding of the world. The early PayPal team worked well together because we were all the same kind of nerd." Except for the office manager, who was female, those first employees were all men and all of similar age and educational background.

Thiel admits in the book that when starting PayPal, he didn't sort through résumés looking for the most talented people. Mostly, he just brought in the buddies he'd worked with at the *Stanford Review.* Levchin, for his part, hired friends and old associates from his time in the computer science department of the University of Illinois at Urbana-Champaign. In fact, Levchin tells me PayPal's first fifteen engineers were "basically lifted" straight from a computer graphics group he ran on campus. "There was never any time wasted on how do you do this sort of thing. We had exactly the same approaches to everything," Levchin says. He points out that these engineers came from a range of ethnic backgrounds but allows that none of them were women, "because we didn't know any."

The idea that these men just happened to be personally connected to the most talented people available is simply ridiculous. Even Rabois acknowledges that "it was almost impossible to get a job [at PayPal] without a connection to the company . . . We were very network-driven in hiring. And they were weird networks." The members of the PayPal Mafia explicitly believed, and some still do, that hiring an ideologically diverse group of people early would slow the company down, when all they wanted to do was move faster. "I don't think you can have first principles debates in a start-up in the beginning," Rabois told me. "In the beginning, it's better to have people who are more similar ideologically than different. Once you have alignment, then I think you can have a wide swath of people, views, and perspectives."

Amy Klement was one of the earliest women at PayPal—not because Thiel or the others hired her, but because she was working at Elon Musk's X.com when it merged with PayPal in 2000. Klement told me, "[PayPal] was a high-intensity, driving culture" full of impassioned debate. Socializing took the form of chess tournaments rather than fratty parties. Employees worked eighteen-hour days, seven days a week, as they worked to build a secure online payments system that could rival the global banking industry. "There were tense discussions, at times anger and slamming doors," Klement said.

But despite their own admission that they were hiring from people they knew personally, Klement confirms that Thiel and other executives often talk about how PayPal was a meritocracy. "We used the word 'meritocracy' a lot, and I do feel like we were very conscious of who was really performing," she said. Klement, one of the few women at the company, became a product manager reporting to David Sacks. "David had a strong point of view on what the product should look like, but I also feel like I would share my points of view and we would work through things."

As the early PayPal staff rose to prominence, Thiel in particular became famous for his strong views. "I think there is this way in which human beings can act in sheeplike, lemminglike, herdlike ways," Thiel once told me in a Bloomberg Television interview. "And I think that's a disturbing truth about human nature that we should try to, try to resist as much as we can . . . I think there is probably something about the general homogenization of our society where people are brought up in increasingly similar ways that probably does limit the amount of creativity one can have."

Obviously, Thiel didn't consider himself one of those doomed lemmings. But how does one find other nonlemmings? Just look for unusual behavior. In his book, Thiel notes with pride that "of the six people who started PayPal, four had built bombs in high school." In our interview, he told me, "There is something that's always quite extreme about the personalities that go into starting a company . . . Having some extreme personalities, I think, is a somewhat good thing."

The beliefs of the PayPal founders—that individual merit is the most valuable metric of human potential and that creativity is deadened by groupthink—have deeply influenced the postcrash tech industry and are consistent with the ideas promoted by Thiel's cohort at Stanford. There are many counterarguments to this thinking, but I'll focus on one of its glaring flaws: Peter Thiel, who champions unbridled individuality, is in fact describing a groupthink of his own. From his Stanford days onward, Thiel has largely surrounded himself with Ivy League, antiestablishment contrarians whose opinions are similar to his own. The *Review* editors might not have been the most popular group at Stanford, but they were a group nonetheless. They took their particular brand of groupthink to PayPal and their subsequent companies, propagating it through Silicon Valley—with consequences far beyond the PayPal walls.

That's why, when Thiel and his cadre advise companies to focus on individual merit in their hiring, we need to look very closely at how they define the term. What are the metrics they use for determining people's "merit"? And why does this particular type of meritocracy seem to reward jobs and stock options only to a razor-thin demographic?

Thiel expresses no regret about the narrow criteria he used in staffing PayPal. "I ended up recruiting a lot of people I'd become friends with at Stanford," he told me; Levchin did the same, hiring from his own alma mater. The co-founders' example was then repeated, Thiel says, by those hiring at the lower levels. "Let's get people like us" became ingrained as company culture. "It was always, you know, is this somebody that we'd want to work with and could become friends with over a long time?" Thiel said. "That was a question we always had in the background."

Levchin, however, admitted to me that his early approach was flawed, recalling a specific moment "where I consciously realized, 'Wait, we are doing something wrong.'" One day his girlfriend (who later became his wife) told him, "If you don't hire a woman now, you will never hire a woman. I would look around the office and say, 'I am not going to be the first woman here.'" By then, hiring had slowed because Levchin was running out of University of Illinois recruits to vacuum up, and he was perplexed about what to do. "We don't know anyone else. We've already hired everyone who looks like us in our little social circle. We realized there was a plateau moment where we had to fix that problem," Levchin recounts. That's when PayPal started to cast a wider net and hired a female head of engineering, Jane Manning.

Manning had all the necessary technical skills, but, more important, she enjoyed Ping-Pong. "I was completely smitten with her," Levchin says. "She came into the interview and said, 'Let's play Ping-Pong,' and I said, 'Hey, that's awesome, she is instantly fitting in.'" But just a few weeks later, Manning left for a job at Google.

Reflecting on her time at PayPal, Manning told me, "The problem was a cultural one, not necessarily a lack of women, but if there were more women, the culture might have been better. There was a certain overconfidence among the engineers. I wanted a little more process that could have protected us from mistakes, something that I think women can be more sympathetic to. I do think there can be a sort of macho all-male environment of 'We don't make mistakes.'" For example, Manning had to fight to get the team to use a bug-tracking system (and one engineer programmed it to play "The Hamster Dance Song" whenever it loaded). The team, conversely, felt they could keep track of whatever they needed to in their heads. On top of this, Manning never quite hit it off with Thiel. "I was uncomfortable with Thiel's political views," Manning told me. "I remember learning that he had met a lot of other early PayPal employees at the *Stanford Review* and really had a moment of feeling that these were not my people."

PayPal did manage to hire more women as the company scaled and acquired women like Amy Klement in the merger with X.com, but the team at the top, the one that would go down in history, was all male. As they cashed out of PayPal and dispersed to start new companies and join or create venture funds, they would wield extreme power and influence in Silicon Valley. Many of the companies they went on to found or be associated with became the most successful and highly valued companies of the decade. Anyone who had boarded the PayPal rocket ship early seemed to have a ticket to unprecedented opportunities and automatic success. Every one of them became very rich. Not one of them was a woman.

A photograph of the PayPal Mafia on the cover of *Fortune* magazine in 2007 pictures the men posing as gamblers with cigars, drinks, and a deck of cards. "It just makes me cringe that there's not one female in that photo," says Amy Klement. "It drives me crazy because there were some really successful women at PayPal." While they might not have been founders, these women, she says, were written out of history.

Did the mythical status the PayPal Mafia acquired perpetuate the idea that successful start-ups were founded by groups of male friends? Was PayPal somehow responsible for this notion that women couldn't or just didn't found companies? "They absolutely created a template because having watched what the PayPal Mafia did and how incredibly successful they were. . . . Why wouldn't you imitate them?" Roger McNamee, co-founder of the tech private equity firms Silver Lake and Elevation Partners, told me. When it comes to the idea of hiring your friends or "people like us," McNamee adds, "they didn't just perpetuate it; they turned it into a fine art. They legitimized it . . . These guys were born into the right part of the gene pool, they wind up at the right company at the right moment in time, they all leave together and [go on] to work together. I give them full credit for it, but calling it a meritocracy is laughable."

THE PAYPAL OCTOPUS

The ultimate reach of the men in that *Fortune* cover photo is astonishing. After the sale to eBay, the PayPal Mafia unfurled like an octopus and deployed its tentacles all over Silicon Valley. Members were forever bonded by what they'd shared. As Thiel told me in our interview, "There's something about the set of us, the set of my friends from PayPal, where this was just an intense experience. And I think that those bonds can probably never quite be matched in their intensity." And as those men dispersed, their relationships became the currency in which they traded. They joined one another's companies, funded one another's ventures, defended one another's controversial public statements, and more.

For Founders Fund, Thiel partnered with two less prominent Pay-Pal co-founders, Ken Howery and Luke Nosek. The partners at Founders Fund invested in their old PayPal buddy Elon Musk's space venture, SpaceX (Musk also co-founded Tesla). Founders Fund, along with Max Levchin and Keith Rabois, invested in the workplace chat company Yammer, which was founded by former PayPal-er David Sacks. Yammer was ultimately sold to Microsoft for $1.2 billion.

The list of "begats" goes on. Sacks went on to become COO of the fast-growing HR software start-up Zenefits. When the founder of Zenefits, Parker Conrad, was kicked out amid accusations of cheating state compliance regulations and creating a bro-y culture that led to "sex in the stairwells," according to an internal memo, Sacks was promoted to CEO. Sacks promptly brought in Peter Thiel as a board member. Even though the valuation of Zenefits was slashed amid the cheating scandal, it still reached $2 billion. (Sacks has since left Zenefits.) And this is just a partial list.

The PayPal Mafia became so dominant that in 2017 Adam Pisoni—an entrepreneur who never worked at PayPal but was recruited by Sacks to be his Yammer co-founder—cited what he called the Mafia's "dynastic privilege" as "one of the major contributors to the lack of diversity" in Silicon Valley. "I am a product of the 'PayPal Mafia dynasty,'" Pisoni wrote in a *Medium* post. "I co-founded Yammer with one of the original PayPal mafia members. Yammer had an easier time raising capital because of our PayPal connection." Yammer, like PayPal, had an all-white, all-male founding team, which hired mostly white men from their networks early, who all in turn benefited greatly from Sacks's Mafia ties. Pisoni continues that it was then easier to raise funds for his next start-up because of his Yammer connection, thus perpetuating the dominance of a selection of white men. Or as Roger McNamee sums it up, "Show me something the PayPal Mafia is not involved in."

Reid Hoffman also acknowledges how much he benefited simply by knowing Thiel. "Because Peter and I were classmates, that ended up being a huge inflection point in my career," Hoffman says. Having co-founded the professional social-networking site LinkedIn (which was funded by the prominent venture capitalist Michael Moritz, who had originally been on PayPal's board), Hoffman has spent a lot of time thinking about how networks can impact diversity outcomes, for better and for worse. "When you're hiring the first twenty people on the team, you don't go, 'Who's the most different from the other nineteen people that we have?' That's not useful," Hoffman explains. "Should it all be white men of a similar socioeconomic class? Well, no, that's more likely to run you off a cliff." The most important thing, Hoffman believes, is that all team members, whoever they are and wherever they come from, cohere quickly on the company mission.

Hoffman eventually sold LinkedIn to Microsoft for $26.2 billion. When I ask him if networking is part of Silicon Valley's gender problem, he says if he could do it all over again, he would go back to his college days at Stanford and network even more, not less, and especially with women, because he's seen the incredible benefit of a single friendship.

Klement agrees that dynastic privilege in tech is a problem. "I think it's gotten worse, where people are hiring from their networks and their friends," she says. "The money flows easily around [the PayPal

Mafia] and hiring flows easily around that group, but I think that's how labor markets work. The elite are connected with the elite . . . It's very logical you're going to invest in people you know and trust more than you're going to invest in people you don't know. We should enable ways to break through and enable others to get in."

Unfortunately, networks like the one created at PayPal are hard to get in once they are established. You have to be one of the gang, a known quantity—much like the real Mafia. The power that these groups wield and the business momentum they create are hard to overstate.

Jeremy Stoppelman and Russel Simmons (both in the *Fortune* photo) started Yelp, which went public with a $1.43 billion market cap. Max Levchin funded Yelp and later joined as chairman. Chad Hurley, Steve Chen, and Jawed Karim came up with YouTube, which sold to Google for $1.65 billion just a year after its founding.

In this particular "meritocracy," whom you know is critical. Michael Moritz of Sequoia, who funded LinkedIn and PayPal, also recruited PayPal CFO Roelof Botha to join Sequoia as a partner after PayPal was sold. One of Botha's first investments was YouTube. Because he had just returned from his honeymoon with several digital videos and no way to share them, he was primed to see great potential in YouTube's fledgling site. Luckily, the founders were three of his old PayPal friends. Botha also funded Xoom, the international payment company started by early PayPal investor Kevin Hartz. Xoom sold to, wait for it, PayPal for $890 million in 2015.

Meanwhile, Youniversity Ventures (now Y Ventures), a fund started by Hartz along with Keith Rabois and Jawed Karim, made an early investment in Palantir, another company co-founded by Peter Thiel. Rabois also worked for Hoffman at LinkedIn and became COO of Square, funded by Sequoia's Botha. He left Square in the midst of sexual harassment allegations involving a male employee (which he denied) and became a general partner at Khosla Ventures. Between his stints at LinkedIn and Square, Rabois also became executive vice president of the social app company Slide, started by Max Levchin and backed by Thiel's Founders Fund. It was at Slide that Levchin learned the hard way that having a male-dominated team like PayPal's wasn't always a recipe for success.

MAX LEVCHIN'S DIVERSITY AWAKENING

Tres, a Mexican bar and restaurant, is located on Townsend Street, in San Francisco's tech-heavy SoMa district, and the staff of Slide assembled there regularly for happy hour. "There was definitely plenty of alcohol," Levchin admits. "If the boys want to go out and do happy hour, who am I to tell them they can't blow off steam?" The introverted Levchin is not one to pound beers at a bar, but many of his employees more than picked up the slack.

Jason Rubenstein joined Slide as a software engineer in 2008, a point when the company was going gangbusters because of the popularity of its social apps and games on Facebook. Employees were pulling long hours, each day trying to beat the numbers they had posted the day before. Every team had a mini refrigerator stocked with beer, Rubenstein remembers. But the occasional beer often turned into groups of people starting to drink at 3:00 p.m., and many of them were drinking to get drunk. According to Rubenstein, one night an engineer got drunk, pushed code at 3:00 a.m., and took down Slide's entire website.

The few female engineers started to feel uncomfortable. "At some point, the alcohol culture led to grabby hands at parties, that sort of thing," Rubenstein recalls. "If someone says no and it keeps happening, that's a problem." A woman who worked at the company told me that Slide felt like a frat house, with an undercurrent of sexism and rumored hookups.

Given that many Silicon Valley start-ups are founded and staffed by young men straight out of college, drinking at the office is common. There's beer on tap at most big tech companies, including Google, Facebook, and Twitter, and you'll often find beer in the refrigerator at small start-ups, to juice those late nights of coding with your buddies. Rubenstein calls Slide's alcohol problem and "ambient sexism" symptoms of "a culture of immature individuals." In these kinds of environments, Rubenstein says, "there are all sorts of comments like 'Gee, that's gay,' or 'Gee, do you have a vagina?' which I've heard far too many times to count."

Looking back, Levchin wouldn't exactly characterize Slide's culture as Brotopia. "I think Slide originally had what I'd call the occasional moral-vacuum culture," he told me. "Different people chose very different interpretations of what was appropriate, or even barely acceptable." His mistake, he admits, was not investing enough time and effort in guiding the culture from the beginning. "That error manifested itself in occasional clashes," he said, and led to some "plain inappropriate behavior" as well as destructive office politics including backstabbing and a general lack of candor.

When he realized his company was destroying itself from within, he took aggressive action. He removed or pushed out the bros on staff ("there were definitely a few," he admits). He apologized to individuals who got "caught in the cross fires," gave some "we're all in this together" speeches to the team, and attempted to reset the culture to get Slide on the right track.

Despite these efforts, the company itself did not succeed, at least by Silicon Valley's lofty standards. Slide cycled through multiple business models and products until Levchin sold it to Google for $182 million in 2010, after raising $78 million from investors and being valued at $500 million in its final funding round. "I could have done so much better. I built a culture that I didn't particularly take pride in being a part of," Levchin told me. He went on to found not only Affirm but another company called Glow, which helps couples combat infertility, and he banned happy hour, in hopes of avoiding his past mistakes.

"Early on, I was very draconian. I said we will not have happy hour; it's a recipe for bro culture," Levchin says. He has eased up slightly on that edict but has also established a core set of values, provided unconscious-bias training, reached out to female coding groups to recruit more women, and set up beneficial work-family policies. "In many ways, I've become much more women and employee friendly," Levchin says.

"Max has an inherent sense of fairness; his fairness compass is superstrong," says Christina Miller, a lawyer who works at Affirm. "Equality is very important to him." Miller attests that, at Affirm, Levchin has built a much more serious, as well as inclusive, culture, one that works very hard to empower women. She also says she has never heard Levchin use the word "meritocracy," not even once. "That's not to say we've never had any HR issues, but most of them haven't revolved around alcohol at all. It's mostly the arrogance of Silicon Valley that's a bigger challenge." By that, she means, in an industry that prizes technical talent, some engineers have a tendency to act entitled.

To build a healthy culture, Levchin, who has been known to wash his own dishes at Affirm, relies on his two decades of company-building experience. "At PayPal, I would argue all of us were so young and running quickly," Levchin says, while at Slide he made far too many "poor cultural choices." "With benefit of hindsight, Affirm is very different," he says.

Thiel has made no such mea culpas. Indeed, in *Zero to One*, he embraces the term "PayPal Mafia," a moniker that is deeply fraught with connotations of misogyny, male dominance, and the brutal exclusion of anyone outside the group. *Zero to One* has now been read by hundreds of thousands of people worldwide, including many would-be entrepreneurs, all hoping to create their own billionaire mafia.

A CRITIQUE OF MERITOCRACY

Believing that they hired on merit from the start, the PayPal Mafia has evangelized that Silicon Valley epitomizes meritocracy. "If meritocracy exists anywhere on earth, it is in Silicon Valley," David Sacks told the *New York Times* in 2014. This echoes Rabois's belief that PayPal's hiring practices were a "perfect validation of merit." I've enjoyed many a debate with Rabois and Sacks on my TV show, *Bloomberg Technology*. And in that spirit, I'd like to closely critique their statements.

The group from the *Stanford Review* claim to have been outsiders, at college and in the tech industry, and they wear that status as a badge of honor. That they became so successful in Silicon Valley in spite of sticking to their contrarian guns is proof, they contend, that they must have done so through merit. But these were young men who started out at one of the world's most prestigious universities. Claiming to be outsiders, in any meaningful sense, is a stretch. Maybe their bombast in the *Review* excluded them from certain clubs and parties, but they were insiders in a way Horatio Alger was not, with the platform of a student publication (albeit a less than popular one) and, more important, access to all the powerful and moneyed connections that elite universities provide.

"I will say I laughed often," Klement says. "When we were talking about the success of PayPal, the theme I would hear from the men was 'We were really smart. We worked really hard,' and the theme I heard from women was 'God, we were lucky.'" Both claims are no doubt true, but it's well documented that luck played a crucial role in the company's success. In 2000, PayPal closed a $100 million funding round as the dot-com bubble was bursting. "You look at all the other companies that tried and failed, all the other companies that didn't close their Series B funding right before the market crashed . . ." Klement's voice trails off. What if the crash had occurred a week earlier, before PayPal had that money in its coffers? The answer comes straight from Sacks, who once wrote that if they hadn't closed that round when they did, the company "would have died."

But the men of the PayPal Mafia succeeded often, with many other subsequent companies. Doesn't that suggest that they earned it through merit?

The concept of meritocracy dates back to the writings of the philosopher Confucius in ancient China. In the second century B.C., the Han dynasty implemented the first known meritocracy (though they didn't call it by that name), promoting government officials based on their performance on civil service exams. As Confucian texts were translated during the Enlightenment, the idea spread to Europe and the United States.

But we didn't have a term for "meritocracy" until the twentieth century, when the British sociologist and politician Michael Young wrote a book in 1958 warning of how dangerous the world's relatively new method of establishing status might be. In his novel *The Rise of the Meritocracy,* Young portrayed a dystopian Britain in which status based on birth and lineage was replaced by status based on education and achievement. Young wasn't advocating for a return to the old system, but he did see grave dangers in the new embrace of meritocracy, eerily predicting that in this new world, status would still be accessible only to a select few: those who had access to elite education. As a result, meritocracy would produce a new social stratification and a sense of moral exceptionalism.

Though Young's book was meant as a cautionary satire, the idea of meritocracy took off, all negative connotations forgotten, as the term for a new equality of opportunity. By the year 2000, at the time of the dot-com boom, the British prime minister, Tony Blair, could be heard extolling the virtues of a "meritocratic" society.

That's when Young penned an op-ed for the *Guardian* in which he confessed he was "sadly disappointed" by his book's effect. "It is good sense to appoint individual people to jobs on their merit," he wrote.

"It is the opposite when those who are judged to have merit of a particular kind harden into a new social class without room in it for others . . . If meritocrats believe, as more and more of them are encouraged to, that their advancement comes from their own merits, they can feel they deserve whatever they can get. They can be insufferably smug, much more so than the people who knew they had achieved advancement not on their own merit but because they were, as somebody's son or daughter, the beneficiaries of nepotism. The newcomers can actually believe they have morality on their side. As a result, general inequality has been becoming more grievous with every year that passes."

"A new social class without room in it for others"? Young wasn't specifically describing the tech industry, but he nailed it. That the winners in Silicon Valley deserve all the prizes they have won is an argument that one hears, both explicitly and subtextually, across Silicon Valley.

Of the many tech billionaires I've met, all have seemed to be very smart, creative thinkers and hard workers. Sometimes exceptionally so. But they've also been lucky. In some cases, more lucky than good. And in many cases, no more good than many others who were less privileged and less lucky.

If Silicon Valley were truly a meritocracy, and opportunities were indeed rewarded according to one's true skill and ability to do the job, that would be great for all workers, men and women. But the reality is, as the PayPal Mafia exemplifies, Silicon Valley is not a meritocracy. More fundamentally, meritocracy is impossible to achieve, because, as Young says, a meritocracy is always based on an imperfect definition of merit and often narrowly defined to favor training, connections, and education primarily available to the wealthy.

Take Stanford. Because Stanford is filled with students with top high-school GPAs and SAT scores, administrators can pat themselves on the back and say, "We only admit the best students. We're a meritocracy." The students are encouraged to think similarly. But is it just a coincidence that the median annual family income of a Stanford student is $167,500 while the national median is roughly one-third that? Did those high-achieving students naturally get high SAT scores, or did they benefit from their parents' paying for tutors and sending them to private schools? Privilege accumulates as you advance in life. If the college you attend is the basis of your future employment networks, then it is impossible to say that your employment success is solely based on merit.

The idea of meritocracy is problematic in other ways. Research shows when companies adopt a "merit"-based compensation system, they can actually become *more* gender biased, awarding promotions and extra money to men over equally performing women. When you are convinced your organization is a meritocracy, the theory goes, you can often forget to do the hard work of rooting out gender and racial biases.

Journalist Megan Garber put it like this in the *Atlantic:* "'Meritocracy' takes as its core assumption, essentially, an equality that does not exist in America. It is romantic rather than realistic . . . We want to believe that talent will triumph, and that hard work will be the tool of that success. Which is to say: We want to believe that opportunity is evenly distributed. But, of course, that great escalator is far faster for some than it is for others. It is harder for some to get to in the first place." As a concept, she adds, meritocracy can speak to the "best of who we are" but also "serve as a justification for the worst."

Many people in Silicon Valley are greatly invested in the "self-made great man" story. But it is a story always told in retrospect, with little acknowledgment of all the factors that actually contribute to success. Personal connections, timing, and access to funding from influential backers can all make or break a start-up. The social ties that come from attending a school such as Stanford or Harvard can provide an enormous head start (one that I too have benefited from). The fact that Silicon Valley is a highly competitive place in which only a handful of companies in each market sector achieve great wealth does not mean that outcomes are based strictly on merit. At no stage of the game are all players on a level field.

If Silicon Valley were a truly level field, we'd have to imagine that a smart person such as Peter Thiel could have had the same impact even if he had not gone to Stanford and if he had been female instead of male, or if he was black instead of white. Of course, we'll never know. We can be pretty sure of one thing, though: alternative Peter Thiel would have had little chance of getting hired at PayPal.

THIEL GOES TO THE WHITE HOUSE

Though some of his views have changed since his *Stanford Review* days, Silicon Valley's philosopher-king is still a firebrand. In 2009, for instance, he wrote an essay in the online ideas journal *Cato Unbound* in which he declared, "I no longer believe that freedom and democracy are compatible."

His political views are clear. "The 1920s," he wrote in that essay, "were the last decade in American history during which one could be genuinely optimistic about politics. Since 1920, the vast increase in welfare beneficiaries and the extension of the [voting] franchise to women—two constituencies that are notoriously tough for libertarians—have rendered the notion of 'capitalist democracy' into an oxymoron."

Let's pause for a second. The man who is one of the main architects of the culture of Silicon Valley in the last twenty years thinks giving women the right to vote has harmed democracy.

With the dream of a capitalist democracy unattainable, Thiel saw a means to escape. The new frontiers were cyberspace, outer space, and "seasteading." In cyberspace, he wrote, you could create communities outside the bounds of the nation-state, and the frontiers of outer space were likewise unlimited, although we needed to be realistic about the time horizon, saying it wouldn't happen before the second half of the twenty-first century. He was perhaps most excited about "seasteading," a word he coined to describe the creation of floating ocean communities dedicated to innovation and freedom and existing outside the laws of nation-states.

Thiel can imagine new communities floating on the ocean or in outer space, but when asked about how to get more women into tech jobs, he says simply, "I don't know what to do about it." Given his belief that women voters are "tough for libertarians" like himself, he may not be particularly interested in the issue in the first place.

By 2016, Thiel was largely downplaying his excitement over seasteading, but he had found another horse to bet on: Donald Trump. His support for the then candidate, first with a $1.25 million contribution to Trump super PACs and the presidential campaign itself and then with a speech at the Republican National Convention, lost him many friends in Silicon Valley. In the speech, he revealed that he was gay (though the gossip site *Valleywag* had reported it years earlier), making him the first person ever to come out at the RNC, but his words also minimized the importance of sexual identity.

"When I was a kid, the great debate was about how to defeat the Soviet Union. And we won," Thiel proclaimed from the RNC podium. Then, in a punch line referring to the recent controversy over transgender rights, he continued, "Now we are told that the great debate is about who gets to use which bathroom. This is a distraction from our real problems. Who cares?"

In thousands of public posts and industry blogs, Thiel was vilified. When there were public calls for him to be taken off the board at Facebook, Mark Zuckerberg himself came to Thiel's defense. "We care deeply about diversity," Zuckerberg posted on Facebook. "That's easy to say when it means standing up for ideas you agree with. It's a lot harder when it means standing up for the rights of people with different viewpoints to say what they care about. That's even more important. We can't create a culture that says it cares about diversity and then excludes almost half the country because they back a political candidate."

It's ironic that Zuckerberg would defend Thiel, the author of *The Diversity Myth,* on the grounds of "diversity." Speaking to college students via a Facebook feed, Zuckerberg went as far as to offer up Thiel as an example of how the company creates a diverse, inclusive environment. "I think you need to have all kinds of diversity if you want to make progress together as a society," Zuckerberg said. Amen to that. But billionaire Trump supporters aren't the only ones who need a diversity champion.

When Trump won the election, to the shock and horror of liberal Americans, that is, most of Silicon Valley, Thiel became the main bridge between the technology industry and a president who was a Twitter fanatic yet declared he sends emails "almost never" and was skeptical of the "whole, you know, age of computer." Most of the tech elite despised Thiel for his role in electing Trump. Yet his contrarian bet on an unlikely political candidate now gave Thiel more power than ever, even among the people who say they hated him.

Not long after the polls closed, Thiel brokered a meeting between the president-elect and tech leaders, including Facebook's COO, Sheryl Sandberg, Alphabet executive chairman Eric Schmidt, and Amazon CEO Jeff Bezos, all of whom had openly supported Hillary Clinton. These tech lords had little choice but to pay fealty (to Trump, and Thiel). Now the contrarian "misfit," who once called the value of diversity a myth, was whispering into the ear of the man holding the most powerful office in the world.

3

GOOGLE:
WHEN GOOD INTENTIONS
AREN'T ENOUGH

I N 1998, WHEN TWO quirky and very academic Stanford students named Larry Page and Sergey Brin wanted to start a search engine business, they needed an office. Like many great tech entrepreneurs before them, they looked around for an underutilized Silicon Valley garage. Through mutual friends, they found a landlord in Susan Wojcicki, who wasn't just any Menlo Park homeowner. An up-and-coming businesswoman, Wojcicki, then thirty years old, had worked as a management consultant at Bain & Company and then in marketing at Intel. She had also recently finished her MBA at the Anderson School of Management at UCLA, and she displayed her business acumen in the rent she charged for the garage: $1,700 a month, which was above the going rate. She also made sure to get a security deposit. When they weren't working, she says she would often find them in the hot tub.

"I wish I could say I had a great eye and I picked them out as students, out of all the students at Stanford," Wojcicki told me in a Bloomberg Television interview. "But it didn't work that way. What happened was I bought a house, and houses are really expensive in Silicon Valley. And I was a student, and so, I wanted someone to help me pay the mortgage."

Over the next year, when Wojcicki came home from Intel, she would sometimes order pizza with Page and Brin and listen to them talk excitedly about their nascent technology. She could see that their search engine algorithm had tremendous potential, even though the two founders had only one employee at the time. Her instinct proved right: a year later, the garage was overflowing with desks and computers, and Google had grown to over a dozen employees. Wojcicki decided it was time to quit Intel and become Google's first marketing manager.

By any Silicon Valley standards, she was an unusual early hire. She wasn't a computer scientist or an engineer. Her background was in business. She was a woman. And she was married and pregnant with her first child.

"I don't think any of them even had a girlfriend, let alone thinking about having a baby," Wojcicki recalled. "But, you know, I told them up front that I was pregnant, and it took them a minute to kind of register that. Then actually they thought about it, and they were like, 'You know what? We're going to build you a day care.' And I said, 'Well, you know, you only have sixteen employees. You're just getting started. You don't have any revenue models.'" Wojcicki laughed as she retold the story. "I said, 'It's okay. I'm glad you're really supportive.'"

Google became, in a little more than a decade, one of the most respected, innovative, and powerful brands on the planet. Its astonishing success compels attention, as does its track record with women—both the good and the bad. Google, in many ways, has gone to great lengths to engage with women. And it's worth examining how the company has benefited from early efforts at gender diversity but more recently has become the subject of both government and employee lawsuits claiming the company treats women unfairly. This is a story about how good intentions can ultimately be defeated.

Google's staff has always been male dominated. In the beginning, however, Page and Brin put effort into hiring a diverse team and gave real power to a number of notably strong, smart women. The cofounders embodied the epitome of what venture capitalists and later public shareholders believed made the greatest tech entrepreneurs: they were "all nerd" with big visions, yet their interest in hiring women, explicitly, set them apart from the tech bros and PayPal Mafia. Whether Google would have achieved the same level of success without hiring these key early women is impossible to know. But what is clear is that several women executives were critical, in those early days, to creating that rarest of technological start-ups: one that turned an actual profit within just a few years.

THE WOMEN WHO BUILT GOOGLE

In person, Susan Wojcicki bears little resemblance to the many brash and often self-promoting entrepreneurs whom I've interviewed over the years. She exudes a quiet, steady confidence. She does not seek the spotlight; it was only in 2016, nearly three years into her current tenure as CEO of YouTube, the video-streaming site owned by Google, that she finally agreed to my repeated requests for a television interview. When I asked probing questions about YouTube's business, she was careful not to reveal any news-making information that could jolt Google's stock price or get Wall Street talking. Analysts estimate that if YouTube were a stand-alone business, it could be worth as much as $90 billion—which, by the numbers, makes Wojcicki one of the most powerful female CEOs in Silicon Valley.

In stories that have been retold about Wojcicki's fortuitous connection with Page and Brin, she is often portrayed as the lucky one, as if Google were always destined for greatness. At the time she joined the company, however, that was far from a sure thing. Dozens of search engines were already vying for the quickly growing number of internet users, and many more competitors were in the offing. To rise above the competition, Page and Brin had to get their product into the hands of consumers, and for that they needed a marketer, not a coder. Marketing was the very skill that Wojcicki brought to the team during the critical early years when Google transitioned from beta to version 1.0. A more accurate story is that in meeting Wojcicki, Page and Brin were lucky too.

Wojcicki was convinced that Google's search algorithms were game changers, but she knew superior code wouldn't matter if nobody ever used it. Google had no marketing budget, so Wojcicki turned to universities, offering them the opportunity to embed the Google search bar free of charge, and the word spread. She was key in launching the first Google Doodle, the now-famous logo designs displayed on the home page for holidays and special occasions. She also gave up her $1,700 in rent and moved the space-starved business out of her garage and into a real office. But her most critical contribution was to help lead Google to develop what may be the best business model in the history of Silicon Valley.

Wojcicki helped pioneer both AdWords and AdSense, two critical revenue streams that bring in tens of billions of dollars for Google today. AdWords allowed advertisers to place ads directly on the search results page, and AdSense enabled website owners to display Google ads that matched their content. Through AdSense, Wojcicki and the team at Google saw the chance to make all content on the web a potential advertising platform for the company. The potential was earth-shattering. "You do the content and leave the selling of the ads to Google," she told Steven Levy in 2003, when he was a reporter at *Newsweek*. She predicted that the new technology would "change the economics of the web."

That proved to be an enormous understatement. Google's new advertising platforms not only changed the economics of the web but also disrupted the economics of the magazine, newspaper, and television industries, and advertising itself.

ABOUT THE SAME TIME that Wojcicki rented her garage to Page and Brin, Marissa Mayer was graduating from Stanford. Though her focus was symbolic systems, an interdisciplinary major heavy on computer science, she'd made it through her undergraduate years without ever realizing that she stood out among her almost universally male classmates. On November 9, 1998, that changed.

On that day, Mayer opened the *Stanford Daily* newspaper to read her favorite columnist, a student named Rachel Hutton, whose "super-witty" musings reminded Mayer of Carrie Bradshaw's on HBO's *Sex and the City*. In this particular column, Hutton dubbed a few dozen of her schoolmates "campus celebrities," writing, "I don't want to connote freaks or weirdos, but just people who seem to draw attention. They're striking." Unfortunately, at least one of the people she drew attention to ended up feeling like a weirdo as a result.

Mayer recognized a few of the "celebrities"—which included the "mean guy at the post office" and the "girls who created their outfits with a Goodwill bin and a couple of staple guns"—but hadn't crossed paths with some of the others. "I was reading through it like, 'Oh I don't know that one, and I don't know that one,'" when all of a sudden, she says, one of the examples was "the blond woman in the upper-division computer science classes." Mayer was perplexed. "I was like, 'I should know this one! I'm in those classes!'"

Then she realized Rachel Hutton was talking about her. "I know it sounds really funny, but I was like, literally, 'Am I really the only blond woman in the upper-division computer science courses?' Until that moment, it was almost like eating the apple in the Garden of Eden or like the emperor's new clothes, and I was just unaware that I was by myself."

The original article is now almost impossible to find. But when I tracked it down, with the help of an early *Stanford Daily* columnist, I found that it refers not to a blonde but rather to an "outstandingly attractive woman in the upper-division computer science classes." Classmates at the time agree that the "celebrity" in question was most definitely Mayer.

After reading that line, Mayer says she suddenly felt very alone: "I started thinking about how many classes am I in a week where I am the only woman or the only blonde or both, and I started paying more attention to it." She also felt extremely grateful to her parents and the many math and science teachers (whose names she can still rattle off) who never once made her feel out of place.

Mayer believes that if even one person had told her how much she stuck out, she might never have ended up on the computer programming track. "All it would have taken was one of those people to say, 'That's unusual for a girl' or 'Not many girls do.' Sometimes giving a voice to the shortage or giving a voice to the fact that most people drop out," Mayer says, "almost gives you as a girl the license to, but I was just lucky." Research backs this up: When minorities are forced to self-identify as minorities, their performance suffers. Sociologists even have a name for this: stereotype threat.

Page and Brin met Mayer as she was finishing up at Stanford and starting a job search. By this point, she was keenly aware of being the odd duck at school and wasn't eager to repeat the experience in the work world. "I went to this one start-up that was eighty people," she told me. She recalls them saying, "'We really want you. You'll be our first woman engineer.' I would have been their fiftieth engineer but their first woman . . . The feeling of walking in the office, the way people looked at me, I knew that it wasn't going to be a good environment for me."

Mayer almost canceled her interview with Google because she had more than a dozen other offers already, then decided, on a whim, to go ahead. From Page and Brin she heard the same refrain. "They were like, 'You'd be our first woman engineer!'" she says. "I remember thinking to myself, 'I've already weighed this option, and I'm not excited about it.'" But the company then had so few employees—only eight when she interviewed—that she kept an open mind.

Meanwhile, Google was putting her through its famously long, drawn-out, no-stone-unturned interview process. "They grilled me for thirteen hours over two or three sessions, then said, 'We really want you and we think it's incredibly important to have women here. We want to get a strong group of women in here early,'" Mayer recalls. "They were very sincere about it, and I will tell you it's very different to join a company where you're one woman of eight versus one of fifty." Google was growing so fast that from the time she was hired to the time she started, the company had already added nearly a dozen more employees, so Mayer became the twenty-first. By then there were six women on the staff including an executive assistant.

One of her first jobs was to help bring AdWords to life, by building the algorithms that would match early Google ads to the search queries users typed in. She also worked on coding the front end, becoming the "gatekeeper" of the minimalist user interface—the single search bar—that was so crucial to Google's consumer appeal. In this, she worked closely with Wojcicki, with whom she shared a design aesthetic. Together, these two women were inarguably key to making Google a standout tech unicorn. The search engine turned profitable in 2001, just three years after its founding. By 2004, the year after AdSense was launched, profit had multiplied fifty-seven times to almost $400 million, on $3.2 billion in revenue.

GOOGLE'S SUCCESS WAS A team effort, but three of the most valuable players were women. With the help of Wojcicki and Mayer's leadership, Google had innovated not just best-in-class technology but an unassailable business model. Now the company just needed to scale it. That job would be given to Sheryl Sandberg. Like Wojcicki, Sandberg didn't have a computer science background. A standout at Harvard, where she majored in economics, Sandberg worked at the World Bank and McKinsey & Company and served as the chief of staff to the U.S. Treasury secretary Lawrence Summers. She came to Google in 2001 as vice president of global online sales and operations, and in that role she worked closely with Wojcicki and Mayer on the projects that exploded Google's profitability.

Sandberg's first assignment was to manage the "business unit," which at the time did not exist, so she built it. She went on to create and manage a massive sales team for both AdSense and AdWords that would serve Google customers around the world. This was happening on the heels of the dot-com bust, when investors were still wary of flashy tech start-ups that could show viral growth in users but not much profit. But in Google, they saw something very different. When the company went public in 2004, it easily raised $1.67 billion, giving it a market capitalization north of $23 billion. The search engine's price-to-earnings ratio was relatively high. So its investors were still speculating. But the fact that the company was already more than doubling its income year over year undoubtedly gave Wall Street confidence.

HOW WOMEN LEADERS INFLUENCED GOOGLE CULTURE

With Wojcicki, Mayer, and Sandberg as critical leaders at Google, the company was an unusual start-up. It is also clear that these women had a meaningful impact on the corporate culture as other women came on board. The same year the company went public, Google hired a Harvard MBA named Kim Scott as a director. Scott's memories of her first years there are remarkable, as Silicon Valley stories go. "All of a sudden my bosses were Sheryl Sandberg and Susan Wojcicki," Scott told me. "I was like, wow, you can really have a vibrant career as a woman and be a great mom too." In Wojcicki and Sandberg, Scott saw two strong, ambitious, and strategic female role models who were willing to take the time to mentor her. As bosses, these women weren't any less demanding of excellence than the top-ranking men, but they did have different styles of management and different ways of achieving that excellence.

From the beginning, Google's culture has always been intellectually intense. Many of the engineers had PhDs, so there existed a quasi-academic, pick-it-apart-and-find-the-flaws atmosphere. There were some yellers, a fair number of combative people, a lot more speaking over each other than listening. As one former executive put it, "There was a lot of IQ and a lot less EQ." It was an atmosphere where, if you didn't have a great deal of confidence in what you were about to say, or weren't in the mood to argue, you might think twice about opening your mouth.

Google's women leaders worked within that culture but seemed to walk a different line from other managers. "Susan was very supportive," Scott remembers of Wojcicki. "But she would tell you exactly what she thought, tell you when you screwed up, and also did a lot of things that made it safe to try something new."

For her part, Sandberg worked to build camaraderie among Google's female employees by kicking off a series of women's networking events, some at the office and some at her home, where she would invite powerful women and men to speak. She also went to great lengths to mentor women in the workplace.

Men also appreciated her management style. "Sheryl had, besides one of the strongest hands, one of the kindest and gentlest," says David DiNucci, one of the first employees on the AdWords team. "Her emotional IQ is off the charts; she knew which people needed a kick in the butt or a pat on the head."

Scott recalls that Sandberg pulled her aside after a presentation. After complimenting her on the positives, Sandberg said, "I noticed you said 'um' a lot. Were you aware of it?" Scott was not, but she shrugged off the comment. "I can tell I'm not really getting through to you," Sandberg then said. "When you say 'um,' it makes you sound stupid, and you won't succeed at Google if people think you're stupid."

Although chastened, Scott was appreciative. "It was like I had been walking around with spinach in my teeth my whole career and no one had told me," she says. Scott went on to teach management at Apple and developed an entire management philosophy and consulting business based largely on her experiences at Google, which she describes in her book, *Radical Candor*.

TRYING TO IMPLEMENT DIVERSITY

As Google grew before and after the IPO, it was desperately in need of qualified engineers. Yet its leaders still aimed to put some focus on hiring women, using a number of unique approaches. For example, each week the company meticulously tracked the percentage of its women engineers. Page noticed that the engineering ranks were filling up with men and pressed his recruiters on why they weren't hiring more women. The team responded by saying that qualified women were hard to find. Not satisfied with that answer, Page insisted he would keep asking until the recruiters found more women. At one point, a recruiter remembers Page ordering the team to stop hiring male engineers until they had hired twenty female engineers in a row.

"They would take disproportionate amounts of recruiters and have them just focus on female hiring," says former Google engineering manager Niniane Wang, who served on the hiring committee for several years. "Recruiters would get upset and feel they were being made to do a harder job," she says. "Finding men was easy. The founders did something really hard and caused grumbling within the recruiting organization in order to achieve this greater goal."

Still, recruiters couldn't source women candidates fast enough. Page voiced impatient disapproval over the lack of progress at a company meeting. "I'm not seeing any movement," one recruiter recalls Page saying. "This is terrible. What are you guys doing?" Page and Brin started kicking around the idea of starting their own school in an attempt to build a gender-balanced pipeline.

"They were very focused," says Sandberg of Page and Brin. "They just cared very much about hiring more female engineers. It wasn't perfect, but no company is."

Wojcicki believes one of the best things about Google's recruiting is that no hiring decision is ever made by only one person. "I think the thing about Google's hiring process is that it's much more committee based," Wojcicki says. "So, let's say you have a bad interview with one person; well, you have a second chance and a third chance and a fourth chance. And so that gives you a better view of that candidate for us from a company standpoint, but I also think it gives that candidate more chances as well."

Mayer went out of her way to back female candidates she believed in. When she interviewed a young aspiring product manager named Laura Holmes, Mayer was impressed. There was only one problem. Google preferred to hire top students from elite schools like MIT, Carnegie Mellon, and, of course, Stanford. Holmes had gone to Stanford but earned only average grades and then dropped out, with just three classes left to complete. "I found CS late, I ran out of money, and I planned it so I could finish my degree in my spare time at community college," Holmes tells me. Google didn't outright reject her. Instead, Holmes says her case was brought before Google's hiring committee multiple times. "The feedback I was getting was 'You seem great; we just don't understand why you didn't graduate,'" she says. Mayer not only encouraged Google to hire Holmes; she saw to it that Holmes received a signing bonus so she could finish her Stanford degree.

Around 2008, Google also established a secret hiring practice to ensure that women engineers did not fall through the cracks. "If a woman failed an interview, a second committee was assigned to review the case," a former Google executive tells me. It was called the Revisit Committee, and it included women engineers who would take a closer look at candidates on the verge of being denied. Eventually, the Revisit Committee started to assess the cases not just of women but of all diverse candidates, and sometimes those applicants would be hired after all. This measure was taken specifically to respond to concerns about unconscious bias in the hiring process, but it was not publicized within the company, to avoid making women feel as if they were getting special treatment and to minimize criticism about "lowering the bar."

Google implemented strict rules stipulating that you could not talk to fellow employees about the interviews you conducted, so as not to sway their opinion or taint the process. One day, Mayer interviewed a fairly senior man in the tech industry. "He was really rude to me," she recalls. "I don't know if it's because I was young or because I was a woman, but I felt it was a little bit of both." After the interview, she sat on a couch and tried to put her thoughts in writing (all Google interviews are documented in detail) but found herself struggling to find the right words to describe what exactly rubbed her the wrong way.

A female colleague sat down next to her, and Mayer confessed she had just come out of a tough interview. Her colleague responded, "You know, I had a tough one today too." They realized they were both talking about the same man and decided to raise the issue with Brin. First they had to explain why they broke the rules by comparing notes; then they tried to describe why they felt this particular candidate might be sexist. "It seems like there could be a gender issue there, and we know how important gender is to you," Mayer recalls saying. Brin suggested having a third female engineer speak to the candidate, and she came back with the same mixed report. Google ultimately passed on the candidate. Mayer says, "It validated that Sergey wasn't going to hire someone who made us feel mistreated."

According to Mayer, Brin later asked her, "'How do we know this isn't happening every day on the interviews you're not on? We could be hiring guys that are going to make you feel mistreated.'" Google then established a policy that all technical candidates had to be interviewed by at least one woman and that the report had to cover not only technical skills but "cultural sensitivities" as well.

Giving women input into all hires carried a downside that Brin was quick to point out. "This means you are going to end up doing a lot more interviews than anyone else," Mayer remembers him saying. "But it's important enough to us that we want to build a strong team." He was right: In return for having a hiring voice, the women had to add these responsibilities to their full-time jobs. Some women felt that participating in so many interviews hurt their performance overall. The more time they spent doing interviews, the less time they spent writing code, which is what reviews and raises were based on. But many women felt obliged to make themselves available anyway, because if they didn't, hiring would slow down. These time-consuming measures would be hard to scale as Google grew. Wang says she received many panicked calls from recruiters because the female interviewer suddenly had to cancel, and they needed someone to take her place.

THE REVISIT COMMITTEE no longer exists as a diversity initiative at Google, but it is far from the only proactive measure the company has taken. Google offers scholarships and internships and runs a summer institute, all reserved for women and other underrepresented groups. The company also conducts research on why young women do and do not choose tech as a career and provides unconscious-bias training to its employees. In 2014, Google launched Made with Code, a $50 million campaign to inspire girls to embrace computer science.

Despite it all, Google struggled not only to get women into the company but also to move them into leadership roles. The search engine battled disgruntlement among employees who believed that Google, with all of these diversity measures, was compromising its rightfully high standards for a seat on the rocket ship. Nancy Lee, who started her career as a lawyer at Google, then became vice president of people operations until retiring in 2017, says the "elitist aspect" of Google's hiring process became especially problematic. "A lot of people thought it was incumbent on them to find a reason *not* to hire someone. This is such an exclusive club that we need to poke and prod a person in such a way as to find any weakness, because so many people want to work here. But that gets a little crazy and you start dinging people for silly things," Lee explains. "I think it hurts women and minorities more because there is a component of unconscious bias, but even absent of that, you have people looking for an affinity and people like them who come from the same backgrounds and can relate to them, instead of the core competencies of the job."

The meritocracy ideal that had started with companies like Trilogy, and was perpetuated by PayPal, was impossible to escape. Yet stereotypes about who made good tech employees (nerds and bros) were pervasive, limiting, and biased in favor of men. Two conflicting narratives developed within the organization. Some believed Google should strive only to be a perfect meritocracy. Others recognized that such an ideal was impossible to achieve in practice. "The underlying principle of meritocracy is that it works as long as your assessment of people is fair and unbiased," Google's former long-time head and senior vice president of people operations Laszlo Bock told me. "The reality is that without support or training nobody is completely fair and unbiased."

MIXED SIGNALS FROM THE TOP

Even when the money started rolling in, Google—unlike, say, PayPal—never became a poster child for bro culture and the hostile-to-women environment that implies. But stories still circulate from the company's early days of Googlers gone wild at raucous ski parties in Tahoe. Office romances and entanglements—including one between Mayer and Page—were tolerated, but no big scandals erupted publicly, at least in the first decade.

As years went by, however, the top executives at Google became insanely rich, and there was increasingly noisy gossip about their love lives. A pattern emerged of executive interoffice relationships, which *The Information* (a subscription-only site that reports on the tech industry) referred to as "something out of a rebooted soap opera—Dynasty 2.0." In the long, hot summer of 2013, executive chairman Eric Schmidt was outed by the *Daily Mail,* a U.K. tabloid, as having had numerous affairs with younger women, including a female television personality who gave him the nickname "Dr. Strangelove." *Valleywag,* a tech industry gossip blog, followed up with a story claiming that

Schmidt's New York apartment was a love nest that had been sound-proofed.

A month later, news broke that Brin, then forty, was having an affair with a junior employee on his Google Glass team named Amanda Rosenberg. To make matters more complicated, Rosenberg's then-boyfriend, Hugo Barra, was a lead executive heading up Google's Android division, who left at about the same time as the scandal broke in the press to run global operations at the Chinese smartphone maker Xiaomi. And to make it even more complicated, Brin was married to Susan Wojcicki's sister Anne, a Silicon Valley force in her own right, heading up the genetic-testing company 23andMe. Fast Company once called her "the most daring CEO in America."

Other sexcapades involving lesser-known but still powerful men at Google never ended up in the media, but became part of company lore. Longtime chief legal counsel David Drummond had an extra-marital affair with a paralegal on his team, Jennifer Blakely, and the pair had a child together. *The Information* reported that in order to address the conflict of interest, Google moved Blakely from the legal department to the sales department and she later left the company, while Drummond remained.

It is hard to say just how the romantic intrigues of Google's leadership affected the rank and file. Some employees have expressed disappointment and frustration at what they described as the hypocrisy of their bosses; the relationships were often secret and when they were exposed it was the women, not the men, who were reassigned. Others have argued that Google has been too permissive of interoffice dating in general, and created an environment that made it easier for employees to traverse dangerous territory. "If you give employees the license to date, the minute you have that license, there are always blurred lines," one former employee told me.

On the other hand, many current and former Googlers are happily married to each other. "Google intentionally tried to create a collegiate culture," says former product manager Minnie Ingersoll, who dated a peer at Google for several years. "Any environment that encourages you to build relationships with your colleagues is going to lead to some romance. Trying to ban something like people falling in love would be both pointless and unfortunate. Of course, we've been seeing the perils of abused power dynamics lately . . . and we all need to have zero tolerance for that sort of behavior. Companies should have clear policies and then create structures that encourage and reward transparency . . . There were HR business partners that were there to help work through real-world individual situations." In 2013, Google began requiring executives to alert higher-ups to relationships that might raise a conflict of interest.

That said, it is a tricky proposition at companies where women are so vastly outnumbered. "Sexism happens anytime when you're in the minority," says former Google product lead Bindu Reddy. "Women become targets because men want to hit on them. There's a lot of attention and that leads to unhealthy situations. This is why having a small percentage of women is really negative."

In 2015, former Google software engineer Kelly Ellis wrote a series of tweets in which she claimed she was sexually harassed by senior leaders at Google. Executives, she tweeted, made comments about her appearance, including one who said, "It's taking all of my self-control not to grab your ass right now." Google employee Rod Chavez, whom Ellis named as one of her harassers in a tweet, left the company that month. In the wake of Ellis's allegations, and Schmidt's and Brin's affairs, the company dramatically reset the bar for what behavior would be tolerated. Google added new avenues for employees to file complaints, shared the numbers of complaints and disciplinary actions taken with the workforce, and started the Respect@ (pronounced "Respect at") program, where executives discussed how to address inappropriate behavior at all levels of the organization. "Yes, at Google," launched separately as a grassroots effort in 2016, was an email list where employees could anonymously submit allegations. "There was an acknowledgment that we needed to tighten it up at all levels of the food chain," says Nancy Lee, referring to how Google handled the well-known dalliances of its top executives all the way up to Brin and Schmidt. "You probably don't know and I probably don't know when the 'shake the shit out of [them]' conversations happened, but they happened. There's shame in that and they don't want it to be their legacy. They think they are changing the world here, and they really are."

Still, the company didn't always properly message how it dealt with bad behavior and, by some accounts, even rewarded it. Reports revealed that in 2014, Andy Rubin, the mastermind behind Google's popular Android operating system, left after engaging in an inappropriate relationship with a subordinate. At the time, Rubin said he left on his own accord, and Google subsequently invested in Rubin's new tech incubator, Playground. In response to the later allegations, a spokesperson for Rubin said that any relationship he had was consensual and did not involve someone who reported to him. In 2016, long-time Google executive Amit Singhal was also permitted to leave gracefully with no mention of his bad behavior. Singhal announced that he would be moving on from Google to pursue philanthropy. It later emerged that he was forced to resign over allegations of sexual harassment (which he denied).

In the meantime, Google continued with its multifronted effort to create a diverse workforce. But as the search engine grew to tens of thousands of employees, those efforts seemed to pay off less and less.

SETTLING AT AVERAGE

In 2017, Google reported numbers much like the rest of the industry's, with women accounting for 31 percent of employees overall, 25 percent of leadership roles, and 20 percent of technical roles, a far cry from fifty-fifty. Despite years of good intentions and multiple company-wide policy changes and initiatives, Google merely settled at average among its Silicon Valley peers, and there was more bad news to come.

That spring, Google's reputation for how it treats women took a significant hit when the U.S. Department of Labor announced that it had clear evidence of "systemic compensation disparities" between male and female employees at the company after reviewing pay data of twenty-one thousand Googlers. "The department has received compelling evidence of very significant discrimination against women," said Janet Herold, Regional Solicitor for the department. "The government's analysis at this point indicates that discrimination against women in Google is quite extreme, even in this industry." The following September, three former female Google employees, including Kelly Ellis, filed a class-action lawsuit accusing the company of paying women less than men for similar work but also putting them on lower-paying career paths. A spokeswoman for Google said, "Job levels and promotions are determined through rigorous hiring and promotion committees, and must pass multiple levels of review, including checks to make sure there is no gender bias in these decisions. And we have extensive systems in place to ensure that we pay fairly."

The government's lawsuit mirrors a complaint I've heard from several Googlers: that the company's efforts to bring women on board wasn't matched with an equally concerted effort to mentor and promote them.

So what went wrong? There are no easy scapegoats—rather, a web of complex problems including an industry that had already crippled its own pipeline, a pile-up of ignorant and bad behaviors, and a perception of meritocracy that led to a lack of urgency around making changes. All of this was amplified as Google's workforce exploded in size over the first decade of the new millennium.

"If I had an intuition about where we introduced problems, it's when you really start to scale hiring," surmises Bret Taylor, who joined Google as an associate product manager in 2003 and was a co-creator of Google Maps. Taylor went on to become chief technology officer at Facebook and knows a thing or two about the challenges of scaling superfast. If a company is growing quickly, he says, there's a critical moment in its life cycle where it needs to expand from a couple hundred engineers to thousands, in order to keep up. If, at that point, you don't already have a diverse team, he says, "it's really hard to change because so much of your culture is built on the people you hired." That is, if you don't have a critical mass of women early, the problem will only magnify as the number of employees grows.

Taylor believes that after Google's IPO, as the company was trying to keep pace with staffing demands, it defaulted to recruiting methods that were more standard in the industry and loosened the requirements for ideal candidates simply because it was hiring so fast. Recruiters went to the same university job fairs as every other tech company and posted their openings on the same websites. The effort that Page and Brin made in the early days of Google to find great women leaders didn't percolate down to other managers in the organization.

"The growth demanded that we move with the velocity that wasn't necessarily as thoughtful as maybe we would have liked in retrospect," says Lee. "The net we were casting was not as wide as it should be and the company relied heavily—as most companies do—on referrals. When someone is referred, they are considered a known entity, so some preference is given to them, but it tends to be the case that our network of friends is destined to continue the demographic profile that we already have."

Some employees also blame the company's approach to retention of women. "I feel like Google cares a lot about diversity, but I feel we have a very singular view as to what leadership means," says Laura Holmes, who was promoted to senior product manager in 2015 and is one of the rare female managers at Google. "I've been coached to be less nice. I have a collaborative style; it works for me. I wish that when we went out to the promotion committee, there was more of a look at results than there was about approach."

It all comes down to what employees perceived as "merit." "The attributes and behaviors and skills that the majority of engineers on the technical side thought people should have—assertiveness, aggressiveness, that pick-it-apart urge, almost the hubris they had, was rewarded," says Nancy Lee. "The things that get undervalued are things like collaboration, willingness to listen. Some of the skills women would bring to bear were simply not valued. Then you say they lack 'merit' and you get the reputation that it's a little brogrammer."

Lee says this "brogrammer" reputation choked the pipeline and discouraged many young women from even applying to Google. "There were so many times that I went to Grace Hopper [the Women in Computing conference] and women said I wouldn't even apply because it's too hard get in and it's a tough environment. Clearly people were qualified and could have tried. They just didn't even think about it."

It wasn't until about 2012, when Google and the advertisers who provide the bulk of its revenue had fully recovered from the financial crisis, that the company had a reckoning of sorts. "There were rumblings in the culture from women because they knew they would be the only ones in the meeting or there would be presentations with no women at all," Lee says. "Diversity was always a priority, but other priorities had eclipsed it."

The bottom line is this: when it comes to its engagement with women, Google gets an A for effort but a C for results. Ultimately, Google always hired and promoted far more men than women, and men dominate the company's most senior roles today. And, while Google's culture was always intense, it appears to have become more monolithic as it grew, rewarding confidence and confrontation.

"In engineering specifically, people can get so caught up in what's right and wrong in a confrontational manner, and they don't put a stop to it," Niniane Wang told me, reflecting on her time at Google. "It can evolve into a culture where people who love arguing are really happy and people who don't love arguing aren't."

The female Googlers I spoke to didn't describe the work environment that early employee Kim Scott experienced, one where new hires were supported and challenged by female managers.

"I've never had a female boss, and it makes me sad to even reflect on that," said Brynn Evans, a user interface designer at Google. "I've worked at Google for about six years, and I just haven't been surrounded by women who are managers. I've just worked with so many men, and I've had crappy male bosses. Crappy and rude." It wasn't until she arrived at Google, Evans told me, that she realized how isolated she was as a woman in technology.

In 2015, Larry Page rebranded the company as Alphabet, now made up of twelve different divisions including Google, Google Ventures (now called GV), and Google X, each of them with its own CEO. At the same time, he set out to find a female CFO for Alphabet and succeeded, hiring the longtime Morgan Stanley executive Ruth Porat. Page also brought in Diane Greene, the co-founder of VMware, to run Google's cloud efforts. The management team of Google's CEO, Sundar Pichai (who was promoted to the role after Page made himself CEO of Alphabet), is some 40 percent women. (YouTube, which Wojcicki runs, is a division of Google under Pichai.)

Still, as of this writing, exactly zero of the Alphabet division CEOs are women. To top it off, representatives from several coding education and pipeline feeder groups have told me that Google's efforts to improve diversity appear to be more about seeking good publicity than having a real effect. One noted that Facebook has been successfully poaching Google's female engineers due to an "increasingly chauvinistic environment."

Most important, Google may also be guilty of a failure to tell the right story about why the company succeeded in the first place. The most commonly shared narrative is that Google's triumph came through innovation—that it was the first to the future. Indeed, the top echelon at Google might have bought into that story themselves. One former Google executive told me that management was never Page or Brin's favorite activity. They preferred to focus on the blue-sky projects—like curing death, and driverless cars. But there was another story to tell: that Google's success had at least as much to do with making bets on strong female leaders like Mayer, Sandberg, and Wojcicki who brought wider skill sets and different management styles to the company in its earliest days. If subsequent managers at Google understood this lesson, that might have quieted the grumbling among engineers who had a narrow idea of what forms of intelligence or training made a Google employee. Early Google had proven that diversity in the workplace needn't be based on altruism or some goal of social engineering. It was simply a good business decision.

THE INFAMOUS GOOGLE MEMO

This brings me to the case of a young engineer named James Damore, who provided a telling clue for why Google's diversity efforts led to only mediocre results. In August 2017, Damore's ten-page missive explaining what he saw as the root causes of gender disparities at the company, now famously known as the Google memo, was leaked to the press. The memo critiqued cultural issues and hiring practices at Google that he found troubling.

In it, Damore argued that there were "biological" reasons that men were more likely to be hired and promoted at Google. He suggested that men have a higher drive for status than women, which compelled them to compete harder for "high pay/high stress jobs in tech." Women for their part were prone to "neuroticism" with higher anxiety levels and a lower tolerance for stress. He also linked to a study that purported to show that "women generally have a stronger interest in people rather than things" and for "empathizing vs. systemizing." Damore added that Google's efforts to improve diversity were discriminatory, lowering the bar, and could actually increase race and gender tensions. Those efforts were just "veiled left ideology" that ignored scientific fact—though Damore's citations, some from Wikipedia, were weak examples in many instances. He failed to attempt to assess the scientific big picture and made several unscientific interpretations and conclusions. Even the researchers he cited disagree with how he used the data.

Google needed to "de-moralize diversity" and "stop alienating conservatives," Damore wrote. "Unfortunately, our culture of shaming and misrepresentation is disrespectful and unaccepting of anyone outside its echo chamber." He characterized Google as a "politically correct monoculture that maintains its hold by shaming dissenters into silence."

At least in terms of that last point, Damore was onto something. Within a day of the memo's leak, Damore's world was turned upside down. Social media exploded with angry commentary. One site, early to the debate, was so overwhelmed with traffic that it shut down. Another site that came to Damore's defense was crippled by a denial-of-service attack from unknown parties. The mainstream media quickly picked up the controversy. "At Google, Memo on Gender and Diversity Sparks Firestorm," headlined the *Wall Street Journal*.

The controversy got so hot that Google's CEO, Sundar Pichai, canceled his vacation and flew back to Mountain View to handle the crisis. Pichai issued a harshly worded rebuke, saying, "We strongly support the right of Googlers to express themselves, and much of what was in that memo is fair to debate, regardless of whether a vast majority of Googlers disagree with it." That said, Pichai continued, "to suggest a group of our colleagues have traits that make them less biologically suited to that work is offensive and not OK . . . The memo has clearly impacted our co-workers, some of whom are hurting and feel judged based on their gender. Our co-workers shouldn't have to worry that each time they open their mouths to speak in a meeting, they have to prove that they are not like the memo states, being 'agreeable' rather than 'assertive,' showing a 'lower stress tolerance,' or being 'neurotic.'"

Internally, Google executives engaged in an intense debate about what to do. Within a few days of the memo's release, Damore was fired.

Pichai promised to hold a company town hall to discuss the situation. But, just thirty minutes before the meeting, he canceled it, citing security concerns (some employees said they were being harassed after their questions were leaked online). The next day—while nuclear tensions ramped up between the United States and North Korea—the most popular article in the *New York Times* was an op-ed calling for Pichai's resignation. It is not an exaggeration to say that, for a solid week in Silicon Valley, this memo was the main topic of conversation.

I interviewed Damore just two days after his firing. He Skyped into our Bloomberg studio from his Mountain View apartment. He seemed a little shell-shocked by the dramatic turns his life had taken, looking a bit like Richard Hendricks, the perpetually bewildered main character on HBO's *Silicon Valley.*

Damore told me the reaction to his memo both internally and externally was deeply unfair. The public reaction, he said, required that he be the scapegoat. He claimed his own boss threw him under the bus. "It's really a shame that no one in upper management could protect me," he said.

I asked Damore if he regretted writing the memo in the first place. "It's hard to regret it just because I do believe that I'm trying to make Google and the world in general a better place by not confining us to our ideological echo chambers," he said. He also doubled down on his belief that everything in the memo was not just true but also "scientific consensus."

Even though Damore links to scientific papers, it is fair to say that the scientific consensus is still out as to whether men and women have biological differences when it comes to traits like status seeking, neuroticism, and a preference for empathizing over systematizing. There are plenty of social scientists who insist that any differences that might be seen in large population studies are a result of culture and upbringing and not biology at all. And literally everyone agrees, including Damore, that population differences—even if they exist— say nothing about an individual's interests or abilities.

Was Damore correct in saying that Google's gender outcomes could be explained by fundamental gender disparities?

Given that we are only a couple of generations into women's full-fledged entry into higher education and the workforce, I believe that cultural stereotypes and biases are a far more likely cause, and there is a vast body of research to back this up. It's research that Google's leaders might have relied on to better explain the company's efforts to get more women in the door, which could have gone a long way toward getting all employees on board and fostering a more welcoming work environment.

Damore's real mistake, however, was more basic. I believe he was asking the wrong question. The assumptions he made in his memo remind me of the makers of those early aptitude tests who assumed good programmers could only be found among egocentric, puzzle-obsessed nerds who "didn't like people." As I've argued earlier, defined that way, women are definitely less likely to be considered good pro-grammers. Damore's criteria were slightly different but hardly broader. Like many in the industry, he took for granted that tech companies like Google should be staffed and led by people who systematize rather than empathize. The better question would be this: What are the consequences, to companies and us all, of assuming that the tech-nology industry should be dominated by one kind of person?

One of the most insightful responses to the memo that I read was posted on *Medium* by Yonatan Zunger, a Googler who happened to leave the company just days before Damore was fired. His point was not just that Damore didn't understand gender but that he didn't seem to have any real insight or understanding about what it took to be a great computer engineer. He took particular exception to Da-more's argument that certain roles at Google were, by nature, limited in "how people-oriented" they could be and that employees should "de-emphasize empathy" in order to "better reason about the facts."

Being coldly rational and solving very specific computational puz-zles, Zunger admits, is part of an engineer's job and a requirement when learning to code and in the early days of one's career. However, it is only after that stage, he says, that the "real engineering" begins. The true job of an engineer is to fix problems that exist in the real world. Those problems *always* involve understanding people. It is a challenge that requires not less empathy but more.

"Essentially, engineering is all about cooperation, collaboration, and empathy for both your colleagues and your customers," Zunger writes. "If someone told you that engineering was a field where you could get away with not dealing with people or feelings, then I'm very sorry to tell you that you have been lied to."

"Anyone can learn how to write code," he goes on. "The truly hard parts about this job are knowing which code to write, building the clear plan of what has to be done in order to achieve which goal, and building the consensus required to make that happen."

The reaction to Damore's memo by both the company's management and much of the rank and file was by and large abject horror. Erica Joy Baker, a former Google engineer, wrote, "What *is* news is that this employee felt safe enough to write and share a . . . sexist screed." Megan Smith, a former Google vice president and the chief technology officer of the United States during the Obama administration, told me the post was not just "offensive" but "incorrect," and that the discrimination that women in technology face day in and day out is "almost class action." The overwhelming criticism Damore received from colleagues seems to prove that he was an outlier at least in terms of his willingness to express his beliefs publicly.

There were, however, some women at the company who came forward to report their suspicion that Damore's assumptions might be more baked into the Google culture than the company would like to admit. Cate Huston, another former Google engineer, declared, "We know when we work with dudes like that. We know when they do our code review. We know when we find their comments on our performance review. We know." I have little doubt that the reason Damore's memo became so famous was because it revealed the toxic assumptions that exist in tech but often remain just out of sight.

BREAKING THROUGH THE SILICON CEILING

Google is a massive organization that now employs over seventy thousand people. Stereotypes of what makes a good leader and a good engineer run deep, and so they do at Google, despite the company's efforts to combat them. Susan Wojcicki wrote an impassioned response to Damore's memo in *Fortune,* acknowledging that while she has felt very supported by Google's founders, she has battled significant resistance from others. "I've had my abilities and commitment to my job questioned. I've been left out of key industry events and social gatherings. I've had meetings with external leaders where they primarily addressed the more junior male colleagues. I've had my comments frequently interrupted and my ideas ignored until they were rephrased by men. No matter how often this all happened, it still hurt."

Still, Wojcicki, Mayer, and Sandberg all broke through the "Silicon Ceiling" in their own way. There are lessons to be learned in the stories we've created about them (or didn't create in Wojcicki's case). These stories deserve our attention because they will have a lasting impact as a new generation of women struggles to climb the tech industry ladder.

Wojcicki is the only one left at Google. As the CEO of YouTube, she's grown revenues by billions of dollars (total YouTube revenues could surpass $12 billion in 2017, according to one third-party analyst) and launched a new TV subscription business to take on Netflix, streaming services, and cable companies. *Forbes* recently ranked her as the eighth most powerful woman in the world. Nevertheless, the media has never gushed over Susan Wojcicki, nor has it picked her apart. What it has done instead is virtually ignore her—an oversight that becomes more astonishing the more you look at her career.

In fact, not only did Wojcicki help pioneer Google's advertising models; she was also the lead in two of the company's most critical acquisitions, including the purchase of YouTube itself—for $1.65 billion in 2006. It's now one of the company's crown jewels. Wojcicki also oversaw Google's deal to buy the online advertising company DoubleClick in 2007 for the more breathtaking sum of $3.1 billion, giving the company a critical opening into the display-ad business.

The first mom on staff, Wojcicki has had five children in her twenty years at Google and has unapologetically made them a priority, priding herself on being home by 6:00 p.m. for family dinners. She doesn't pretend to be a supermom. When I met her for the first time, at a speaking engagement in 2015, and marveled at her ability to run You-Tube while raising five kids, she frankly volunteered that she had plenty of help at home.

One job she hasn't delegated is breast-feeding, and she's even open about that. When she attended the World Economic Forum in Davos in 2016, she stored two containers of her breast milk on the snowy ledge outside her hotel window and tweeted a photo of the setup with the comment "One advantage of the cold weather at #Davos2016 is it's easy to store breast milk. No freezer required."

The Davos tweet is one example of Wojcicki's overall approach to work and family: she doesn't seem to separate her mom and executive mom personas. She has talked openly about being the "mom of Google," nurturing company projects and taking pride in how the company grew and matured. And she thinks the time constraints of motherhood have made her a better executive.

"When I'm in the office, I am really, really focused and I'm prioritizing," she told me. "I can't stay there until midnight. I can't work weekends." Because of the time pressure, she says, she isn't tempted to waste the company's time on problematic projects. "Let's just forget about all those other things that are growing slowly; they're not going anywhere. I don't have time for that. I'm gonna focus on the big ideas, and we're gonna get them done *now*," Wojcicki told me.

Despite her impact on Google, and her profound effect on the worlds of advertising and publishing, Wojcicki is largely unknown outside the tech industry. Google her name, and the number of results is hardly impressive: about the same as an average baseball player and fewer than many entrepreneurs who are far less successful than she is. In an American culture that has glorified and glamorized internet pioneers, Wojcicki's story remains largely untold. That's partly because she deliberately chooses to keep a low public profile. But even if she doesn't sing her own praises, why haven't others taken notice and told her story? As a journalist, I can think of one reason: it's easier to get a story printed or aired if it fits a preconceived idea. The story of the internet, the media has decided, is the tale of internet start-ups driven by brilliant nerds or bros of a certain age. The story of a brilliant woman who every day manages to prioritize both her work and her family just doesn't fit that stereotype of the high-rolling, risk-taking genius tech revolutionary.

THE RISE AND FALL OF MARISSA MAYER

Only forty-two (as of this writing), Marissa Mayer has received a lot of press in the first half of her work life. Reporters frequently note her blond, fashion-conscious, all-American beauty. Mayer seemed comfortable in the spotlight, happy to step in as a spokesperson for Google's media-shy founders. For many years she flourished at Google before being pushed out of Page's inner circle after a reorganization in 2010. She went from being search product head to vice president of location and local services, a change that many industry observers saw as a step down. Page's reasons were never clearly spelled out, but insiders report that over the years Mayer had become a sharply polarizing figure whose colleagues either loved her or couldn't stand her. Mayer often had a strict vision she would try to implement, and it often rubbed people the wrong way. Of course, being prickly and uncompromising has often been a lauded attribute for male leaders in tech. "Steve Jobs had a very top-down thing going on for him, and that worked for Apple," Laura Holmes said. "Did it work better for Apple because he was a man? I don't know, so it's kind of hard to say."

In June 2012, about a year after she was moved out of the inner circle, Mayer arranged a meeting with Sergey Brin. The quirky Google co-founder wheeled into her office on Rollerblades (twenty minutes late, in typical Brin fashion), and Mayer told him the news: she was leaving Google to become CEO of Yahoo. Brin was magnanimous, wished her luck, and famously told her to "be bold."

But Mayer had already been bold. In accepting the Yahoo offer, she was leaving the rocket ship that was Google to try to save an iconic company that was in a death spiral. She became the youngest of just twenty women CEOs running Fortune 500 businesses at the time.

Just a few hours after the official announcement, the news got even more interesting. That was when the world learned Mayer was also the first woman to become CEO of such a large public company while pregnant. For months, she had chosen to keep the pregnancy a secret from most; she didn't even tell Brin in their resignation conversation. But by late afternoon, Mayer decided it was safest to announce this twist before the rumor mill got started (she was already twenty-eight weeks along). She decided to call the journalist Pattie Sellers, known for hosting *Fortune*'s Most Powerful Women Summit, but had to ring her multiple times before Sellers finally returned her call. "I've got a story for you, and you need to write it right now," Mayer said. In the story, Mayer revealed not only that she was pregnant but also that she planned to take only the briefest of maternity leaves in order to focus on Yahoo. As the news shot around the world, journalists, pundits, and fellow moms instantly weighed in to suggest she was shirking her responsibilities as a mother, a business leader, or both. *Forbes* wrote, "New Yahoo CEO Marissa Mayer Is Pregnant. Does It Matter?" and "The Pregnant CEO: Should You Hate Marissa Mayer?," while *Fortune* ran the headline "Marissa Mayer's Brief Maternity

Leave: Progress or Workaholism?" One blogger quipped, "Marissa Mayer becomes CEO of Yahoo and proves women cannot have it all."

If Mayer had been a man expecting a child, none of those stories would have been written. The press probably wouldn't have thought it was important; in fact, journalists very likely wouldn't even have known.

Does Mayer think she was treated differently by the press and industry analysts because she was a woman? "Anything that's odd or unusual gets more scrutiny, and I think it got more scrutiny because it was odd or unusual. The pregnancy, being a woman, it's correlative, not causal," Mayer told me when I met her in 2016 at Yahoo headquarters. "Is it because people like to scrutinize women more? No, it's because people like to scrutinize."

By that point, Mayer had been leading the company for four years and pointed to new revenue streams that she had grown to $2 billion. She had, however, spent big on poor acquisitions and ultimately failed to turn the company around. When she and I spoke, Mayer had recently struck a deal to sell what was left of Yahoo to Verizon, but there were complications. Hackers had compromised one billion user accounts (in 2017, it was revealed all three billion accounts were affected), and the deal was in peril. Despite the stress, however, Mayer seemed as calm and in charge as ever; it was just another high-stakes moment in a life that has been filled with them.

In those years, she had given birth to her first child, a boy, and, in another headline-sparking move, set up a nursery for him at her office. She'd also had a pair of identical twin daughters in 2015, then just a year old. Even though Mayer has made it clear that she doesn't feel the press treated her unfairly, I wondered aloud if all the negativity about her choices around work and motherhood had ever gotten to her. If all the criticism ever hurt her feelings.

"Overall, no, I was really pretty blind to all of it. Every now and then, you just sort of have to let the pettiness end," Mayer reflected. "There were literally hundreds if not thousands of articles, prime ministers commenting on my maternity leave. I didn't say it was appropriate for people in your country or anyone other than me, but I just chose to rise above it." She adds, "I don't think [the criticism] comes from an angry place."

But didn't it bother her that everything she said and did seemed to be taken as some kind of broader social statement about working motherhood?

"I'm not trying to do that. I'm trying to say this is what's right for me, given my circumstances," Mayer told me. "I had been planning a six-month maternity leave at Google; it would have been glorious. There was no way I could have come to Yahoo for two weeks and be gone for six months. Life changes, and in the moment, I needed to come back more quickly."

What Mayer doesn't say is that it was a no-win situation. Had she taken a longer maternity leave, no doubt she would have been criticized for imperiling Yahoo's future, or even for accepting the job in the first place. When she set up an office nursery so she could be closer to her baby, she was accused of setting a double standard by enjoying a privilege not available to lower-level employees. When Mayer ended Yahoo's work-from-home policy, available to all but frequently used by employees who were mothers, billionaire Richard Branson told me she would be on the wrong side of history. What got buried in the avalanche of coverage was the rationale for Mayer's decision: that some Yahoo employees (both men and women) had not appeared in the office for some time and she questioned their productivity—something Mayer needed to increase, across the company, if Yahoo was going to stop spinning around the drain. It seems unlikely that a new CEO who swept in and changed Yahoo's policy would have drawn much notice, much less criticism—assuming that new CEO was a man.

In the spring of 2017, the business wires lit up again with news about Mayer. With Verizon's $4.5 billion purchase of Yahoo about to close, she was expected to step away from the company. Over her time as Yahoo CEO, the stock price more than tripled, thanks in large part to the company's lucrative investment in the Chinese e-commerce giant Alibaba, yet Mayer seemed to have acquired even more detractors. Her payout package, estimated to be close to $190 million, was widely criticized.

Of our three Google heroines, Mayer, in my mind, is the one who most attempted to step into the stereotype of the rock star entrepreneur, which had been mostly reserved for men. That she wasn't able to turn Yahoo around like Jobs turned around Apple after his return in 1997 has engendered the story that this woman didn't have the right stuff. Here's another story that might be told: Mayer took a grand risk and may have done the best anyone could have, after being dealt a losing hand.

LEANING IN

Sheryl Sandberg's impact on both tech and our cultural conversation about women in the workplace has been more dramatic than both Mayer's and Wojcicki's. I suspect that the full impact of her influence is still gaining force. In 2007, Sandberg—who was then still a VP at Google—was considering a job as a senior executive at the Washington Post Company. Then she met Mark Zuckerberg at a holiday party. After several meetings, dinners, breakfasts, and phone calls, she joined Facebook as its COO, Zuckerberg's number two, in 2008. Google's top brass discussed with Sandberg the possibility of her becoming the search engine's CFO, but the opportunity at Facebook was bigger.

Letting Sandberg go was a big mistake.

Facebook pre-Sandberg had a classic Brotopia reputation. One particularly cringe-inducing video interview with Zuckerberg circa 2005 shows the mostly male Facebook staff doing keg stands in their Palo Alto office. It was known as a boys' club where the fastest way to get ahead was to become Zuckerberg's buddy. One former employee said that Facebook was "basically a frat" before Sandberg showed up. Clearly, Sandberg's hire was part of an effort to bring some maturity to the organization.

In her first years at the company, Sandberg built Facebook's business model from scratch, and it is now Google's biggest competitor in the advertising business. Under her direction, Facebook's revenues multiplied nearly a hundred times between 2008, when Sandberg signed on, and 2016, when the company generated $10 billion in profit. She also immediately started counting the number of Facebook's female engineers and started a speaker series for women at the company, inviting guests like Gloria Steinem—similar to the events she had organized at Google.

In 2010, Sandberg gave a now-famous TED talk in which she called out the lack of women leaders in business and government and called on women in the workforce not to "lean back" prematurely in their careers. Two years later, the *Atlantic* published an article by the public policy expert Anne-Marie Slaughter titled "Why Women Still Can't Have It All" in which she attacked Sandberg directly. "Although couched in terms of encouragement, Sandberg's exhortation contains more than a note of reproach," Slaughter wrote. "We who have made it to the top, or are striving to get there, are essentially saying to the women in the generation behind us: 'What's the matter with you?'"

Slaughter's article came out when I was seven months pregnant with my first child. The subhead summarized her point: "It's time to stop fooling ourselves, says a woman who left a position of power: the women who have managed to be both mothers and top professionals are superhuman, rich, or self-employed."

As I read it, with growing trepidation, I began to doubt my ability to succeed as a working mom. Slaughter had quit a high-profile, demanding job in the State Department (under Hillary Clinton) because her family needed her. Maybe, I thought, I would have to quit my job too. That night, I went to bed and cried myself to sleep, even though crying is the worst thing you can do when you're going to be on television the next day.

In the morning, I re-watched Sandberg's TED talk and her commencement addresses at Barnard College and Harvard Business School. I took notes. Then I mustered up the courage to email her. Though I'd reported on Sandberg's work at Facebook, we had never met in person and she might have had no idea who I was, but for some reason I felt compelled to thank her for putting herself out there on this sadly controversial subject. I had no idea at the time that she was busy writing *Lean In,* a book that would become an international phenomenon.

I gasped aloud when, thirty seconds later, Sandberg's reply hit my in-box. She offered her congratulations on my pregnancy and gave me her cell-phone number in case I ever wanted to talk. Three weeks later, Sandberg and I connected and she shared many of her thoughts on work and family now chronicled in *Lean In.* I even got a taste of the "radical candor" that Kim Scott had experienced with Sandberg at Google. I never really came close to quitting my job, but my conversation with Sandberg gave me the motivation and confidence I needed to stop questioning myself so much. She made me truly believe that not only was it okay to want to be a working mom, it was actually possible to do a good job at both work and home.

By the time I called on Sandberg again to ask for an interview for this book, *Lean In* had become an international bestseller. Thousands of "Lean In circles" had sprouted around the world, where women would gather to share their stories. But the book also created a cottage industry for writers—virtually all of them women—to critique the advice Sandberg was offering. "Why I Hate Sheryl Sandberg," "The False Promise of Sheryl Sandberg's Theory of Change," and "Why I Won't Lean In" were just a few of the headlines in prominent newspapers and journals. Many of the writers proclaimed that Sandberg, a billionaire, simply couldn't understand the plight of regular moms who are struggling to get food on the table. Some writers targeted both Sandberg and Mayer simultaneously, as in Joanne Bamberger's 2013 *USA Today* column "The New Mommy Wars": "Mayer and Sandberg, even if they have good intentions, are setting back the cause of working mothers."

A front page *New York Times* article quoted a female business consultant who said that Sandberg was "blaming other women for not trying hard enough," and *New York Times* op-ed columnist Maureen Dowd wrote that Sandberg "has co-opted the vocabulary and romance of a social movement not to sell a cause, but herself." The *Lean In* backlash became so powerful that many commentators were happy to criticize the book while openly admitting that they hadn't read it.

It was the mother of all pile ons. And, in my view, undeserved. Sandberg acknowledges that not every woman wants what she wants; in the book, she stipulates that many women are not looking to juggle a family and a career or ascend the corporate ranks. She was speaking to the women who wanted to succeed at both. As one of them, I can say she inspired me: I now go out of my way to give other moms the same pep talk when they feel the same self-doubt. Sandberg made me realize how powerful women can be when we help each other.

Sandberg lived through something of a replay when she published her second book, *Option B,* written after the tragic death of her husband, Dave Goldberg. In the midst of the deepest despair, Sandberg picked herself up and went back to work in ten days. Some bloggers said it was too soon. She started dating again after about ten months. Again, everyone seemed to have an opinion.

These writers are all entitled to their reactions (as are the many writers—and readers—who found merit in both books). Work, family, death—all of these arouse strong emotions and go to the very core of who we are as a society. And as a woman, I know how easy it is to get defensive when being judged about career and parenting choices. That said, there is something about the media's desire to tear down

Mayer and Sandberg that suggests something very broken in America. Our culture just does not understand how to deal with extraordinarily successful women. No one expects the media to treat Mayer and Sandberg with kid gloves, but the most vitriolic critiques they received were out of proportion to what these women were communicating. We just don't do this with men.

If we feel compelled to tear down the handful of superstar women in tech, who will want to go down that path? Who will want to be the next pregnant CEO? Who will want to share her hard-earned career advice with the rest of us?

You could argue that Sandberg's role at Facebook and the platform she has created with *Lean In* give her greater influence than almost any other woman in our world. When we spoke, she made a passionate case for more women in tech and acknowledged that when it comes to hiring and retaining women, Facebook and the industry have a long way to go. "People in tech are having a lot of impact on our culture," she pointed out. "The next person in my role at Facebook will likely have a technical background. In addition to that, technical skills are increasingly important for women in any industry. Whether you go into retail or construction or banking or anything, technical skills have become more and more important. And I think will continue to be more important, so I think it really matters that women get technical experience and technical degrees."

I asked, why aren't women advancing faster in Silicon Valley specifically? "Some women are told they can't. Others are told they shouldn't. Across the board, women don't get the support they need," Sandberg said. "Women are held back by a lot of things—including sexual discrimination and harassment. In addition, a lot of what's hurting women now are the insidious, constant, smaller things. Every day things happen that can really quickly add up." Maybe your boss interrupts you or gives credit for your ideas to someone else. It is difficult to complain because often the boss isn't even aware of the behavior, Sandberg said.

I've met with so many women in Silicon Valley who feel that it's worse than that. They feel as if they are leaning in with all their might and it's not working for them. One prominent female executive told me, "No matter how hard you lean in, you're not going anywhere if the door is nailed shut."

So I asked Sandberg if she agrees that some women in the industry may find themselves in especially toxic waters. "I totally agree with that. I always did," she replied. But waiting for the environment or attitudes to change isn't an acceptable option for Sandberg. "Women in leadership will help create the environment for more women in leadership," she said. It may sound like something of a catch-22, but Sandberg doubled down. "Women will create the institutional change we need."

I believe this will happen. How quickly depends, in part, on how the stories of women like Sandberg, Mayer, Wojcicki, and others are told and understood by the next generation. There may be cracks in the Silicon Ceiling, but it is far from shattered.

4

THE TIPPING POINT: WOMEN ENGINEERS SPEAK OUT

O N FEBRUARY 19, 2017, a young engineer named Susan Fowler published a scathing blog post about sexual harassment she had experienced while working at Uber. She posted it on her personal blog, but it almost immediately went viral. Social media exploded with rage at the Uber empire, a frequent target of user animosity. The tech press and the mainstream media soon followed. Fowler stayed mostly silent. She didn't talk to the press until seven months later, when she spoke to the *New York Times,* and a few days later, sat down with me to give an interview for this book.

I met twenty-six-year-old Fowler for breakfast at a diner near her home outside San Francisco. She was seven months pregnant with her first child and still trying to come to grips with her new role as the whistle-blower of Brotopia and defender of women in technology. "It's been really overwhelming," Fowler told me. "I just kind of let it play out in its own way because I knew I was just showing the tip of the iceberg. There was so much more that was coming." Fowler joined Uber in November 2015 as a site reliability engineer, or SRE, part of a team that was responsible for keeping the massive app up and running. Fowler did not have the typical Silicon Valley pedigree. The daughter of an evangelical preacher, she is the second-oldest of seven children, born and raised in Yarnell, a small town in rural Arizona. "We were very poor," Fowler told me. The family lived in the church parsonage and her mother homeschooled the children until Fowler turned twelve. At that point, Fowler said she started working full-time in minimum-wage jobs to support the family. She was a nanny and a stable hand, among other low-wage jobs. She kept reading every night, even designing her own high school curriculum. She thought she could never catch up, but managed to get into Arizona State University on a scholarship, then transferred to the University of Pennsylvania, where she studied math and physics. It was in a physics lab that she discovered coding. "They would get data from running these giant experiments and you have to write code to analyze the data and look for new particles. And I *loved* it. It was so wonderful, straightforward, and logical." She debated going into academia, but instead decided to try her luck in Silicon Valley.

Getting a job in technology, as a woman with an unconventional background, wasn't quite so straightforward. "I got a lot of doubt in all my interviews, like, 'Oh, you're not a real computer science student,'" Fowler recalled. "Even now, people will say, 'Are you a real engineer?'" After she worked at a couple of start-ups, however, a recruiter reached out to her about a job at Uber. She said the company told her the engineering team was 25 percent women. "There weren't any women in my physics lab, or at the companies I had already worked at, and so I thought that would be amazing." The only problem is, it wasn't true. At one point, women accounted for less than 6 percent of her team. And things got weird almost immediately.

On Fowler's first official day of work (after a couple of weeks of training), her new manager made a pass at her over the internal company chat system. He was in an open relationship, he told her, and his girlfriend was having an easy time finding new partners but he wasn't. "He was trying to stay out of trouble at work, he said, but he couldn't help getting in trouble, because he was looking for women to have sex with," Fowler wrote. "It was clear that he was trying to get me to have sex with him."

"It was just too absurd," Fowler recalled. "You just don't proposition your subordinate for sex, like ever, but especially not on their first day on your team." Fowler said she took screen shots of the messages and reported the manager to the human resources department immediately. To her surprise, she was told that this was her manager's first offense, so he wouldn't get more than a warning. Plus, he was a "high performer," so they didn't want to punish him for "what was probably just an innocent mistake."

Fowler believed she had no choice but to transfer to another department. As she met more women engineers within the company, she realized many had stories similar to her own, some involving the very same manager who had come on to Fowler—meaning her case had most certainly not been his first offense. When she pointed this out to HR, Fowler said, the representative simply denied it. "It was such a blatant lie that there was really nothing I could do," she wrote. Eventually, the offending manager left the company, though it was unclear why.

All of this played out, Fowler reported, against a department culture that had, at that time, devolved into a "game-of-thrones political war," with managers openly fighting and undermining each other, leaving projects abandoned and priorities unclear. "We all lived under fear that our teams would be dissolved, there would be another re-org, and we'd have to start on yet another new project with an impossible deadline," Fowler wrote. "It was an organization in complete, unrelenting chaos."

What happened to Fowler next is not simply offensive but petty and ridiculous for a company that had by then expanded to thousands of employees around the world.

Hoping to work in a "less chaotic" department than her own, Fowler requested another transfer but was told it would not be granted due to "undocumented performance problems." That bewildered her, because the performance reviews she had seen had been exemplary and there were other teams that wanted her. Her next review was positive, so again she tried to transfer. At that point, she was told she was still not eligible, because her performance score had been retroactively recalibrated. Fowler says HR explained that she didn't appear to have an "upward career trajectory" and needed to prove herself as an engineer. This explanation was particularly suspect, given that Fowler was publishing an engineering book, *Production-Ready Microservices: Building Standardized Systems Across an Engineering Organization*, and had spoken at major tech conferences—quite impressive for a rank-and-file employee. Fowler says she went home and cried. The newly negative review would not only hurt her take-home pay but also disqualify her from continuing in an Uber-sponsored graduate computer science program at Stanford that she had been attending.

At a later point, Fowler overheard her manager boasting that while other teams were "losing their women engineers left and right," his team still had some. She implied that he deliberately blocked her transfer out of the department in order to make himself look good. In the meantime, the number of women in Fowler's part of the organization was dwindling. When she confronted a director at an all-hands meeting about it, "his reply was, in a nutshell, that the women of Uber just needed to step up and be better engineers," Fowler said.

The rank sexism wasn't the company's only problem. "There was a lot of day drinking and a lot of weird shit. It was usually people that were managers or tech leads doing the inviting. They would be like, 'Oh, everyone, let's go get drinks' or 'let's go to a strip club.'" After going out a couple of times, Fowler told me she just kept her head down and coded. "The culture was just so fucked. It just led me to want to be disconnected to the point where I'm just going to get my work done, go home, and not interact with anyone."

In perhaps the most ludicrous incident Fowler described, Uber ordered leather jackets for all the men on the engineering team but not for the women. When Fowler complained to the head of her section, he emailed her, saying that because there were so many men, Uber could get a discount. But he couldn't get a bulk discount on the women's jackets, because they needed so few of them, so they could not justify placing an order for Uber's female engineers. "I replied and said that I was sure Uber SRE could find room in their budget to buy leather jackets for the, what, *six women* if it could afford to buy them for *over a hundred and twenty men*," Fowler wrote. "The director replied back, saying that if we women really wanted equality, then we should realize we were getting equality by not getting the leather jackets." After all, he continued, it would not be "equal or fair" to give women jackets that cost more than the men's; therefore the women should look for other jackets at the same bulk-order price.

Fowler forwarded "this absurd chain of emails to HR," and a meeting followed. "The HR rep began . . . by asking me if I had noticed that *I* was the common theme in all of the reports I had been making, and that if I had ever considered that I might be the problem," Fowler wrote. A week later, in a one-on-one meeting, her manager stated that she could easily be fired for making these complaints because California is an "at-will" employment state, meaning employees can be terminated at any time without cause. At that point, Fowler decided to leave—and had an offer within a week.

What makes Fowler's rendition of her Uber experience even more compelling is that she is not entirely negative. She closes her post by talking about how proud she is of her team. "We loved our work, we loved the engineering challenges, we loved making this crazy Uber machine work," she wrote. The reader can't write her off as a complainer who could never be happy. In the aftermath of the blog post, Fowler claimed that a "smear campaign" had been launched against her that aimed to dig up dirt on her by contacting the people she knew. Uber denied being behind any such campaign.

Fowler's post put Uber once again at the epicenter of public backlash. A couple of weeks earlier, a wave of users had deleted the app over perceptions that Travis Kalanick was aligned with newly elected President Trump. And before that, Kalanick had caught flack for making a joke in response to a question about his own "skyrocketing desirability" in *GQ* magazine, saying, "Yeah, we call that Boob-er," referring to "women on demand." But the worst for the Uber CEO was yet to come.

Over the next few weeks, my colleagues at Bloomberg released video of Kalanick getting into an unflattering argument with an Uber driver. *Recode* revealed that Uber's new head of engineering, Amit Singhal, had left Google after being accused of sexual harassment. A story broke in *The Information* about several Uber executives, including Kalanick and his then girlfriend, visiting an escort-karaoke bar in Seoul. That evening in 2014, four male executives reportedly picked female escorts out of a lineup. Uber found itself at the center of a firestorm, accused of creating a hard-charging culture of sexism and male entitlement.

Fowler's story and the ensuing tsunami of bad press struck a nerve in the Valley. As if on cue, a few weeks later, the *Atlantic* published a cover story titled "Why Is Silicon Valley So Awful to Women?"

BREAKING BREAD WITH WOMEN ENGINEERS

As it happened, the *Atlantic* revealed its cover story the same evening I had invited a dozen women engineers to my house to discuss this very question. With the Fowler story on everyone's mind, I knew there would be no lack of opinions.

The women made small talk in my entryway until Postmates arrived at the door with our dinner on demand. We each filled a plate and squeezed into a circle on my living room floor. The group was diverse in terms of age, sexual identity, race, and career background. In attendance were current and former employees of Uber, Google, Apple, and Facebook as well as various start-ups. Some were graduates of schools such as Stanford and Harvard, others had gone to less elite schools, and at least one had not finished college. Upstairs, my husband had finally managed to soothe our screaming newborn—a distraction that a couple of mothers in the group sympathized with—and the room quieted.

My first question got straight to the point: "What do you think of Susan Fowler?"

After a few moments of silence, and a little encouragement from me, the women began to weigh in.

"It's frustrating to hear so many people say, 'Wow, this is so shocking,'" began Tracy Chou, a thirty-year-old former Pinterest engineer who had moved to working on her own start-up. "It's like, we've been telling you this for a long time. And it's not isolated to Uber. Travis embodies a lot of the things that are easy to hate, so it makes Uber a target, but I don't think the things that came out of Susan's post were that unique."

Fowler's story had been pretty horrifying. She had, after all, been propositioned for sex on her first official day at the job and had received no support from the HR department. Yet the group expressed immediate and unanimous agreement with Chou's assessment. Lydia Fernandez, an Uber software engineer, piped up forcefully from my couch: "The only people I know who were shocked were men."

The crowd groaned in agreement. Ana Medina, a twenty-three-year-old engineer who also worked at Uber, said, "It's easy to question, do I even belong here? Because so much crap happens day by day." Medina had worked on the SRE team with Fowler at Uber and backed up the legitimacy of her story.

Leah McGowen-Hare, an executive at Salesforce, likened the shock she heard from men in response to Susan Fowler's post to the horror expressed by white liberals after the 2016 U.S. presidential election. "Hearing people's reaction to Susan and all the men, like, 'Oh my God, it's happening!' was sort of like when Trump won the election and white people were like, 'Oh my God, racism is still alive.' Big surprise! Nothing shocks me. I've been through it as a woman. I've been through it as an African American."

If Fowler's post had contained nothing very surprising, I asked, then why had it gone viral? Chou suggested that Fowler's story had had such an effect because it was impossible to brush off—not because her claims were so shocking, but because she was the perfect victim. "She is a white woman who . . . has the technical credibility of releasing a book and had all the proper documentation [of her harassment]," Chou said.

A young Google engineer, Lea Coligado, agreed. "She is in a good position [to defend herself]. If she were a woman of color, it would have been a lot harder for her story to come out. The angry black or angry Hispanic woman trope would have come out."

Though they were fully cognizant of Fowler's various advantages as a poster child, none of the women suggested that Fowler didn't deserve support or credit for coming forward. As the evening continued, and every one of the twelve women in my living room shared a story, or several, about the abuse and discrimination she had suffered or witnessed, what became clear was that the decision about whether to come foward was usually a very difficult one. While Fowler might have been the perfect victim, most people are not, and the stakes in such a decision are gut wrenchingly high. Is refusing to stay silent about unwanted sexual advances worth risking your reputation, your career advancement, your livelihood? In the harassment stories these women told me, what one woman called the "little things" often felt too small to report, but they happened constantly and added up quickly. The big things were often embarrassing and scary, and people found it hard to come forward when there was little promise of a positive resolution at the end.

UNWANTED ADVANCES, 24/7

When I asked if anyone in the room wanted to share a "Susan Fowler" type of experience, Laura Holmes, senior product manager at Google, was the first to speak up. She hesitated as she started to tell the story, as if gathering courage, then continued in a steady tone.

It was the summer of 2008, just as a new wave of tech companies, including Uber and Airbnb, was about to take off. Holmes, then a computer science student at Stanford, got an internship at a hot new photo-app start-up in San Francisco named Cooliris. One evening, she and her co-workers went out for drinks at the Ruby Skye night-club. Around 2:00 a.m., Holmes informed one of the male engineers that she was about to go home. Apparently, he had had too much to drink. "He was about six foot three, and he told me I was not going to leave," Holmes recalled. "He put his hand around my neck and tried to choke me."

As Holmes recounted this story, there were a few gasps from the women in the living room and then silence. This wasn't some sick joke, Holmes went on; this man was angry. Fear overtook her. "I im-mediately burst into tears," Holmes remembered. A bystander inter-vened, and the man's grip was broken. Holmes never told anyone else at the company about it. As is common among Silicon Valley start-ups, Holmes said Cooliris did not have a human resources depart-ment. Instead, she buried that moment and went back to work the next day. It was the most dramatic, but far from the only offensive, incident to occur during her internship.

Sexist behavior often comes from the top, and in Holmes's telling that was the case at Cooliris, where the young CEO, Soujanya Bhumkar, gave the entire staff copies of the *Kama Sutra,* an illus-trated guide to sexual positions. Holmes said Bhumkar would often joke, "Thank God we don't have an HR team," a phrase that other employees at the company took up and repeated. One day, Bhumkar also passed out toothbrushes imprinted with the company's core metrics. "He said, 'So you can think about our metrics when you wake up in the morning,'" Holmes recalled. "And he made a joke that he would print them on condoms so we could think about them at night." Bhumkar then held up a three-pack of condoms, though he never did pass them out. I reached out to Bhumkar several times for his reaction to these comments, but he did not respond.

Holmes, who hoped to become a product manager at Cooliris, was told to make special efforts to build alliances with the engineers, so she scheduled some collegial lunches. While she was walking to the restaurant with one particular engineer, things got very uncomfortable.

"He said, 'I'm offensive, I bet I can offend you,'" Holmes remembered. Because she was "trying to be one of the bros," she decided to play along. "He gets close to my face and says, 'You're so fucking dumb, and you don't know shit. The only thing you're good for is being taken out to the back parking lot and being raped.'" Yep, she told him, that sure was offensive.

"It was only the two of us. I was thinking that 'oh, this is what the industry is like. This is bad. I didn't sign up for this, but I guess I better get used to it,'" Holmes said. "Things were pretty atrocious, and I could have filed a lawsuit . . . But at the age of twenty-three, I didn't want to be the whistle-blower; I didn't want to be defined by this." Her tone was almost apologetic, but as she looked around the room, it was clear that no one present was going to second-guess the difficult decision she had made. No ambitious, hardworking woman wants to be defined or thwarted by a few boneheaded men they have little choice but to work with.

Holmes's story broke the ice. For the next three hours, each woman told her tale.

Chou spoke up next, describing her experience as an intern at Google in 2007. "I was hit on every other day," Chou said. "One person, eleven years my senior, that I had to work on a project with asked me, 'Do you want to go watch a movie in the conference room? We'll close the doors, turn out the lights, and pull the blinds.'" He even made her a T-shirt with his name on it and left it on her desk.

"People didn't take me seriously," Chou said. "I just felt like I was kind of their pet intern and that I wasn't there to actually get anything done." She said another male intern once told her she looked tense and offered her a massage, adding that the massage would be better if she lay down.

While Chou didn't complain at the time, those experiences built her resolve to see that the industry changed. In 2013, when she was an engineer at Pinterest, she attended the Grace Hopper Celebration of Women in Computing and heard Sheryl Sandberg speak. "Sheryl was talking, and she had one line about how the numbers of women in tech were dropping precipitously. I just thought, 'Who has any numbers? How do you know they are dropping? No one has any numbers.'" In that moment, Chou realized that it was crazy for this data-driven industry not to track and publicly release such statistics. And she felt it was time to hold companies accountable.

After the conference, Chou wrote a *Medium* essay demanding that top tech firms release statistics on the gender breakdown of their employees. With her employer's permission, Chou revealed the percentage of Pinterest's engineers who were women (12 percent at that time), putting the pressure on other tech companies to keep the ball rolling. Like Fowler's post, Chou's essay became the talk of the Valley. It took some time, but most of the major tech companies ponied up. In 2014, Apple, Google, and Facebook revealed their diversity data, and, unsurprisingly, the picture was dismal. Not only were women outnumbered, but in the most critical and most senior positions they were grossly outnumbered. The women who do work at these companies are generally more junior, a trend that preserves an old boys' club power dynamic that often works against the young women's advancement.

The import of the numbers that Chou had forced the industry to reveal was something that every woman in the group was familiar with. Because engineering teams are often made up of only a handful of people, there's often just one woman, if that, on every team. These women are alone in large groups of men all day long, alone at company off sites and at social gatherings after hours. During our evening together, many of the women in my group reported being bombarded with sexual advances, no matter how hard they tried to convey that they were not available or not interested.

"You get sexual advances and people hitting on you 24/7," said Ana Medina. "First of all, it's emotionally draining because you have to be turning down people every damn time." Then, if something goes wrong, especially while socializing outside the office, it's difficult to report. "You can't go to HR and say, 'I was drinking with so-and-so, and this thing happened.'"

And employees in these companies spend a lot of time drinking. Medina confirmed Fowler's account of Uber employees using and abusing alcohol. Uber, she said, provided kegs of beer on multiple floors. For a while, the kegs were open twenty-four hours a day; then the company started a new policy, locking the kegs until 6:00 p.m. But the rules were never too rigid, and sometimes the kegs would still be open the following morning. "We would start drinking in the office as early as 12:00 or 1:00 p.m.," Medina said. "Teams had their own bars; people had their own bottles. Sometimes you'd start drinking from people's own supply." Managers were flexible, Medina added: "As long as your work was getting done, it didn't matter where the fuck you were or how hungover you were or what you did that night . . . There were times we'd leave the office [midday] and just never come back."

Medina admitted that she probably shouldn't have been drinking during work hours, even if her team members were doing it and the culture condoned it. But she joined Uber as a software engineering intern when she was twenty-two, and few people make their best choices right out of college. Uber's drinking culture "was free drinks and fun," she said—except that during these benders with co-workers, she said, she was often subject to their sexual advances. "People were drunk and persistent, and a lot of the people were people I was close with as engineers. Having engineers come ask you if they can take you home or say they would like to cuddle with you, that was the awkward part. I'm way too nice, and I let it slide on a daily basis."

Many of the women pointed out that declining to drink with the boys is a double-edged sword. If women don't participate, they're seen as uptight and not team players. And they risk missing out on group-bonding time, which may cost them personal and political capital within the organization. If they do participate, they're considered not serious and, worse, risk being sexualized or, as in Holmes's case, even assaulted.

As the conversation continued, there were some moments of levity. The women lamented male engineers staring at their breasts during interviews or at their behinds when the women turned their backs to write code on a whiteboard (a standard practice in tech known as whiteboard coding). "I always worry they are looking at my butt, and try to dress as not sexual as possible," said Kristen Beck, a researcher at IBM. "But then you're turning your back. I know I've got a good booty but still." A few women laughed. But, really, none of this was funny at all.

THE "ELEPHANT IN THE VALLEY"

Until recently, there hasn't been any way to quantify the harassment, sexism, and amorphous "bro culture" in the tech industry. People could dismiss misogynistic stories like Susan Fowler's as one-offs, exceptions and not the rule. But in 2016, a group of industry insiders, in conjunction with Stanford University, published a survey of women and their experiences at Silicon Valley workplaces. The "Elephant in the Valley" study (yes, that's its real name) found that of the more than two hundred women respondents (most of them having had at least ten years' experience), the vast majority—90 percent—reported witnessing sexist behavior at industry off sites and conferences. Sixty percent said they had personally been sexually harassed or received unwanted sexual advances, most of the time from a superior. Bear in mind, according to the study authors, 25 percent of the women surveyed were C-suite level; 11 percent were founders.

These women also reported the "little things": 84 percent of those surveyed said they'd been called too aggressive at work; 66 percent have felt excluded from social or networking activities because of their gender; 59 percent felt they had not gotten the same opportunities as their male counterparts. Most said questions that should have been directed to them were asked of their male peers instead, and almost half have been asked to do lower-level tasks such as taking notes or ordering food, jobs that male colleagues are not asked to do.

In addition to these statistics, the "Elephant in the Valley" surveyors collected hundreds of heretofore unpublished anonymous stories they agreed to share with me. With the help of an incredibly patient researcher, I spent hours organizing these stories into categories that included "sexual harassment," "porn use in office," "bro culture," "rape jokes," and "assault."

The data dump came in the form of a massive spreadsheet including around 250 accounts of women in tech. Their stories were an exhausting read, for both their volume and their emotional content. The largest number of complaints, by far, fell into my category of sexual harassment—inappropriate and unwanted come-ons by co-workers, bosses, or superiors. One woman working among a hundred male engineers reported being hit on repeatedly, with one engineer telling her, "If I was 20 years younger I would rock your world." There are several reports of unwanted kisses and gropes, and even of men showing up at the homes of their female colleagues expecting some form of sex and refusing to leave when asked.

Off-color remarks and sexual jokes were also a common theme in these accounts. Apparently, at tech firms, comments and jokes about sexual behavior, Viagra, porn, and even rape seem to fit right in. One woman reported, "I was walking with some male colleagues around the office at lunch, and when we found ourselves in a remote area of the building with a sketchy old door, one of them said, jokingly, 'Quick! Grab her legs, let's rape her!'" Many women had also had the uncomfortable experience of seeing male co-workers watch porn while at work and hearing them rate women in the office based on sexual attractiveness.

According to the stories, things often get really dicey at company off sites or social events. One woman said her company's designated happy-hour location was Hooters, where she listened to her boss complain about his wife. There are tales of strip clubs, of course, accounts of uncomfortable come-ons whispered into women's ears at parties, and one report of being groped in a hot tub at a company retreat. Many women felt they had no choice but to participate in these events and one reported that "only those who would party and drink excessively with the CEO on Friday nights would get promoted."

After reading dozens of the anonymous "Elephant in the Valley" stories, I noted that the women spoke in a surprising tone: more exasperated than outraged. Like the dozen women I had gathered in my living room, they were tired of the toxic culture they worked in and tired of having to explain it to those who somehow managed to ignore it. It is because of their endurance and courage, I believe, that we have reached a cultural tipping point. From here on out, ignorance of the problem can only be willful. Reactions like "Gosh, I didn't know *this* was going on" and "Is it really that bad?" are simply no longer credible. Or acceptable.

TO SUE OR NOT TO SUE

San Francisco employment lawyer Therese Lawless has taken on hundreds of discrimination cases in Silicon Valley; in 2015, she joined the legal team representing investor Ellen Pao in her lawsuit against the storied venture capital firm Kleiner Perkins Caufield & Byers. Lawless has represented plaintiffs in a variety of industries but says tech is among the worst offenders. The stress I felt after reading through all the "Elephant in the Valley" stories was nothing compared with what this lawyer endures daily.

Lawless is ethically bound not to share any specifics, but she did reveal the broad strokes of a few frightening examples from the tech industry. One client was sexually assaulted in the bushes at a company off site by a married colleague. In another instance, a man showed up at a female colleague's hotel room. He said, "Just five minutes, five minutes. I just want five minutes." When she refused to have sex with him, he began to masturbate in front of her. Generally, Lawless said, her cases involve "individuals of power using their power over women to get them to get involved with them, promising them things."

Her clients, Lawless added, almost always have trepidations about moving forward with lawsuits: "Women are often afraid to speak out because they're single, or they're supporting a family and they are fearful that if they speak out, they will be marred for life, have a scarlet letter, and never be employed anywhere. Women don't want to be the poster child."

Many of the women who consult Lawless decide, in the end, not to go public, even if they have the makings of a successful criminal case. The woman assaulted in the bushes, for example, decided not to pursue legal action out of a mixture of embarrassment and fear of backlash at work. Lawless often has to tell clients that prosecutors are reluctant to take "he said, she said" cases that they don't think they can win. She's seen prosecutors drop cases even when there was DNA evidence and signs of physical abuse.

Civil litigation is more successful, on average, but it is no sure thing. Often abusers will settle the complaints without a public trial on the condition that the court documents be sealed and that participants not talk publicly about the accusation. The legal term for this court-imposed silence is perhaps the most unfortunate in all of juris-prudence: the "gag rule." Silicon Valley companies routinely ask em-ployees to sign nondisclosure and nondisparagement agreements as part of employment contracts or settlements, meaning that women can face legal action if they speak out. Stories of harassment and discrimination live on in whispers or are simply never told.

Lawless proudly told me of one case she litigated where the abuser was fired and the female victim stayed in her job, though admitted such an outcome is rare.

What made the difference in the case you won? I asked.

"There were very powerful women in that firm," Lawless told me, "and they didn't like what they saw. They called their partners on it and said, 'This can't be.'"

SURVIVING ALL THE "LITTLE THINGS"

One of the women at my home that Sunday evening had a unique per-spective: Lydia Fernandez has seen the tech industry from both a man's perspective and a woman's, because she is transgender. I had first met Fernandez in 2011 when she was an intern with Code2040, a program that helps recruit blacks and Latinx to Silicon Valley and places them at established tech companies. At the time, Fernandez presented as male. It wasn't until 2014, just before she took a permanent job at Uber, that she came out as transgender and changed her name to Lydia.

Given that Fernandez had begun her career being seen as a man, she was particularly sensitive to what she called the "little things" she had to put up with, now that she was seen as a woman. The difference in how she was treated was "night and day," she told the group, then rendered her verdict: "I've sat on both sides of this table; this game is rigged."

For example, while presenting as male, Fernandez said, she was rarely interrupted. When she started presenting as a woman, however, men suddenly began cutting her off midsentence. Fernandez was taken aback. "It ran contrary to twenty years of [my previous] life experience," she said. Slowly but surely, she rebuilt her confidence, and soon she was back to her old self, the firebrand always ready to speak her mind; if someone cut her off, she called him on it. Confronted that way, Fernandez said, "people would double take. They are not used to a woman being like, 'Let me finish speaking.' I've had female colleagues who've said, 'You speak your mind more than any woman I've ever met.' What I've got [that most women don't] is two decades of people saying, 'Yeah, your opinion is worth hearing.'"

The rest of the women in the room clearly identified with Fernandez's description of the "little things"—the small, daily insults that build up over time. These interactions are not necessarily intentional or malicious, but they have a cumulative effect. When I used the term "mansplaining," which had just recently entered the lexicon, every woman there seemed to instantly know what it meant, and they gave me many examples.

One start-up engineer said that her male colleagues routinely question her programming, force her to revise it, then realize that her original version was best. When she critiques their work in the same way, her comments are routinely ignored. "It feels like everything that I do is wrong," she said. Her feeling is backed up by research. One study found that women's code on the open-source software community GitHub was approved more often than men's, but only if the gender of the coder was hidden. When women were identified openly, the acceptance rate of their code went down. One former engineer at Facebook recently collected data showing that female engineers received 35 percent more rejections of their code than men. Facebook's head of infrastructure told the *Wall Street Journal* that the discrepancy was based more on an engineer's rank than gender, revealing another problem: the lack of women in senior engineering roles. One engineer said that working at a big tech company is "kind of like Russian roulette," meaning that a great manager can really make women feel valued, while getting a bad manager means you're screwed.

The women in my living room told me that men who had positive things to say about their contributions too often expressed them in a patronizing way, saying, "Wow, that's *actually* a really good idea." They also complained that they are routinely sexualized, as when men comment on their outfit choices. These are the subtle slights that women experience daily, sometimes five to ten times per day.

The point isn't that any one comment or incident is going to push a woman out of tech or make her miserable at work. It's the constant emotional labor that she has to perform, day after day, just to keep her job and do her work. Often, women will not immediately blame sexism if they feel they are being mistreated or overlooked, rather they question themselves. "Did I do something wrong? Or, was I not clear enough?" they might think. These concerns wear constantly on self-esteem. Pushing against a stereotype is emotional labor that men, white men in particular, don't have to perform. Instead, they can use that energy to focus on being a great engineer. Women and minorities, on the other hand, start and end the day at an emotional deficit. It is this "death by a thousand cuts" phenomenon that wears women down—not because they are weak, or because they can't keep up, but because they are doing a whole extra job.

THE DOUBLE (AND TRIPLE) MINORITIES

In Silicon Valley, all women are fighting an uphill battle. But what about black, Latina, and Asian women? What about trans women? What about disabled women? These people are often excluded from conversations about diversity in tech because they don't have the same reality as white, cisgendered, able-bodied, upper-middle-class women. They are not just fighting implicit and explicit sexism, but sometimes two or three other isms as well, including racism, ageism, and classism. Just 2 to 3 percent of Google and Facebook employees, male and female, are black; 4 to 5 percent of them are Latinx, compared with a national population that's 13 percent black and 18 percent Latinx. People of color are a small fraction of all workers in Silicon Valley, and an even smaller fraction of that fraction are women. No wonder, then, that once we turned to the subject of life as a Silicon Valley "double minority," the discussion got very emotional.

Leah McGowen-Hare, who has two and a half decades of experience in the industry, broached the subject first. In the late 1980s, she'd wanted to be a dancer, inspired by Irene Cara in that decade's hit movie *Fame*. "My father said, 'I'll give you two years to be a dancer,' and I twirled away," said McGowen-Hare. She started college as a dance major but, ultimately, at her father's urging, switched to engineering. She joined PeopleSoft in the late 1990s and stayed on through the company's takeover by Oracle. If being a black female engineer is rare in Silicon Valley today, it was almost unheard of when McGowen-Hare started her career.

"I'm sure things were said to me, things were done that I could have escalated to another level. But I was just grateful to have a job and sold myself short in some ways," she said. "Being twenty years old and not being able to call it or name it and not wanting to blacklist myself or my career—I took it in stride and kept it going."

Nearly thirty years later, not much has changed for the female engineers who constitute a minority in Silicon Valley, even though women, overall, are a majority in this country. If "little things" happen to white women engineers five to ten times in a workday, women who are also members of a second minority—or a third minority in the case of Fernandez, who is also transgender—can double or triple that number.

"For many years, I've been sitting on the sidelines, navigating through, watching it, doing my due diligence to make a powerful impact and change," McGowen-Hare said. Yet the number of black men and women in technology is still close to zero, and McGowen-Hare said even her most progressive colleagues don't understand how big a problem that is. "The day after the 2016 election, I come into work, I'm hurt, I'm distraught. All the women are crying and can't get themselves together in meetings, crying, eyes welling up." That reminded her of the previous summer, when three young black men had been shot by police in one week. At that time, McGowen-Hare didn't feel she could display her feelings openly the way the women upset by the election were now doing. "I had to go into a bathroom stall because I couldn't keep it together and everyone else acted like nothing was happening," McGowen-Hare recalled. "The level of empathy for the black community wasn't there. The white women could just show their emotions in the workplace in a way that I don't feel like I could."

McGowen-Hare said she applauds the recent surge in discussion about gender bias in Silicon Valley, but she feels something is missing: "As a woman, I'm thrilled. But as an African American, I'm put out. I'm not feeling it. If you don't address racial diversity, you're going to end up with fifty women and fifty men, 100 percent white." McGowen-Hare said she tries to focus on the positive. "I want girls to see me and say, 'She's there so I can be there.' I want to represent opportunity, not limitation."

Across the room, Shola Oyedele agreed that the way diversity is being defined is one-dimensional. "I've been in spaces with women who only want to talk about gender bias but not racial bias and won't stick up for me in the workplace," Oyedele said. The child of Nigerian immigrants, she grew up in a mostly black neighborhood in Maryland before attending Stanford University. "When I went to college, which was predominantly white, I had a lot of trouble in school, and it took me a long time to figure out what it was. Until then, I hadn't really realized that I was black and what that really meant," Oyedele said. "I'm from an immigrant family, so most of what I learned about race and slavery came from school. Because of the way I look, I have to take on a history that's not completely my own," she added. "There's so much resistance to women and minorities in tech. For me to get the same recognition as my peers, I have to do a great job *and* show why I'm worth being here. Being just as good isn't enough; you have to be exceptional."

Part of being exceptional is that sometimes behavior that's standard for the group is contraindicated for you. "I personally think that I should have never been drinking with my co-workers. I think it's a line that should never be blurred if you're a minority or double minority, because you're going to get treated different," said Medina, who is Latina. "Most of these people are going to be white males. I think you get looked down on. They think it's a power thing: you're supposed to stay there and make sure they have a good time, and they are allowed to say whatever they want to you. Those power dynamics just come out when alcohol or drugs are involved."

Medina said that even though she had a prestigious job at Uber, one of the most highly valued companies in Silicon Valley, she still often "felt like shit . . . The fact that you constantly need to prove yourself everywhere you go because you're a minority—it's tiring. People keep questioning my technical capabilities, even as I continue to stack more jobs on my résumé."

As the women talked, I realized that Vanessa Farias had been mostly silent. Farias, also Latina, had been an emergency services coordinator before she enrolled in a mid-career coding class that was part of an apprentice program at Adobe, where she then became an engineer. Her voice broke as she started talking for the first time, and she paused to gather herself as her eyes welled up.

"I actually like my job, but on the hard days I ask, why am I even here? Am I worthy of it?" she began. "Ultimately, I want to pave the way for others. My father was a janitor his whole life. For me to bitch about a bad day . . . ?" Her voice trailed off. Farias drives an hour and a half to San Francisco every weekday, often leaving as early as 4:45 a.m. to beat the traffic. But once she's in the office, she questions whether her colleagues actually notice her. "When I see someone who's Hispanic or black, I know they see me," she said. "I don't feel like anyone else really sees me sometimes. If this is a movement, it's moving way too slow."

In Silicon Valley, if you're not a white man, your identity is a ball and chain, from which you cannot escape. White women in tech have one kind of burden. Latina women have another. Black women, yet another. Asians are generally well represented in the field but under-represented in leadership, adding another wrinkle to the story. Tracy Chou once wrote this about the "uncomfortable state of being Asian" in tech: "It's not as 'good' as being White, but it's certainly 'better' than being Black or Latin@, and it's good enough that we don't complain about the erasure of our individual identities and work ethic and personal successes, we don't complain about the bamboo ceiling, we stay quiet on issues of race."

And aside from race, there are so many other facets of one's identity that can leave women feeling even more isolated. "Not only am I a double minority," said Medina, "the fact that I dropped out of school, forget it. It's even worse." Medina never completed her college degree but networked heavily via Twitter to find her way into the tech crowd.

Simply hiring more white women isn't going to solve Silicon Valley's diversity problem. If this industry is supposed to represent the future, there must be room for talented people who are not young, straight, white, well educated, childless, and male.

BRILLIANT JERKS

In the weeks following the dinner, the post-Fowler pressure on Uber to moderate its hard-charging, masculine culture didn't let up, nor did the press scrutiny. Kalanick apologized over and over again as the negative stories stacked up. Following the publication of Fowler's sexual harassment claims, the company launched what it promised would be two sweeping investigations into both individual allegations and the company's overall culture, and Uber hired former U.S. attorney general Eric Holder to lead the effort. Kalanick said in a statement that what Fowler described was "abhorrent and against everything that Uber stands for and believes in."

Employees didn't necessarily blame "TK," as they affectionately called him, for all of the company's culture problems. "I think to a certain extent he wasn't aware of what was going on because he was so focused on getting more VC money," one employee told me. "He just trusted other people to run it . . . and all of a sudden we have a fire that is just burning. At some point, it translated to a lot of assholeyness." The culture wasn't necessarily malicious, this person said, but several people didn't intervene in bad situations when they could have: "I think there is a small number of people acting really poorly and a lot of people with bystander syndrome, a lot of people seeing it happen and not doing anything." Employees felt optimistic that TK had publicly taken responsibility, but they wanted to see him take action. (In fact, I've heard some people say that if Travis Kalanick wasn't "an asshole," Uber never would have soared to a $70 billion valuation. But nobody stops to think that if he were less of "an asshole," the company might be worth twice as much.)

Others pointed to the executives Kalanick chose to surround himself with, including Amit Singhal, the former Google executive who left the search engine amid sexual harassment allegations; Ed Baker, who resigned in the midst of reports he'd been seen making out with another employee at a work event; and Emil Michael, who accompanied Kalanick to that escort-karaoke bar in Seoul. Though Kalanick had once promised to "grow up" (after video was leaked of him getting into a petty argument with an Uber driver), his immaturity could not be blamed on his age. In 2016, he turned forty.

Tasked with assisting Holder's investigation, Uber board member Arianna Huffington publicly announced the company would stop hiring "brilliant jerks." Uber's newly appointed head of HR, Liane Hornsey, told the *New York Times,* "What has driven Uber to immense success—its aggression, the hard-charging attitude—has toppled over . . . And it needs to be shaved back." The company was saying all the right things, but for some employees it was too late.

After Fowler's post made the rounds, Uber employees grew increasingly incensed and started collecting digital paper trails and lodging their own complaints with HR and Kalanick himself. Previously, many hadn't reported questionable incidents, because they felt the HR department was "broken," as one employee put it, and nothing would change. Ana Medina wrote Kalanick a lengthy missive describing what she found to be a "sexist and toxic work environment" at Uber in which women got passed up for promotions, sexual comments were overlooked, and bad managers were tolerated. Medina was especially angry because she knew something about the Fowler case that hadn't been included in the blog post: that several Uber employees had gone to HR on Fowler's behalf to complain about the manager who originally made a pass at her but he still held on to his job. "That guy was a major creep. It took forever to get him fired," Medina tells me. "We were aware of it and extra people went to HR for her and shit didn't happen."

As the weeks passed, Medina grew increasingly frustrated that the investigation seemed to be moving so slowly and opaquely while employees scrambled to cover up anything that might incriminate them. She emailed Kalanick asking for a one-on-one meeting, to which she says he responded, "Sorry, I'm already meeting with other fearless women"—a reply that left Medina, who had spent a great deal of time helping to recruit other female and Latinx engineers for Uber, feeling as if she had been used and taken for granted. "I was just like, 'What the fuck,' I was only asking for fifteen minutes," Medina says. Later, however, she was invited to a listening session with a few dozen female engineers and the CEO in April, nearly two months after Fowler's original post.

Kalanick showed up late and ended up taking the seat next to Medina. He bowed his head and nodded as the women spoke. When it was her turn, Medina says she turned in her seat and confronted

Kalanick directly. "I said, 'This is the shit that has happened. People who were involved in the claims from Susan's post, they are still at the company. Why aren't we suspending them? Why aren't we hearing more from the investigation?'" Kalanick acknowledged a need for greater transparency. Then Medina got personal. She told Kalanick, "The only way I haven't burnt out the last few months is going home and getting stoned every day." She says he responded, "Oh, Ana, I've never smoked weed. Maybe you should smoke me out for the first time." Medina was shocked. "I'm telling the CEO, 'Hey, I'm doing drugs so I can survive working here,' and that's what he says?"

What she was trying to tell Kalanick was that her Uber experience had plunged her into a very dark mental state. She often felt nauseated and unable to eat, and she was throwing up every other day. She couldn't make time to see the right doctors, because she was working so hard. "I was on edge. I was hating my life. I was suicidal on and off," Medina reveals. "I had come up with an entire suicide plan, and I was okay with doing it. A lot of it was, I don't matter, no matter how hard I try, who I talk to, nothing's going to change."

During the first week of June 2017, Medina took a medical leave of absence and bought a one-way ticket to Minnesota to visit a friend. As her plane was landing, she received an email that the release of the results of Uber's sexual harassment investigation had been postponed. To Medina, it felt like another broken promise. "That took me into a really bad spiral. I felt more suicidal and extra pissed off. I was like, I can't believe this is happening." That evening, she checked herself into the emergency room at the Mayo Clinic in Rochester, Minnesota, where she was hospitalized for ten days. "One of the things I kept on saying was 'I don't feel human. I have no sense of emotion. No passion to do anything or create.' I just felt blank and empty." Medina was diagnosed with severe depression and anxiety. "Coming to terms with that, it took a while," she says.

While Medina was in the hospital, *Recode* published an email Kalanick had sent to employees ahead of an Uber employee party in Miami in 2013. The email began, "You better read this or I'll kick your ass." Kalanick went on to share these guidelines for interoffice hookups: "Do not have sex with another employee UNLESS a) you have asked that person for that privilege and they have responded with an emphatic 'YES! I will have sex with you' AND b) the two (or more) of you do not work in the same chain of command. Yes, that means that Travis will be celibate on this trip. #CEOLife #FML." (Translation: "Fuck My Life.")

My Bloomberg colleague Eric Newcomer also reported the questionable handling of a rape case involving an Uber driver accused of sexually assaulting his passenger in India. According to the report, Kalanick and his top deputy, Emil Michael, discussed their belief that the case was a conspiracy, engineered by Uber's local rival, Ola. An Uber employee who oversaw operations in India obtained a copy of the victim's medical report and told co-workers that the records revealed no physical harm, though *Recode* reported sources said it appeared she had been sodomized. Even after the driver was convicted, Kalanick questioned whether the woman had actually been raped.

That same month, Uber finally revealed the results of its external investigation. The law firm Perkins Coie investigated 215 claims, including 47 cases of sexual harassment, 54 of discrimination, and 45 of unprofessional behavior. As a result, 20 employees were fired. The company also released findings from Holder's report into the broader culture. Uber's board adopted the report's long list of recommendations, which included providing additional training for managers, revising the company's values, limiting alcohol in the workplace, banning relationships between employees and managers, and requiring the company to interview women and minority candidates for open jobs. Emil Michael left the company. Kalanick held on to his job but announced he would take an indefinite leave of absence. Just days later, Uber investors delivered a letter to Kalanick in person, asking him to formally step down. After a few hours of deliberation, Kalanick resigned. Later Kalanick was sued by one of his earliest backers, Benchmark, for board control. The firm claimed that Kalanick was consumed by his own "selfish ends." A Kalanick spokesperson said the suit had no merit. After a tumultuous search process, Uber's board of directors hired Expedia's CEO, Dara Khosrowshahi, as the ride hailer's new chief executive.

"Susan Fowler's story has been a catalyst for meaningful, positive change at Uber," a company spokesperson told me. "We're grateful for her courage to speak out, which has led to major cultural shifts across the company. These improvements—which include an equal-pay review, a revamped performance review system, a more robust HR team, and expanded diversity and inclusion resources—are all part of our efforts to create an environment where everyone feels safe and respected."

LOOKING BACK OVER THE controversy she kicked off, Fowler told me she never once fathomed that her blog post could take down Travis Kalanick, but she felt it was the only way that Uber's culture could ever improve. "Thinking they are above any sort of moral decency, that comes from the top," Fowler told me.

Fowler was still trying to figure out how to use the platform she now finds herself thrust upon. She has been named to *Vanity Fair's* New Establishment list and *Fortune's* 40 Under 40. "People are listening and people want to hear what I have to say and I don't want to squander that. I want to use it for good," Fowler told me. "What does that look like? How do I use this to make change?" After Uber, she accepted a job at the payments tech company Stripe, was writing another book, and had sold the rights to a movie based on her life that would be written by Allison Schroeder, the screenwriter behind *Hidden Figures*.

Fowler, with the help of her lawyers, also filed an amicus brief in three Supreme Court cases (none involving Uber) arguing that employment contracts that set up roadblocks to class-action suits and force disputes to be resolved in private violate federal labor laws.

"There's a legal way to cover up illegal behavior," Fowler told me. "We need to make sure the legal system can be the advocate for women. It's not fair to expect women to have to come forward and take all the risks themselves."

She also revealed that she was having a baby girl. "I don't want her to have to deal with the same crap. She shouldn't ever have to work at an Uber, or ever have to worry about being retaliated against or discrimination."

WHAT THEY DO FOR LOVE

At the time I held my dinner for women engineers in the spring of 2017, none of us knew for certain that we were at a cultural turning point. We couldn't have guessed that Fowler's post had begun a chain of events that would lead to the dethroning of one of tech's most powerful CEOs. Such radical change seemed impossible. As the discussion started to wind down, the mood was distinctly somber, and I could tell the women were emotionally exhausted by sharing so many depressing stories. But I had one last question.

These women had stayed in the game, but there are countless others who quietly leave the industry every day. In fact, women exit the tech industry at a rate 45 percent higher than men. Had any of the women in the room ever considered leaving technology altogether? The answer was a resounding yes. And yet they were still here.

Ana Medina had barely survived an extreme case of burnout, and now she had another job offer. Yet she was hesitant to give up on Uber. "I'm not a quitter. I don't want to let go. Part of it is, being a minority in tech at such a strong company inspires other people to think if [she] can end up at a top ten company, so can I." A few months later she made an even bigger statement and sued Uber (while she was still employed but on medical leave), along with two other Latina engineers, for gender and racial discrimination.

Tracy Chou had a different reason for staying in tech. "When I was a year into working at my first job, there was a period where I was crying myself to sleep every night," she said. "I just didn't think I belonged. That experience of being ignored. One of my co-workers would just turn and look at the wall and not acknowledge I existed. But I loved being an engineer, having people use what I made all the time."

"Why am I in this industry in spite of all of it?" said Uber's Lydia Fernandez. "If I wanted an easy career, I would have gone and worked in high-frequency trading and not come out for another ten years. But I'm interested in . . . making things faster and more efficient, and working on what I'm doing looking like this." Fernandez gestured at her skirt and long pink hair. "The rest of the world can go fuck themselves."

5

SUPERHEROES AND SUPERJERKS: THE ROLE OF THE VENTURE CAPITALISTS

"**M**Y NEMESIS!" SIR MICHAEL Moritz declared loudly, the moment he saw me. We were both guests at *Vanity Fair's* 2016 New Establishment Summit, and I had successfully, if awkwardly, avoided eye contact with him during cocktails. When I discovered that we had been seated directly across from each other at dinner, I briefly contemplated moving the place cards. Now Moritz had arrived at our table and found himself opposite perhaps his least favorite journalist in Silicon Valley.

"Why is she your nemesis?" asked a CEO seated beside us.

"I'll let her explain her way out of this one," Moritz said as he grudgingly took his seat. In my defense, let me say this: It wasn't what I had said about Moritz that had brought him headaches. It was what he'd said about himself.

A year earlier, I had conducted a wide-ranging TV interview with Moritz about his recently published book, *Leading* (which he co-wrote with the famed former Manchester United manager Alex Ferguson), and his near-legendary Silicon Valley career. He had arrived alone that day, a few minutes late, without the typical army of public relations handlers—surprising for a man who is, arguably, the most successful investor in Silicon Valley history. Moritz made his fortune investing early in companies like Google and Yahoo; now his firm, Sequoia Capital, is among the most sought-after venture capital out-fits in the world. Moritz stepped back from day-to-day duties at Se-quoia in 2012 due to what he called a "rare, incurable medical condition" but remains very engaged in the firm to this day. In 2013, he was knighted—for his success in investing and generous charitable giving—yet on the TV set he displayed none of the airs you would expect from one of the world's wealthiest men.

As soon as Moritz began to answer my questions on camera, I re-alized there was nothing casual about him. He speaks slowly, choosing his words carefully, like a painter selecting colors from a palette. Most of his answers to my questions were sharp and insightful. Which was why his comments about the absence of women partners at his ven-ture capital firm were so jarring.

At the time of the interview, the number of Sequoia's female invest-ing partners in the United States was zero (though there were three in China and two in India). When I asked Moritz about Sequoia's respon-sibility to hire women, he responded, "We think about it a lot. I like to think and genuinely believe that we are blind to somebody's sex, to their religion, to their background." He went on to give the typical Silicon Valley answer: that too few women elect to study the sciences, so there-fore the pool of hirable women is much smaller than the pool of men.

To my ears, this explanation was too glib. Yes, women are underrep-resented in the STEM pipeline. But Sequoia is a relatively small firm (with about a dozen U.S. investing partners at the time), and no one disputes the fact that there are thousands of exceptional women working in tech (though still not nearly enough). Sequoia couldn't recruit just one? Perhaps, I suggested, Sequoia might not be looking hard enough.

"Oh, we look very hard," Moritz said, bristling. He then noted that it had just hired a young woman from Stanford into a junior position. "And if there are more like her, we'll hire them. What we're not pre-pared to do is to lower our standards."

This was the line that would haunt him for the foreseeable future. The Silicon Valley chattering classes exploded, as did the mainstream media. *Vanity Fair* proclaimed, "Here's some news for all the many smart, driven, capable young women interested in working in technology: apparently, you don't exist." For the next several months, industry folks stopped me everywhere to express their horror at what Moritz had said. The idea that Sequoia had never hired a woman because the firm couldn't find even one who met its high standards was just plain ridiculous. One female venture capitalist, Jennifer Fonstad of Aspect Ventures, told me Moritz's words would be "his epitaph." Bijan Sabet, a co-founder of Spark Capital, put it this way: "When you make a lot of money, you either become a superhero or a superjerk."

The irony is Moritz himself didn't study the sciences on his way to becoming one of the most powerful VCs in the Valley. Born in Wales, he earned a history degree at Oxford and an MBA at the University of Pennsylvania's Wharton School. He then became a San Francisco–based correspondent for *Time* magazine, where in January 1983 he published a controversial piece on Steve Jobs. Then, in the mid-1980s, Don Valentine, founder of Sequoia, who was one of Apple's original backers, offered Moritz a role as an investor at the firm. Despite his lack of a technical background, Moritz was promoted to full partner in short order.

"I'm a history major, knew nothing about technology, nothing about Silicon Valley," Moritz told me in our TV interview. "Eventually, through a stroke of great luck, a fellow who had started Sequoia, Don Valentine, took a risk on me." Later in the interview he added, "I think it's very difficult to tell from somebody's background whether or not they'll be successful in the venture business."

Moritz isn't the only venture capitalist in Silicon Valley who didn't need a computer science degree in order to succeed, among them Peter Thiel of Founders Fund (BA in philosophy, plus a JD, early investor in Facebook) and Peter Fenton of Benchmark (also a philosophy BA, plus an MBA, early investor in Twitter). What about all the others? On the heels of my interview with Moritz, the entrepreneur and angel investor Sukhinder Singh Cassidy took a close look at the *Forbes* Midas List of standout venture capitalists in 2015 and discovered that 61 percent of the top male investors had a STEM degree. All but one of the few women on the list had STEM backgrounds.

Putting those numbers a different way, Cassidy is telling us that the absence of a STEM degree is not the deal breaker Moritz (and many others) make it out to be, because almost 40 percent of the top male investors do not have that background. The excuse that VCs aren't hiring women because there are not enough of them getting science and computer degrees just isn't valid.

In the midst of the backlash to our interview, Moritz sent me an email with what he called a clarification. "I know there are many remarkable women who would flourish in the venture business," he wrote. "We're working hard to find them and would be ecstatic if more joined Sequoia or other firms." Sequoia Capital followed up with a tweet from its official account: "We need to do better."

A few months later, Moritz managed to give new life to the controversy while taking questions from journalists at the San Francisco Exploratorium, saying, "We're not going to run an affirmative action [program]. And I happen to think it's an insult to a woman we hire, a black we hire, or a Hispanic we hire, to feel like they're coming to work at Sequoia because of their gender or their race. The people who want to come to work for us want to be the very best." He again mentioned the "spectacular" female analyst Sequoia had recently hired: "If she had five sisters we'd hire them all!"

Moritz's comments dogged him, illustrating the almost comical difficulties late-career VCs have in navigating this unfamiliar terrain. But even if you judge Sequoia only on its actions, Moritz and his colleagues would fail the loosest diversity tests. Sequoia didn't hire a single female U.S. investor in the firm's first forty-four years.

As part of a panel discussion just before our awkward dinner, Moritz was asked—again—to clarify his "lowering standards" remark.

This time his answer was more polished: "It makes zero sense to exclude 50 percent of the human race who've got some of the smartest brains around . . . the more the merrier."

Beth Comstock, vice-chair of General Electric, who shared the stage with him, was prepared to speak her mind. "Diversity fuels innovation," she said emphatically. "It's just that simple. And part of the challenge is people want to hire people like themselves." She continued, "Who's setting the standards? Are you working hard enough to make the standards wide and inclusive and have the right access? . . . You got to work really hard to hire people who don't agree with you, who don't look like you . . . You have to say, bring me enough women and diverse candidates . . . flood the zone with better candidates . . . There are no women in software who can do this? That's absurd. Keep looking until you find them!"

After that public scolding, it was understandable that Moritz was less than delighted to find, only a few hours later, that I was his dinner companion. After I explained to our CEO tablemate why Moritz had branded me his nemesis, he politely offered that he felt he understood exactly what Moritz had been trying to say. "See?" Moritz said to me, as if his words had been validated. "We discriminate against all dummies equally."

Moritz and his firm would soon receive another black eye. Sequoia's partner Michael Goguen became the talk of Silicon Valley when a former stripper named Amber Laurel Baptiste slapped him with a $40 million lawsuit claiming he kept her as a sex slave for thirteen years. Although Goguen denied the allegations, claiming he was being extorted, Sequoia fired him as soon as the case went public. Insiders at the firm insist they knew nothing about his extracurricular affairs. While Goguen's relationship with Baptiste wasn't related to his job, the Valley's intense interest in the scandal, I believe, came from the feeling that Goguen's sexual behavior was emblematic of a cavalier attitude toward power and sex that existed inside many VC firms. There was a swirl of rumors about the behavior of venture capitalists across the industry, and I was often told off-the-record stories, but it would take another two years for many of those stories to break.

WHY FEMALE VCS ARE SO SCARCE

Though venture capitalists make their names by betting on massive technological innovation, their own business has changed little over time. The first VCs in America were the wealthy families of the late nineteenth century—the Vanderbilts, Rockefellers, and other dynasties who invested in high-return undertakings such as railroads, steel, and oil; they also funded some of the earliest tech entrepreneurs, including Alexander Graham Bell. The industry became more organized in the 1940s, when the first venture capital firms were formed. Then, in the 1970s, it became clear that there were great fortunes to be made in the emerging field of technology, and an entire subindustry of tech-focused venture capital firms was spawned. Sequoia Capital and Kleiner Perkins Caufield & Byers set up shop in 1972, just a year after the microprocessor was born. These firms were all-male—with many partners who were former employees of chip companies such as Intel and Fairchild Semiconductor—but as women became full participants in the post-1970s workforce, they started seeking a place for themselves at this rich table.

Few of them found one. By 1999, women accounted for just 10 percent of partners at venture capital firms, and that number actually *declined* over the next fifteen years, to 6 percent in 2014. VCs have had little incentive to change. Two of the top firms in Silicon Valley, Sequoia and Benchmark Capital, made billions of dollars before hiring any women partners at all. Why mess with a good thing? In other words, while investors expect the start-ups they fund to take extreme risks, VCs themselves have chosen to take very few chances in how they run their own firms. Unfortunately, one company that did make changes became something of a cautionary tale.

Sequoia and Kleiner reached the top of the VC hierarchy by roping "unicorns," that is, making early investments in companies that later reach the billion-dollar valuation mark. During the dot-com boom, a top partner emerged at each firm: Moritz at Sequoia and John Doerr at Kleiner. As the men who led their firms' investments in Google and served on the search engine's prestigious board of directors, they delivered the lion's share of the returns and thus became the most influential partners within their respective fiefdoms. As such, they closed deals with investors and entrepreneurs, spoke at industry conferences, and had the greatest sway over internal hiring and operations.

After it became clear that Google was going to be huge, Moritz and Doerr took different approaches to finding the unicorns of the next decade. Sequoia stayed small and lean, making early investments in some of tech's biggest hits, such as YouTube, Airbnb, and WhatsApp. Most founders dream of getting a check signed by Sequoia and the contacts and bragging rights that come with it.

Kleiner, on the other hand, changed its approach, scaling up in staff size and widening its investment focus to include new energy and clean tech—changes made largely at the behest of Doerr. Among the slew of new partners hired were big names such as former vice president Al Gore, the famed former Wall Street analyst Mary Meeker, and the esteemed doctor Beth Seidenberg; the new junior partners included a number of promising women. Doerr continued to push recruiters hard to find more women, even when other partners didn't agree it should be a top priority. With these new hires, Kleiner became one of the most gender-diverse top-tier venture capital firms in Silicon Valley.

Despite its ambitious expansion, over the next decade Kleiner's reputation suffered. The firm failed to invest early in some of the most successful web 2.0 companies such as Facebook and Twitter (though it invested in both at a later stage and a much higher price tag); Kleiner even found itself playing catch-up to the hot new venture capital firm on the block Andreessen Horowitz. Then came the biggest blow yet. On May 10, 2012, Kleiner was sued for gender discrimination by an employee named Ellen Pao.

Pao had joined the firm as Doerr's chief of staff in 2005. She came with an electrical engineering degree from Princeton as well as a JD and an MBA from Harvard and had already worked at several tech companies. At Kleiner, she was promoted to junior investing partner but didn't make the cut for senior partner when the firm decided it was time to downsize. Pao charged that she was denied partnership because of her gender, while the firm maintained she simply underperformed. Pao's work ethic was never in question. She put in so many hours that at one point Doerr wrote to her, "Please, please, really take a real leave. You deserve it!" Nonetheless, many current and former Kleiner employees agree that Pao, however hardworking, was an unremarkable investor. Current Kleiner partner Beth Seidenberg says of Pao, "She was always quiet in meetings. She never spoke up. She didn't take a seat at the table. She did a lot of things that do not serve women well." (Pao later told me she didn't get opportunities to take a seat at the table.) Still, Doerr continued to be Pao's champion, asking other partners to give her more time to prove herself.

But things got messy. Pao had a romantic relationship with a married junior partner, Ajit Nazre. It was consensual, by all accounts, but then soured. Pao reported to her managers that Nazre was harassing her and excluding her from important emails and meetings. A few years later, Nazre also hit on another female junior partner, Trae Vassallo, once showing up at her hotel room wearing a bathrobe and carrying wine. When Vassallo reported this to the firm, Ray Lane, a managing partner, allegedly joked that she should have been "flattered" by Nazre's attention. In court, Lane denied making that comment but admitted he did not handle the complaint appropriately.

After an internal investigation into Nazre's behavior, he was fired, but in the meantime several incidents that built Pao's case piled up. One senior partner gave her a book of erotic poetry by Leonard Cohen on Valentine's Day. She also claimed two male partners (Ted Schlein and Matt Murphy) and a CEO (Chegg's Dan Rosensweig) discussed porn stars and their preferences for sex workers on a private plane ride to a business meeting, which she later wrote about in vivid detail in her memoir, *Reset*. Schlein, Pao writes, said he preferred "white girls—Eastern European, to be specific." Pao also alleged that women at the firm were excluded from all-male ski trips and dinners. Specifically, she claimed a male partner, Chi-Hua Chien, suggested that women not be invited to an upcoming dinner hosted by partner Al Gore, because they "kill the buzz."

On the stand, Chien denied saying this but confirmed that an all-male dinner did occur at Gore's home and that the number of guests was limited because of the size of his living room. Chien also testified that he often invited Pao to get-togethers that might lead to deal flow but she was too busy to attend. Kleiner's attorneys presented multiple emails that showed Chien inviting Pao to meetings he thought she might find interesting. The implication was that Pao chose to pass on critical social opportunities that might have advanced her position within the firm.

WHETHER PAO WASN'T INVITED, or chose not to attend, or was invited but didn't feel welcome, her experience is a stark reminder that venture capital partnerships are deeply competitive and political. Not only do you have to persuade the most desirable entrepreneurs to choose you and your firm as backers; you must also convince every single partner who may be less enthusiastic about that start-up than you are. Plus the more money you get to invest in your companies, the less there is left for others. When the final vote on the deal happens, you need to wield serious influence in that room, and whether you've got it depends on several factors: your track record and your partners' confidence in you, of course, but also how smart you are about pushing your agenda through the organization. If you don't have sufficient personal and political capital, it can be hard if not impossible to succeed. Pao claims that she advocated for the firm to invest in Twitter earlier, but couldn't persuade another partner to agree.

When promotion time came, Kleiner promoted three men to senior partner. Pao and Vassallo were passed over. Pao didn't think that it was a coincidence. In a letter to John Doerr in 2012, she wrote, "The two people who have made recent complaints of discrimination, harassment, and retaliation—have been . . . relegated to more junior status." She also expressed her disappointment and called for change. Later that year, she filed her suit.

It's useful to compare Pao's career at Kleiner with that of Aileen Lee, who joined Kleiner in 1999 as an associate partner, also working very closely with Doerr. Colleagues tell me that Lee was more successful than Pao because she worked harder to build personal relationships and was ultimately promoted to senior partner. But Lee left Kleiner just before the downsizing that sparked Pao's suit got under way to start her own seed fund. Now, assessing her own chances of becoming a managing partner at that time, Lee says, "I don't think I would have gotten a seat at the table. Internally, [Kleiner] had changed a lot and I wasn't happy. We had gotten big. Seed was an important new category where I felt like I could have a chance to repot my plant."

Lee won't speak specifically about Pao's case against Kleiner, but I asked if she herself ever felt she was treated differently there because she was a woman. "It's confusing how much was boys' club and how much was just mismanagement," Lee said. "I think VC has been a boys' club, and even if many of those boys have great intentions, many of them don't realize the privilege that they have being male and mostly white and how things they do or say may unintentionally make others feel excluded or uncomfortable or discouraged. At the time, I didn't think of a lot of those things as bias. I just thought, 'Oh, there's a cool kids' club, and I'm not in it.'"

Lee added that when women aren't invited to male-only social events, or don't attend, they often don't know what they're missing. "You don't realize they trade deal flow and talk about what they've learned and what's a hot deal," Lee said. "When that hot deal is raising their next round and someone says, 'Who should we call?' Someone says, 'Oh, how about Jeff?' And Jeff gets the deal." When I asked Lee if she felt that these circumstances qualify as gender discrimination, she paused, then said, "I think most women at VC firms, most women in business, if they wanted to could probably put together a case." When Lee was on maternity leave, for example, her seat on the board of the solar company Miasole was eliminated. The company had decided to change its board structure, reducing the number of Kleiner's seats from two to one. Doerr, the other Kleiner board member, kept his seat. No one called Lee to inform her of the change, and she found out on her own when she returned.

Ellen Pao ultimately lost her case against the firm. The Pao jury cleared Kleiner of any wrongdoing, including gender discrimination and retaliation. But in the court of public opinion, Kleiner's reputation was badly damaged. Pao's story appeared on the front page of the *New York Times,* and the tech blogs had a field day reporting the salacious details and mocking the firm's poor management.

Despite the controversy surrounding the trial, when I told Doerr I was writing a book about the challenges facing women in technology, he quickly agreed to talk to me.

"A partnership is a family business. It's like improv," he told me. "There's an ensemble. The cast takes risks, and if someone is in trouble, your partners are there to help you do better." In Doerr's recounting, his efforts to help Pao advance within the firm had backfired, leading him to believe that he should have more carefully considered his partners' pleas to move Pao into an operating role at one of the companies Kleiner had funded. Doerr speculated that had he acted differently, he might have avoided the lawsuit altogether. "If we had transitioned Ellen a year earlier, if I had listened [to my partners], I don't think we would have gone through the trial." It is a thought Doerr has lost sleep over for many nights since.

In 2016, Doerr stepped back from his investing duties at Kleiner but as chairman remains focused on recruiting. He says he hasn't given up on working on tech's diversity issues. "I think the problem begins early. Yes, there is a pipeline problem. Yes, there is a leaky bucket problem. Yes, there is a hidden bias problem. Yes, there is a role model problem," he told me. "You have to get up and work harder every day to prioritize and source outstanding candidates that are going to cause the culture of your organization to reflect the world you want to win in."

While Kleiner Perkins is still working to rebuild its reputation post-lawsuit, Pao's reputation has evolved considerably in the two years since the verdict. After the trial ended, I would often hear Pao discussed as a cautionary tale.

Many women I spoke with applauded her bravery, but some who felt they had been victims of gender discrimination took her experience as a warning. They vowed they would never sue, because they didn't "want to end up like Ellen Pao."

The case also weighed on VC firms. "[Kleiner] got seriously burned in this very, very public way that makes everyone else have a natural excuse: 'Oh, hey, Kleiner was trying to do the right thing, and look what happened to them,'" Greylock's Reid Hoffman told me in 2016.

When I spoke with Pao about a year after the verdict, she said she wouldn't recommend that other people pursue legal action if they can help it. "If you think people will listen, you should try to change from within, if you have the energy for the path you want to take," Pao told me. "But I tried to change from within, and it did not work."

By fall 2017, however, amid a deluge of sexual harassment and gender discrimination allegations in Silicon Valley and beyond, Pao herself seemed to feel differently. I asked if she thought she might win her lawsuit in today's climate. "I don't know that we would be here if

I hadn't filed my suit. We've changed the conversation. No longer are women forced to defend themselves. It's a much easier experience to say, 'I've been harassed, I've been discriminated against.' People believe it. If it hadn't been for all these women who have come after me to share those stories, we wouldn't be where we are today."

THE POST-PAO EFFECT

In this new climate, some VC firms have slowly started to recruit and hire more women. Some seem to be doing so at the point of a gun, afraid to be called out publicly. Others believe that doing so will be a competitive advantage. Chamath Palihapitiya told me that his firm, Social Capital, beat out Sequoia for a recent deal with a female entrepreneur: "Just yesterday, those fucking bozos, we ran circles around them and did a deal from right under their nose . . . they're going to ask, why did they not see it?"

Palihapitiya claimed to see an opportunity where other investors haven't, to hire partners—both men and women—from a variety of ethnic and religious backgrounds. (His wife, Brigette Lau, as well as one other woman are investing partners.) "We have more empathy in the room," he asserted. "These people are making really emotional decisions about who they connect with." Palihapitiya has built his firm's brand, in part, on trying to rectify the visceral inequality in Silicon Valley. Whether it will be more than marketing bluster remains to be seen. (The firm lost a key male partner to Kleiner in 2017.) Though Sequoia's returns still dwarf those of newer funds like Social Capital, Palihapitiya declares that the next decade will see a shake-up in the VC hierarchy. Exploiting the perceived weakness of one of his largest rivals, he calls Sequoia's partners "a bunch of soulless milquetoast bros"—and says they have created a massive blind spot by not hiring women: "There is no excuse for that kind of stuff if your goal is to win."

Other firms have a similar strategy. Canaan Partners was the first of the big firms to hire not one, not two, but three female general partners: Maha Ibrahim, Wende Hutton, and Nina Kjellson. In meetings with female CEOs and founders, says Ibrahim, "You can almost see their surprise . . . when they sit across the table and say, 'I've never seen a firm like this. I can have a voice here. I can be heard.'" In her view, however, the rest of the industry isn't changing so fast. "The bias exists. It's going to exist for a long time. We have umpteen stories we can tell you. It's a sad situation," she says. "The only thing we can do is just dig in."

Some firms seem less motivated by potential profit than by the desire to do what they see as the right thing. When LinkedIn's co-founder Reid Hoffman joined Greylock Partners in 2009, he tells me, the conversations about hiring a woman were already under way. "Everyone agreed strongly that it was embarrassing that we didn't have women partners, and it was kind of like saying, 'Are we part of the problem?'" Hoffman says. "We decided that we were going to go to the ends of the earth to recruit a female partner. We would not stop making it a weekly partnership discussion until we had one."

Greylock then made a critical decision: it redefined the talent pool it would draw from. Did every partner really need to have a technical background? In those conversations, "we mentioned Mike Moritz and his dumbass comments on women. He's got a literature background, and, you know, no one disagrees he's a pretty damn good VC," Hoffman points out. As part of the search, Hoffman says, he had a conversation with every powerful woman he knew about potentially joining the team as an investor. Greylock pursued a few female candidates who turned it down. Then the firm discovered Sarah Tavel, a philosophy major from Harvard who had also worked as a junior VC. Tavel might not have studied computer science, says Hoffman, but she had something else Greylock decided was key: "company-building" experience at Pinterest.

Tavel doesn't believe an engineering background is essential to a venture capitalist's success. "Would my life be easier if I was technical? Yes," she says. "But the more senior I get, the less it matters." In fact, she believes the analytical rigor of her philosophy studies prepared her perfectly. "When you're investing in a company, you have hypotheses that you're assuming," Tavel says. "I believe this is the way the world's going to evolve, this is the product for that world and this is why, and if you believe those things, this is going to become a big company."

Before Pinterest, Tavel worked as an analyst and, later, as an associate at Bessemer Venture Partners, where she was often the only woman in the room. "I was the youngest person; I was the smallest person. You feel the physical difference especially because everybody's voice is literally stronger than yours. It was intimidating in a way I was totally unprepared for, and I blamed myself for being intimidated by it," Tavel says. "There were three other analysts, all men, and they were chummy with the male partners in a way that I didn't feel comfortable [being] . . . It could have been about sports, or it didn't even have to be a male topic, but it was the way in which they had that conversation that didn't feel natural to me." Still, Tavel stepped up to the plate and ultimately co-led Bessemer's investment in Pinterest, where she later became one of the discovery site's first product managers.

A year after I spoke with Tavel, she made news in the venture capital industry by jumping ship from Greylock to Benchmark, another firm that had yet to hire a woman. Tavel had only positive things to say about her former Greylock colleagues but explained that she felt Benchmark's smaller, more intimate team was a better fit. On the one hand, it was encouraging to see another top, all-male firm welcome a woman. On the other, it was discouraging to see two firms fight over the same woman, rather than expand the overall female-partner pool.

As for Sequoia, it did hire its first woman partner, a year after I interviewed Moritz on TV: Jess Lee, a Stanford computer science major who was the CEO of the fashion site Polyvore. Other partners at Sequoia spent years recruiting her and actually offered her the job before Moritz's controversial comments, but she did not accept immediately. At the time, she was working for Yahoo's CEO, Marissa Mayer, a long-time mentor, after the company had acquired Polyvore, and it took a great deal of persuading before she agreed to leave for Sequoia.

"One of the things that really mattered to Jess was knowing she wasn't hired because she was a woman," said Sequoia partner Roelof Botha. Botha, who co-leads Sequoia's U.S. operations, told me that he personally works very hard on finding new partners and that over the last three years he has interviewed more than 150 people, including a few dozen women. Sequoia has typically hired its partners from its portfolio companies. (Remember Botha came from PayPal, which Sequoia backed.) In order to find women and other exceptional candidates, Botha is now looking beyond the obvious suspects and casting a wider net, which is how he discovered Lee.

"The industry and Sequoia need to do more, and we're taking action to help move the needle. We still have a long way to go," Botha said.

In 2016, Sequoia launched a mentorship program called Ascent that pairs women in technical roles with senior women across the industry (though one female founder who was asked to join the program as a mentor said she felt as if Sequoia was asking her to do free work, while the firm took all the credit). Botha has also been working to add more women to Sequoia's super-secretive "scout" program, a large group of mostly entrepreneurs who unofficially refer deals back to the firm, then get a cut. It's an ingenious way to get deal flow, but once again male dominated. When the *Wall Street Journal* compiled a long list of known Sequoia scouts in 2015, only 5 out of 78, or about 6 percent, were women. By September 2017, the number of female scouts had jumped to 25 percent.

Still, women have a long way to go before they can have even close to an equal voice at the venture capital table. Though many firms now claim they are working hard at gender diversity in hiring, Hoffman believes that not all the firms are as serious as they would like observers to believe. "I've seen more explicit sexism [in Silicon Valley] than I've seen explicit racism," he says, noting that he's spotted one reliable clue that a firm may be a boys' clubhouse: "super-attractive reception-ists." It's "bullshit," Hoffman says. The attractiveness of the assistants out front, he insists, is a direct indicator of which firms have problems in the way they treat women. "Literally, from the offices I've gone to, it's a one-for-one match."

HOW MALE VCS DEAL WITH FEMALE FOUNDERS

In Silicon Valley, the power of the top-ranked venture capitalists can-not be overestimated, because while all money is good, all money is not created equal. From a start-up's point of view, the best money comes from the top firms, because their initial investment ends up delivering a lot of other benefits. For example, a business funded by Sequoia or Andreessen Horowitz during the initial Series A round will likely have little trouble finding follow-on investors for its Series B. But money isn't the only advantage that flows from having a top firm on your team. The right VC can also open doors to key power players within both the Silicon Valley ecosystem and the larger business com-munity. Marc Andreessen's personal relationship with Mark Zucker-berg might, for example, be critical to an entrepreneur launching a company in any area where Facebook does business. VC firms also help with hiring, because they know the best talent in the Valley. And if the time comes for an IPO or sale, they can connect you to the best bankers and law firms around. If entrepreneurs are the princes of Silicon Valley, a few dozen VC partners at a handful of firms are the kingmakers. Every founder wants the top VCs' helping hands up to the throne, but each investor makes only one or two investments a year, so the competition is crushing.

Most venture capitalists are men, and they most often back male entrepreneurs. In fact, men run 92 percent of VC-backed companies nationwide. What may be more surprising—and discouraging—is that even firms with female partners back the same (small) number of female founders as all-male firms do, according to one Bloomberg report. Some believe this is because female VCs worry about being accused of bias in favor of female entrepreneurs and also do deeper due diligence to avoid making mistakes, feeling as if they have more to prove. Either way, female founders lose. In 2016, VCs invested a little over $58 billion in companies with male founders, while female founders received just $1.46 billion. The average size of an investment in a company led by a man was about $10.9 million, up from $9.7 million the year before. Women-led companies received $4.5 million on average, actually *decreasing* from $6.1 million over the same period.

Female entrepreneurs, including Katrina Lake, the founder of Stitch Fix, an online personal shopper that went on to become one of the most promising start-ups in the Valley and went public in 2017, often lament the challenges of raising money from mostly male investors who may not connect with them easily or appreciate business ideas that cater mostly to women. (And some of the businesses they do fund benefit from sexist behavior. Think trolling on Reddit and Twitter.)

Lake is a no-bullshit, straight-talking CEO who grew up in Minneapolis and San Francisco, the daughter of a public-school teacher and a doctor. She was always surrounded by strong women, Lake tells me at Stitch Fix's buzzy San Francisco headquarters, including a grandmother who fled an arranged marriage in Japan and encouraged her granddaughter to march to her own beat. As such, Lake had her own iconoclastic sense of style. In high school, you might have found a teenage Lake wearing green cargo pants or baggy jeans and neon raver boots. "Surprisingly, it didn't stop me from making friends," Lake jokes.

When she arrived for her freshman year at Stanford, Lake thought she wanted to be a doctor. She enrolled in premed classes and scored highly on the MCAT. This was just as Facebook was starting to take off with its soon-to-be-iconic founder. "Mark Zuckerberg . . . had quit Harvard and would go to parties at Stanford," Lake recalls. "That was what I thought of as an entrepreneur. Someone who coded in their basement."

At school, she gravitated toward economics and abandoned medical school for management consulting. After graduation, she joined the Parthenon Group, where she focused on retail and restaurants and realized that many retail businesses either don't have or don't effectively use customer data. She then became an associate at a small venture capital firm, in hopes of finding a retail start-up she might like to work for. After meeting hundreds of entrepreneurs, she didn't find a single company appealing as an employer, but she also realized that not all founders actually look like Mark Zuckerberg.

"That was inspiration," Lake says. Finally realizing that she could simply create her own dream company, Lake went to Harvard Business School, which is where she hatched the initial idea. She'd read about an online service that connected men to personal shoppers, and she decided to take a crack at something similar for women. She teamed up with the wife of a Stanford classmate, Erin Morrison Flynn, who had worked as a direct merchant at J.Crew, and the pair began by asking classmates, friends, and friends of friends to fill out style profiles to indicate what kind of clothing they liked and needed. Then they bought a bunch of pieces at retail, on their credit cards, and started delivering boxes of clothes to their first "customers," who reimbursed them for the clothes they liked, leaving them to return the rest. They didn't make any money but did get a feel for how the business could work: they could style customers to their satisfaction, even if they didn't know them personally and even if the customers didn't recognize the brands they were receiving. Eventually, they started sending five items per box, which Lake refers to as their "fix," because people who like the service get addicted. Hence the company name, Stitch Fix.

Stitch Fix started to take off thanks to an initial investment from her mentor and fellow entrepreneur Sukhinder Singh Cassidy (whom Lake had met during an internship at Polyvore). Lake and Flynn later parted ways. "We had a good partnership . . . the company was scaling and we were going in different directions," Lake tells me. *Forbes* reports there was an ownership dispute, a lawsuit, and a settlement and ultimately Flynn left the company. Though Stitch Fix had successfully raised a Series A, the next round of fundraising proved much more difficult.

In the fall of 2012, Stitch Fix was running out of money. Customers kept coming back, suggesting that an online personal styling service could be something big. The company needed to scale, which meant it needed cash. But even though Stitch Fix's revenue growth was promising, some fifty VCs passed on investing. Those who gave an explanation suggested they just didn't want to invest in a women-focused business or simply didn't understand the opportunity. "One investor literally in the first minute said, 'I don't know why anyone would ever want to receive something like this,'" Lake says. "In a lot of cases, men aren't going to see the same thing [that women see]."

Investors generally do see women's businesses differently than their founders do. One VC told me, "I'd love to fund more women, but I just don't want to fund another e-commerce company!" This comment points to the same issue that some VCs have complained to me about privately: that too many women choose to start companies in sectors where growth is expected to be lower, such as e-commerce and parenting, rather than in areas with huge growth potential, such as artificial intelligence. A lot of low-growth businesses are viable; they just don't have the kind of enormous upside that excites investors who are successful enough to pick and choose. In 2011, *Mashable* reporter Jolie O'Dell tweeted, "Women: Stop making startups about fashion, shopping, & babies. . . . You're embarrassing me." Her comment triggered the typical social-media uproar, but there is some truth to it.

In a comprehensive survey in 2017, *TechCrunch* found that 31 percent of start-ups with a female founder focused on e-commerce. Other sectors popular among women were education, health care, and media and entertainment. But the vast majority of venture capital in 2016 went into fintech (meaning financial tech, such as apps that disrupt banking and retirement planning), security, genetics, augmented and virtual reality (VR), and artificial intelligence, in addition to an outsize amount in transportation (dominated by funding of Uber, Lyft, and other ride-hailing services). These numbers indicate a big mismatch between ideas that attract mostly male VCs and ideas that attract female entrepreneurs.

Is this a true gender gap? Maybe, but not necessarily. There is evidence to suggest that women choose lower-cost-of-entry, lower-growth sectors simply because they have fewer resources available to them. Not only are women less likely to receive venture capital than men, but they are also less likely to have business loan and credit applications approved. That said, the data also shows that women ask for smaller amounts of credit and hesitate to take on more debt. The author Sharon Hadary, who has closely studied entrepreneurship, says men tend to set bigger goals for growth while women focus instead on making their business sustainable. Hadary believes the problem is twofold: "First, you have women's own self-limiting views of themselves, their businesses and the opportunities available to them. But equally problematic are the stereotypes, perceptions and expectations of business . . . leaders."

Supporting Hadary's view is evidence that venture capitalists talk about male and female entrepreneurs differently. In one study of a group of investors (including five men and two women) discussing future funding decisions in Sweden, male founders were more likely to be described as "young and promising," while young women were described as "inexperienced." Being cautious was viewed as positive for men and negative for women. Ultimately, women were denied funding more often than men, and when they did receive it, they got 25 percent of the money they requested, whereas men received 52 percent.

The data clearly also shows that when a woman walks into a pitch meeting, she is already at a disadvantage. In one study in which women and men voiced the same slide presentations word for word without ever showing themselves, investors funded male-voiced ventures 60 percent more often than female-voiced ventures. When entrepreneurs presented in person, attractive men were particularly persuasive, whereas good looks didn't give a woman an extra edge, even if she said the same thing as the man who came before her. Sarah Thébaud, a sociology professor at the University of California, Santa Barbara, has found that both male and female investors tend to have lower expectations of women entrepreneurs and systematically perceive them as less competent and skilled.

Thébaud writes in *Newsweek*, "On an aggregate level, this dynamic suggests countless ideas that could have blossomed into successful businesses and benefited the economy never did, simply because the individuals who pitched them weren't the 'right' gender . . . This finding suggests that when a man proposes a business idea, he can typically expect others to respond on the basis of a simple risk-benefit calculation, the kind any venture capitalist might make when deciding whether to help finance a project. But when a woman proposes the same idea, she can expect others to simultaneously be looking for cues that she in fact possesses the types of skills and traits needed to make a venture a success—abilities she's often assumed to lack because of her gender." In essence, investors are prone to selling women entrepreneurs short.

"There is not a single woman that I can think of in this industry that is publicly labeled as a 'visionary' or a 'genius,'" Rent the Runway CEO Jennifer Hyman told me. "There are dozens and dozens of men in the country where those adjectives are used. Because we label men as geniuses and visionaries, we give them a lot more chances, we allow them to fail a lot more times, and we make excuses for things that we wouldn't make excuses for, for women . . . Unless we change the public vernacular of how we lift up and recognize women and how we all give women the same sorts of chances . . . we are not going to see that change."

VCs will argue that many female entrepreneurs are guilty of underselling themselves. Investors have told me that women often focus on pitching their skills, data, and metrics rather than selling a big vision, something men are more comfortable doing. That vision may be grandiose and nearly impossible to achieve, but it sure sounds good. Investors want to fund outsize successes, and telling a good story is critical. That's why you will often hear investors say they fund people instead of ideas. VCs want to believe in an entrepreneur's idea, but they want to believe even more in that entrepreneur's willingness to think big and drive to succeed at any cost. That said, if investors are already predisposed to doubt that women have what it takes to deliver a big return, would they believe a woman who said she could? VCs want to hear a visionary pitch, the story of a billion-dollar opportunity that will justify the financial risk required to make it happen. But if a woman does make a visionary pitch, VCs are prone to doubt that she will be able to bring that vision to life. With men, they are more willing to believe that the sky's the limit.

On top of this, VCs generally spend years working closely with the handful of founders they've chosen to fund, helping them make the dream a reality. Given that level of commitment, it's no surprise they want to bet on companies they are truly passionate about. But here's the catch-22: because most venture capitalists are men, they are likely to be more passionate about ideas that appeal to, well, men. When Lake was raising her seed round, she noticed that a fair number of little league coaching apps were getting funded. "I'm like, how big of a business is that? Seriously, a T-ball league? But your target audience is these VCs who manage their sons' T-ball league," Lake says. "There's bias that gets introduced in terms of what people's passions are, what people's interests are . . . what industries people understand, and what they personally feel an affinity toward. I do think there ends up being a bias against where women are the primary opportunity."

When VCs do fund women, however, they often do right by them. Julia Hartz co-founded Eventbrite with her husband, Kevin, the early PayPal board member. Sequoia backed Eventbrite and Roelof Botha joined the board. When Kevin stepped down as Eventbrite's CEO in 2016, Julia became one of the few female chief executives in Silicon

Valley. "You start to think, okay, there are a million different ways I could fail here," Hartz says. "So you look for signs of people who are going to support you or people who are going to judge you." Sequoia definitely fell into the first category, Hartz says. She visits the firm's offices monthly to discuss strategy with Botha. "I get the sense that I'm not a sideshow [for them]," she says. "I'm not somebody that they are even trying to exploit. I'm like any other CEO, and they are there to help." As for Moritz's comment that hiring women would involve lowering the firm's standards, Hartz says, "It certainly runs counter to what I'm experiencing."

Adi Tatarko, CEO of the home design company Houzz, says her Sequoia investors have been very understanding of her working-mom issues—for example, when she has to schedule around her sons' birthdays and basketball games. "I'm not trying to protect Mike [Moritz] or anyone else there or being diplomatic here," Tatarko says. "I have had lots of discussions with them, and they are truly looking for more, to do more, to invest more, to support more, and bring more relevant women forward."

Ultimately, Katrina Lake secured Series B funding for Stitch Fix from Benchmark, and one of its general partners, the acclaimed investor Bill Gurley, joined her board. Gurley discovered Stitch Fix via his assistant who was spending an inordinate portion of her income on a personal styling service. As soon as he met Lake, he was impressed. She is "nutty smart," Gurley told me in May 2016. Fifteen minutes into her presentation, he asked for more details on the startup's cash flow. "She opened up her laptop and said 'Let's look,' and she had a three-year-forward financial model, balance statement, income statement, and cash flow statement. I've never seen an entrepreneur do that in twenty years," Gurley said.

In just a few years, Stitch Fix became one of the most promising e-commerce companies in Silicon Valley. In 2017, Stitch Fix filed for an IPO and revealed that it was profitable with $977 million in annual sales and about six thousand employees. Other female entrepreneurs hoped Lake would prove to all venture capitalists that they should be investing in more women. That same year, however, a disturbing scandal made it clear that one insanely successful female founder would not change an entire industry—not when that industry had a much bigger problem than it had ever admitted with male investors sexually harassing female entrepreneurs. And Lake was one of the most prominent victims.

THE PREDATORS IN VC

In 2013, an investor by the name of Justin Caldbeck, of Lightspeed Venture Partners, led an early investment in Stitch Fix and became a board observer. Multiple sources who were close to Lake at the time say that Caldbeck initially provided invaluable help to the promising start-up, including recruiting new Stitch Fix executives. But at some point he made Lake feel so uncomfortable that she asked Lightspeed to remove him from the board. The following year, Caldbeck left Lightspeed, ostensibly because he wanted to start his own fund, Binary Capital. Lake was asked to sign a nondisparagement agreement, mandating that neither party ever speak of what happened.

Jeremy Liew, a managing director at Lightspeed, told me, "Justin was with us for a few years. He made some excellent investments, and we mutually decided he would not be part of Fund 10," that is, Lightspeed's next fund. To some industry insiders, that was code for "he got fired." Others I spoke to had never heard rumors of Caldbeck's being disciplined for questionable behavior. Caldbeck and his new partner, Jonathan Teo, were able to raise $125 million for Binary Capital's first fund, including a personal investment from Lightspeed partner Ravi Mhatre. Binary made several investments over the next two years. In the meantime, several female entrepreneurs discovered, by talking among themselves, that they weren't the only ones Caldbeck had sexually harassed.

Caldbeck had walked on to the Duke University basketball team, got an MBA from Harvard, worked at McKinsey, Bain Capital Ventures, and then Lightspeed. He was once described to me as a "Walking LinkedIn," an investor who can make an introduction to anyone and everyone. "He is an aggressive personality," one female entrepreneur told me. "He gets deals done and gets to the right people. He is just a hustler." Turns out Caldbeck didn't just hustle deals.

In 2010, former Googler Niniane Wang started a co-working space for elite entrepreneurs called Sunfire. Sequoia, Benchmark, and other VC firms backed Sunfire in exchange for the opportunity to visit the office and interact with high-potential founders. Bain Capital Ventures, where Caldbeck then worked, was also a sponsor, and sent him as the firm's representative. Every Thursday, Sunfire held drinks at a nearby bar from 6:00 to 7:00 p.m. One day, Caldbeck told Wang he wanted her opinion on a fashion start-up and asked if they could discuss it in person after the weekly drinks, saying he had a meeting beforehand. By the time he arrived, everyone had left but Wang. When she started to talk about the start-up, Caldbeck stopped her. "Let's not talk about work," he said. He went on to grill her about her dating history and comment about outfits she had worn that he thought she looked good in. "He asked to move to a booth," Wang told me. "He sat so his body was touching my body. At one point, I agreed to let him embrace me." When Caldbeck drove her home, he kept pressuring her to let him spend the night. Finally, she says, she managed to persuade him to drop her off and leave her alone.

Wang said she felt ambushed. "I had no mental preparation that this could or would happen, so I had not at all emotionally prepared for what to do. It's a serious issue to terminate a relationship with a financial backer. I felt trapped. In a personal situation, I could say no more forcefully, but I was worried that it would have financial consequences for other people," including the other entrepreneurs who shared space at Sunfire.

After that night, Wang said, Caldbeck pursued her relentlessly, texting and calling at odd hours and suggesting they could have a secret relationship. "I just kept saying no, and then eventually he switched to sending me lots of work messages at inappropriate times." Caldbeck continued to visit the work space, which made Wang even more uncomfortable. She never reported Caldbeck's behavior to Bain Capital, but later decided not to renew Bain's sponsorship. "I always worried that if I said anything, it would cause damage to others, not just to myself, but to others I cared about, and that always gave me a lot of pause," Wang says.

Eventually, Wang confided in a fellow female entrepreneur and discovered that the other woman had also had an uncomfortable experience with Caldbeck. "Oh, he's harassing me too," she said. A few years later, Wang heard about yet another woman with a Caldbeck story. "I continued to hear rumors about other women," she said, but Caldbeck was getting away with it. "There seemed to be no consequence," she told me. "His fund continued to get bigger and bigger. I knew that Justin was continuing to harass more women, and he seemed to be getting more and more bold." Seven years after her first encounter with Caldbeck, she said, "I felt that I had to stop him." Wang told her story to Reed Albergotti, a reporter at *The Information*, and spent hours persuading other women to speak to him as well. In all, six women came forward alleging bad experiences with Caldbeck, but none of them would allow Albergotti to use their names. Wang says the editors at *The Information* decided they needed at least some of the women to speak on the record. "The only way to get this article published was to use my real name," Wang said. "I had nothing to gain and a lot to lose." Still, Wang concluded that her harassment by Caldbeck had already been so painful that she was willing to suffer a little bit more to expose him, plus she was at a strong place in her career, having been a star at Google, the chief technology officer of the online design marketplace Minted, and more recently founded a company called Evertoon.

Wang decided she would go on the record and persuaded two other entrepreneurs to do so as well: Susan Ho and Leiti Hsu, the co-founders of the travel start-up Journy, both of whom said they had been sexually harassed by Caldbeck. After a fund-raising meeting, Ho says Caldbeck sent her a text message at 1:00 a.m. asking to meet up. She hesitated to meet with him again but decided she had no choice. "We were in a place with our business that was make or break," Ho told me. Assuming safety in numbers, Ho asked Hsu to accompany her. Midway through the meeting, Caldbeck grabbed Hsu's thigh under the table. "Like out of nowhere," Hsu later recalled, explaining to me, "It was just like, wow, the trope of the wealthy, powerful Silicon Valley investor is real—the one that grabs your thigh." Hsu says she casually shook his hand off.

When *The Information* published the allegations against Caldbeck, naming Wang, Ho, and Hsu, the statements from Caldbeck and Binary Capital were surprisingly confident. Caldbeck said, "I strongly deny *The Information*'s attacks on my character. The fact is, I have always enjoyed respectful relationships with female founders, business partners, and investors." Binary Capital said the allegations were "false" and that while *The Information* had "found a few examples which show that Justin has in the past occasionally dated or flirted with women he met in a professional capacity, let's be clear: there is no evidence that Justin did anything illegal and there is no evidence that any of his investing decisions were affected by his social interests."

In the hours after the article went live, the Silicon Valley Twittersphere, which is normally quick to pile on, was quiet. Wang's worst fear—that she would convince other women to risk their careers and no one would care—seemed to be coming true. Some women did immediately back her. Sarah Lacy of *PandoDaily* wrote a post begging, "Where's the outrage?" Ellen Pao sent Wang a message applauding her bravery. When a few VCs tweeted condemnation of Caldbeck's behavior, Pao retweeted them, adding, "We drive women out of tech if we don't speak up."

The following day, Reid Hoffman spoke up in a big way with a lengthy blog post titled "The Human Rights of Women Entrepreneurs." Hoffman wrote, "This is entirely immoral and outrageous behavior," so why the lack of outrage? "Folks may think: well, that's bad behavior but not my problem. If you think that, and work here in venture, think again," Hoffman continued. "We all need to solve this problem. If you stay silent, if you don't act, then you allow this problem to perpetuate." In his post, Hoffman proposed something other women in tech had suggested to me, building "an industry-wide HR function" that would presumably govern interactions between investors and entrepreneurs and keep individual companies from burying allegations. He also asked that investors who stand against this behavior speak up online and include this hashtag: #DecencyPledge.

Several investors responded, including Roelof Botha of Sequoia, who tweeted, "At Sequoia we support the #DecencyPledge." Hoffman's call to action sent a strong message to female founders that they mattered and led to the airing of some of Greylock's own dirty laundry. Internally, it emerged that Greylock's COO, Tom Frangione, had an inappropriate relationship with a female employee. Within three days, Greylock investigated, and Frangione was asked to resign. The firm called it a "significant lapse of judgment" that was "inconsistent" with its values. "If you're going to talk the talk, you have to walk the walk, and we all moved very quickly on it," Hoffman told me of the Frangione incident. He also says the partners held a meeting in which they told staff that if anyone knew of any more untoward behavior, they should feel comfortable enough to report it immediately.

In the days that followed, the story of sexism in venture capital that I had been following for more than a year became a moving target. Several of the women who came forward were women of color. "It's fucked up and a bit dark," one female entrepreneur told me. "They're taking advantage of those who are the most vulnerable." Things everyone had whispered came out into the open. Investors whom I had been tipped off about as being "bad guys" were exposed. I had spent months trying to persuade women who had confided in me to go on the record. Most felt too ashamed, intimidated, or downright petrified to talk publicly. But after Caldbeck's public takedown, my in-box was suddenly full of emails from women wanting to openly tell their stories about the investors who had invited them back to their hotel room, tried to kiss them, or even just made a creepy comment about their lipstick. They felt emboldened, empowered, and, to be frank, fed up.

And slowly the real story emerged: that most women who have tried to raise money in Silicon Valley have not just one or two stories to tell about how someone made them feel uncomfortable but too many stories to count. "Whether it be a snide comment or just a hug that's a little too grabby," Hsu says, "this is just stuff that happens all the time."

A week after the Caldbeck revelations, Katie Benner at the *New York Times* published a story in which two dozen women came forward about several different prominent investors. Susan Wu, a longtime entrepreneur, told the *Times* that she had a bad experience not only with Caldbeck but also with the billionaire venture capitalist Chris Sacca, who she said had once touched her face at a party in a way that made her feel uncomfortable. Sacca preempted the article with a lengthy post that he published hours before the *Times* story broke that included the phrase "I am sorry" five times. He later disputed Wu's particular account but admitted that he had played a role in the industry's larger problem with sexism. "There is no doubt I said and did things that made some women feel awkward, unwelcome, insecure, and/or discouraged," Sacca wrote.

Another entrepreneur, Sarah Kunst, told the *Times* that Dave McClure, a co-founder of the early-stage venture fund 500 Startups, had also made unwelcome advances toward her. After talking to her about a potential job at 500 Startups, McClure sent Kunst a text message, saying, "I was getting confused figuring out whether to hire you or hit on you." McClure also responded to the allegations with a long-winded apology; his was titled "I'm a Creep. I'm Sorry." He said he had already been removed as CEO of 500 Startups, due to the allegations, but that he would remain at the company to focus on fiduciary obligations to investors. For the female CEO Cheryl Yeoh, that apology fell short. She published her own account of how McClure, who was an investor in her company, got her drunk at a gathering of tech folk at her apartment.

Of that night, Yeoh wrote, "Dave kept pouring scotch into my glass . . . suddenly, everyone except Dave decided to order a cab . . . I quickly asked if Dave wanted to leave like the rest of them but he said no. Perplexed, I offered him to crash on the couch or the guest room and proceeded to show him the guest room. Then I went into my own bedroom but Dave followed me there, and that's when he first propositioned to sleep with me. I said no . . . At this point, I led him to the door and told him he needs to leave. On the way out, he pushed himself onto me to the point where I was backed into a corner, made contact to kiss me, and said something along the lines of 'Just one night, please just this one time.' Then he told me how he really likes strong and smart women like me. Disgusted and outraged, I said no firmly again, pushed him away, and made sure he was out my door." As Yeoh's post went live, a female partner resigned from 500 Startups, alleging the firm had tried to cover up the allegations against McClure. That same day, McClure left the firm for good. It was becoming clear that bad behavior in the industry had long been tolerated, ignored, or not taken seriously. And everyone wondered how many investors had yet to be exposed, how many never would be, and how many women would remain silent.

"Usually, the accused knows so many more stories than what has been reported because the people who come forward are the people who did not give in, did not have sex," Wang says. "The VCs put out these heartfelt apologies . . . and people fall for it. You hear people say, 'Well, he groped her, but it's not that bad.' Well, it *is* that bad."

Toward the end of the summer of 2017, the venture capital firm DFJ (originally named Draper Fisher Jurvetson) launched an independent investigation into alleged misconduct by one of its co-founders, Steve Jurvetson, a longtime friend of Elon Musk, and a Tesla and

SpaceX investor. Then, in October, female entrepreneur Keri Krukal publicly posted on Facebook: "Women approached by a founding partner of Draper Fisher Jurvetson should be careful. Predatory behavior is rampant." Shortly thereafter, Jurvetson left the firm and took a leave of absence from the boards of Tesla and SpaceX. In a Facebook post, he said he had departed due to "interpersonal dynamics" with his partners and implied that the allegations involved personal, rather than professional, relationships. "It is excruciating to learn just how quickly, in one news cycle, people conclude that because I have left DFJ there must be some credence to vicious and wholly false allegations about sexual predation and workplace harassment. Let me be perfectly clear: no such allegations are true," Jurvetson said. Whatever happened, men in technology were finally being held accountable.

Just a few weeks later, I published a *Bloomberg* article in which multiple women claimed they were sexually assaulted or harassed by yet another prominent investor, Shervin Pishevar. In December 2014, Pishevar, an early Uber backer, attended the company's "Roaring 20s"–themed holiday party with a pony, wearing a Santa hat, on a leash. But that wasn't the only stunt he allegedly pulled. Pishevar, then forty years old, also approached Uber employee Austin Geidt (then thirty), put his hand on her leg, and moved it up her dress, according to a current colleague and a former colleague. Geidt squirmed away, the colleagues say.

Pishevar, a major Democratic party donor who raised money for President Obama and hosted a fundraiser with George Clooney for presidential candidate Hillary Clinton, was one of Uber's most influential backers; he maintained an especially close relationship to cofounder Travis Kalanick. Geidt, who joined Uber as its fourth employee and its first woman, was in charge of launching the ride-sharing company in new cities at the time. A person with firsthand knowledge of Pishevar's behavior toward Geidt confirmed the holiday party account. Though Geidt declined to comment when the story broke, it's clear Pishevar was in a position of power. He had recently co-founded his own venture fund, Sherpa Capital, and the futuristic tube transportation company Hyperloop One. Pishevar, through his lawyer, denied the allegation and told *Bloomberg* that he and Geidt always maintained a "friendly, professional relationship." His representatives also directed us to speak with someone else who had attended the party, and asked not to be named, who claimed that Pishevar couldn't have touched anyone that night because he had a drink in one hand and the pony leash in the other. The "pony defense" was widely mocked on social media.

Five other women also told me that Pishevar used his influence to pursue unwanted sexual encounters with them, but declined to reveal their names, citing fears that he could retaliate and destroy their careers. One of the women, an entrepreneur, told me that Pishevar started hitting on her at a dinner meeting to discuss investing in her company, then forcibly kissed and groped her later in the evening. Another woman who works in the tech industry said she met Pishevar for dinner in 2013 to discuss career opportunities. He invited her back to his home, where, she said, "He basically jumped on me, tried to put his tongue down my throat, and I stopped it." Also that year, a third woman, who Pishevar had hired to work for him, says he repeatedly tried to pressure her into having sex with him. Though she told him she was not interested in a romantic relationship in a Facebook message shared with me, he booked one hotel room for the two of them on a trip. That's where she says he tried to perform oral sex on her until she convinced him to stop. "It felt really wrong, and it was really confusing at the time," she told me. "I just remember his big body on top of me. I was young enough to be his daughter." At the Web Summit conference in November 2013, where Pishevar spoke onstage with Tesla CEO Elon Musk, a fourth woman says she went to an afterparty that Pishevar had organized at a hotel. There, she said, she found herself alone on the couch with Pishevar and another man. Pishevar, she said, was holding a phone—it's unclear who it belonged to—and was smiling as he was showing her photos of genitalia of women they claimed to have slept with. A fifth woman says Pishevar hired her company to work for him in 2015. He invited her to a party in Los Angeles where, she said, he force-kissed her, then, in the weeks that followed, tried to bully her into dating him.

In response to these allegations, Pishevar's representatives said, "We are confident that these anecdotes will be shown to be untrue." At the time, he was already in the midst of fighting press coverage of his arrest in London in May 2017 after a woman accused him of rape. London police say he was "released under investigation" but not charged. His lawyer confirmed that Pishevar was "detained briefly" but "categorically denied" the sexual assault allegation, saying, "He fully cooperated with the police investigation which was exhaustive and detailed. In July he was informed that no further action would be taken against him and he was 'de-arrested' [a British legal term]." Pishevar also sued a so-called Republican opposition research firm that he accused of spreading false information about him in a smear campaign. The firm said it never conducted work on Pishevar and called his claims "delusional." It was by far one of the most dramatic tales yet of misbehavior by powerful men in Silicon Valley.

JUSTIN CALDBECK RESIGNED FROM Binary Capital three days after *The Information* article was published and updated his initial statement. "Obviously, I am deeply disturbed by these allegations. While significant context is missing from the incidents reported by *The Information,* I deeply regret ever causing anyone to feel uncomfortable . . . There's no denying this is an issue in the venture community, and I hate that my behavior has contributed to it." Binary Capital's fund-raising was halted, and the firm effectively started to shut down, and Caldbeck's partner, Jonathan Teo, who had initially supported him, also offered to resign.

At the height of the scandal, Ann Lai, a former employee of Binary Capital, filed a lawsuit against the firm for post-resignation harassment. Lai said she left the firm because of a sexist environment that involved inappropriate conduct with other female staff members and routine comments about her attractiveness and that of female founders looking for funding. After her departure, she alleges in her lawsuit, the harassment began, and she presented to the court detailed messages in which Caldbeck threatened to make sure "she would never work again" if she spoke poorly about the firm. She claimed that Binary also threatened to withhold her share of the profits from its investments. The suit also claims that Binary falsely told Lai's potential new employers that she had been fired for poor performance and that Lai—who had three Harvard degrees, including a PhD in engineering—had trouble finding a job as a result.

One doesn't have to look too closely at how Binary operated to figure out how the fund was run. Caldbeck and Teo spent big to transform a former brewery into their new office, which featured a long marble bar. "They wanted their office to look like a high-end club or residence. They didn't want it to feel like a traditional work space," designer Ariel Ashe told *Architectural Digest* in a feature about the new location. "There is a focus on entertaining as they wanted to be able to throw parties in the space." Caldbeck and Teo were well known among entrepreneurs and investors as the "party VCs" who made frequent trips to Las Vegas. In fact, the pair met in Vegas while Caldbeck was dancing with Teo's executive assistant from Benchmark Capital, where Teo worked at the time. It was a match made in Sin City heaven.

Someone close to the firm told me the partners had an informal rule that Caldbeck wasn't allowed to meet female entrepreneurs at a bar after 5:30 p.m., because he simply couldn't be trusted not to cross the line (Caldbeck denies this). The same person said that when Caldbeck was confronted about coming on too strong to certain women, he would mutter things like he had "only asked her to dinner" and "chicks are so dumb." I've seen multiple sexually explicit text messages sent by Caldbeck to a woman he has harassed in which he employs obscene language to describe pleasuring himself while thinking about her.

As the Caldbeck saga unfolded, *Recode* added Katrina Lake's name to the list of women he had made uncomfortable. Lightspeed, his employer at the time, tweeted, "In light of what we have learned since, we regret we did not take stronger action." Lightspeed partner Ravi Mahtre immediately forfeited his original investment in Binary.

Three months after his resignation, I met Caldbeck with my colleague Mark Milian to ask about these charges. Caldbeck was somber and contrite, and admitted that he had repeatedly screwed up, referring to his former self as "unselfaware me." He said he was writing letters of apology to all of the women who came forward (though he had yet to send them). He would not comment on the record about specific allegations, including any interactions with Katrina Lake.

A few days later he followed up with a statement promising to become a "beacon of accountability," and help "ignite honest self-reflection and positive change." His new mission will involve speaking to college students. "Through intense therapy and lots of research on sexual harassment, I had a realization that behavior that is defined as sexual harassment in the workplace is common behavior amongst many college men . . . This behavior is often referred to as bro-culture. My focus moving forward is to help eradicate the bro culture and create a positive change for women by elevating consciousness in men."

I'd find such a mea culpa much more compelling if it had come *before* the public shaming. Was "lots of research" really necessary for such basic insights? His statement alone reveals just how cloistered and cut off certain powerful men in Silicon Valley can become.

THE FOLKS WHO COULD FORCE THE VCS TO CHANGE

While Lake also won't comment on her experience with Caldbeck, she raises a good point: that there are zero guidelines governing the relationship between venture capitalists and entrepreneurs. Typically, venture capital firms are too small to have a human resources department, and there's no industry code of conduct. VCs maintain that they are under pressure to behave appropriately because their entire careers rest on their reputations. If they do anything stupid, entrepreneurs will tell other entrepreneurs, who won't want to take their money. The argument is that's enough to prevent bad behavior. But there's enough documented bad behavior to suggest that given the tremendous power differential between venture capitalists and the founders who desperately need their money, this disincentive has little effect. There is only one group of people in Silicon Valley who have more power than the VCs, enough power to punish them for bad behavior toward women, and that is the limited partners (LPs), the individuals and groups who provide the money that VCs dole out to everyone else.

"The only thing that VCs are measured on, their success, is 100 percent measured on returns," Lake told me. "There is nobody who is holding them accountable to conduct business in a good way . . . They just need to make a lot of money for the LPs. How they do it matters less to the LPs."

To explain: LPs fund VCs, and VCs fund entrepreneurs. (Sometimes VCs invest a small portion of their own money into their portfolio companies depending on the firm's policies.) Either way, the money that LPs provide to VC funds is critical. This capital comes from pension funds, school and family endowments, high net-worth individuals, hedge funds, and the like. Just as start-ups raise money from venture capitalists in exchange for equity, general partners (GPs) at VC firms raise money from limited partners in exchange for the promise of big returns over a certain period of time, usually ten years or so.

Whether Binary's LPs knew of Justin Caldbeck's reputation is an open question. One LP faulted Lightspeed for not sharing the full story of his departure, but that person admitted the firm re-upped an investment in Binary even after hearing rumors about his falling-out with Lake. Several LPs said they had approached Caldbeck about the rumors; when he denied them, they took him at his word. Another LP told my colleague Sarah McBride that over three dozen reference calls were made about Caldbeck and Teo, and "we have never had reference checks that were so enthusiastic." Some find this a little hard to believe. When I started writing this book, a full year before Wang stepped forward to *The Information*, Caldbeck's behavior was already an open secret.

I sat down with Kirsten Green of Forerunner Ventures in 2016, long before the allegations against Caldbeck were published. She told me simply, "We don't do business with them." And she said she had told many LPs the same thing. "When they raised that fund so fast, it was like, what? They're fun guys. Do fun guys help you raise a fund? In an environment where there's plenty of people to put your money with, I'm not sure why you need to put your money there." Canvas Ventures partner Rebecca Lynn told me, "I don't think all LPs knew but I think some of them knew. They thought it was great he was in the party crowd. All these guys were known for a long time and no one cared. You could have made a couple phone calls and you would have known."

Part of the problem is that LPs themselves are competing to get their money into the best VC funds. From 2014 to 2017, venture investors in the United States raised $130 billion from LPs to deploy into start-ups. One LP told me, "I just want the best GPs. I don't care who they are; I just want the best returns. Some of the best GPs aren't the best people, but they drive the best returns."

When I started researching where the money comes from, I expected to learn that most Silicon Valley LPs were also white and male. I was surprised to find far more women sitting around the tables of limited partnerships than at venture capital firms. For example, the chief investment officers of many of the institutions with the most prestigious endowments are women, from the Smithsonian to the Metropolitan Museum of Art. And they're not interested in policing the industry's bad boys.

"There are a lot of women in the LP community, but all of us would say the same thing," says Joelle Kayden, founder of Accolade Partners, a limited partnership that invests in a variety of different venture firms including Accel and Andreessen Horowitz (two firms that had no female investment partners as of 2017). "We'd like to see more women [at venture capital firms], but if you stuck a gun to our heads, we'd invest based on returns." Kayden's job, after all, is to deliver returns to her own investors.

When Kayden and I spoke, Sequoia had just hired its first female partner and Benchmark had yet to do so. It was in that context that Kayden told me, "Part of the problem is [those two firms] have the best returns in the entire industry. What are you going to do, not invest in them? I'd die to be in those funds; I wouldn't turn them down because they don't have a woman. I will do whatever it takes to have great numbers."

WOMEN GOING THEIR OWN WAY

So, if the people funding the VC industry won't force change, the industry won't change unless it changes from within. These days, more women investors are taking matters into their own hands. When Aileen Lee worked at Kleiner, she was assigned due diligence on the firm's investment in the high-tech motorized scooter the Segway, which, in retrospect, was greatly overhyped. She took herself for a spin and quickly realized the scooter had several drawbacks (it was expensive and required training to use, and there was nowhere to hang your purse, briefcase, or groceries). "I had instincts leading me to believe the product wouldn't be a hit. I wish I'd voiced these concerns more effectively, but I was working with such legends, and I thought they knew better."

Every investor has a list of woulda, shoulda, coulda's, to be fair, but had Lee spoken up, she might have saved Kleiner a lot of money— that is, if the legends had listened. A few years later, Lee suggested the firm make a seed investment in a quickly growing ride-hailing company called Uber. At that time, however, Kleiner didn't typically invest at such an early stage. Later, she encouraged the partners to meet with Uber's then-CEO Travis Kalanick as he was raising the Series B, but there was little interest. Given the juggernaut that Uber became—despite its cultural issues—clearly this was a missed opportunity. (Again, Kleiner later invested in Uber at a much higher valuation.) Lee started to believe she might have more success by striking out on her own.

With the blessing of Kleiner, Lee started raising money in 2012 for her own seed fund, Cowboy Ventures. Seed investing was a new, risky category, but Lee was optimistic she'd get enough money, because she had built relationships with other investors who introduced her to the right LPs. Still, it wasn't easy. At one meeting, an LP asked whether she had kids. She replied that she had three. "He was like, 'Whoa, how is this going to work? Are you going to run the fund *and* have the kids?' I'm like, 'No, I'm going to get rid of them,'" Lee joked.

That particular fund ended up investing in Cowboy Ventures anyway. "I was kind of torn. Should I take their money? They clearly have a weirdness about me being a working mom," Lee recalls. But she thought, "I'm going to kick ass, and maybe all their weirdnesses will go away."

Lee's firm is in its early days, but she has been quietly building a well-respected brand; she even coined the now widely used term "unicorn" to refer to start-ups with billion-dollar exits. In 2016, she added her first unicorn to the Cowboy portfolio, when the razor-subscription start-up Dollar Shave Club (which Lee had invested in initially at Kleiner and again at Cowboy) sold to Unilever for $1 billion. How did Lee manage to see the potential in a service that was mostly for men? "You don't need men for razor deals and women for tampon deals," she points out.

Still, while women like Lee are blazing new trails in venture capital, barriers remain to busting into one of the most exclusive boys' clubs in the business world. In 2014, a journalist got wind of a secret all-male club of venture capitalists called VC 21, consisting of male partners from a variety of firms, including Kleiner, Accel, and Greylock. Once club members realized the press was on the scent, they invited a few female investors to join, and the bad PR was averted. VC 21 was later rebranded as the Venture Social Club.

An email to club members in March 2017 touted an all-expenses-paid stay at the Rosewood hotel in Menlo Park and an "over the top" long weekend at the Montage on Maui, "complete with sunset cruises, ocean fun and private dinner experiences." Members have also told me of similar trips, involving stays at spectacular mansions, sporting events such as heli-skiing, ridiculous amounts of drinking, and elaborate dinners accompanied by $200 bottles of wine. All of this luxury is sponsored by various banks, law firms, and limited partners, all of whom want access to top deals. "They've been sponsoring people for years, and they're paying for everything, right down to the massages," says one member.

These sponsors are footing the bill because a lot of business is getting done. The offhand gossip over drinks, the ten minutes on a ski lift—all can have billion-dollar consequences. Chance encounters and opportunities unavailable to all the women who weren't invited into the club.

On the club email chain, members discuss deal flow and congratulate one another on big exits. These messages involve a fair amount of backslapping, including bro-ish comments such as "You're the fucking man, drinks on you!" and "You're awesome! Baller!" one member explains. It's an atmosphere in which many women would feel uncomfortable; still, it's great that some female VCs are now members. It's not so great that they have missed out on these networking opportunities for most of the last ten years.

When I asked female investors what they thought of the Venture Social Club, most just rolled their eyes. "What it seems like from the outside is you have a country club that only invites certain members," one female VC said. "I kind of say, 'Fuck them.'" Then she reconsidered. "Tell me what it's about and tell me that it's not discriminatory and I'll think about it." All VCs know if they want to get ahead, they have to play the game that's on the field.

Then again, maybe the game is starting to change. Kirsten Green of Forerunner was named VC of the Year by *TechCrunch* in 2017 (she also invested in Dollar Shave Club and Jet.com, which was acquired by Walmart for $3 billion), and she doesn't fret too much that she'll miss opportunities because she's not hanging out with the guys. "I don't want to be left out of deals because I'm not going on the guys' trip to wherever, but at the end of the day, I don't want to go on the guys' trip," Green says. "Maybe we [female VCs] just need to have some of our own stuff." To that end, Green recently bought a bunch of box seats to see the comedian Amy Schumer and invited other industry women. "I think there are some really cool women in this business that I like a lot and want to do business with," she says.

As for Aileen Lee, she now hosts an annual gathering of powerful women at her home, where the husbands and partners of the guests don suits and pass out the drinks. At the most recent event, Chamath Palihapitiya kindly served me some sparkling water.

In case her intentions weren't already clear, Lee dubbed the event Ladyfest.

6

SEX AND THE VALLEY: MEN PLAY, WOMEN PAY

bout once a month, on a Friday or Saturday night, a select group of the Silicon Valley Technorati gather for a drug-heavy, sex-heavy party. Sometimes the venue is an epic mansion in San Francisco's Pacific Heights; sometimes it's a lavish home in the foothills of Atherton or Hillsborough. On special occasions, the guests will travel north to someone's château in Napa Valley or to a private beachfront property in Malibu or to a boat off the coast of Ibiza, and the bacchanal will last an entire weekend or longer. The places change, but many of the players and the purpose remain the same.

The stories I've been told by nearly two dozen people who have attended these events or have intimate knowledge of them are remarkable in a number of ways. Many participants don't seem the least bit embarrassed, much less ashamed. On the contrary, they speak proudly about how they're overturning traditions and paradigms in their private lives, just as they do in the technology world they rule. Like Julian Assange denouncing the nation-state, industry hotshots speak of these activities in a tone that is at once self-congratulatory and dismissive of criticism. Their behavior at these high-end parties is an extension of the progressiveness and open-mindedness—the audacity, if you will—that makes founders think they can change the world. And they believe that their entitlement to disrupt doesn't stop at technology; it extends to society as well. However, few participants have been willing to describe these scenes to me without a guarantee of anonymity.

Sex parties are just one aspect—albeit an impressively excessive one—of today's sexually open Valley culture. Everyone, it seems, is experimenting with their sexual lives and relationships. A thriving hook-up culture is fueled by apps such as Bumble and Tinder. Open relationships are common and there is an active polyamorous community. For the large population of young heterosexual men in tech making six figures, there is also the pay-for-sex scene that includes strip clubs, easy access to online escorts, and a new type of prostitution promoted by numerous "sugar daddy" websites where men pay women regular stipends for their companionship.

If this activity was just relegated to personal lives it would be one thing. But what happens at these sex parties—and in open relationships and at strip clubs as we'll see later—unfortunately doesn't stay there. The freewheeling sex lives pursued by men in tech—from the elite down to the rank and file—have consequences for how business gets done in Silicon Valley.

SEX PARTIES OF THE TECH AND FAMOUS

From reports of those who have attended these parties, guests and hosts include powerful first-round investors, well-known entrepreneurs, and top executives. Some of them are the titans of the Valley, household names, men whose faces have graced the covers of tech and business magazines. Billionaires abound. The female guests have different qualifications. If you are attractive, willing, and (usually) young, you needn't worry about your résumé or bank account. Some of the women work in tech in the Bay Area, but others come from Los Angeles and beyond, and are employed in symbiotic local industries such as real estate, personal training, and public relations. In some scenarios, the ratio of women to wealthy men is roughly two to one, so the men have more than enough women to choose from. "You know when it's that kind of party," one male tech investor told me. "At normal tech parties, there are hardly any women. At these kinds of parties, there are tons of them."

Over the last two years, numerous sources have told me that this culture has become rampant, though this has been the hardest chapter of this book to report by far. Many potential sources, especially women, abruptly canceled meetings with me the day of. Others asked me not to reveal their names, fearing retribution.

Still, I believe there is a critical story to tell about how the women who participate in these events are often marginalized, even if they attend of their own volition. One female investor who had heard of this culture before I approached her told me, "Women are participating in these parties to improve their lives. They are an underclass in Silicon Valley." A male investor who works for one of the most powerful men in tech put it this way: "I see a lot of men leading people on, sleeping with a dozen women at the same time. But if each of the dozen women doesn't care, is there any crime committed? You could say it's disgusting but not illegal; it just perpetuates a culture that keeps women down."

To be clear, there is a wide range of parties for experimental sexual behavior. Some, devoted entirely to sex, may be drug- and alcohol-free (to encourage safety and performance) and demand a balanced gender ratio. Others are very heavy on drugs and women and usually end in group "cuddle puddles," a gateway to ever-so-slightly more discreet sexual encounters. The path by which women are lured into these sex parties differs. One female tech worker told me she fell into a high-flying, open-minded crowd after attending a party for the Bravo reality show about Silicon Valley. "I was invited to some villa in the city, I had just graduated from college, and it sounded cool and glam-orous," she said. That took her on a series of unexpected adventures, including a sex party where several tech founders and engineers were in attendance and food was being served off the bodies of naked women. A few years later, this same woman met an investor who was trying to sell off some of his shares in a multibillion-dollar start-up on the secondary market. She introduced him to prospective buyers and received a commission for her efforts. The pair started dating, and the investor took her to exclusive dinner parties, one of which ended up being a sex party. When I asked for more details, she grew quiet. Talking about these events to anyone on the outside, she said, is "seen as the ultimate betrayal."

Men show up only if directly invited by the host, and they can bring as many women as they want, but guys can't come along as plus ones (that would upset the preferred gender ratio). Invitations are shared via word of mouth, Facebook, Snapchat (perfect, because messages soon disappear), or even basic Paperless Post. Nothing in the wording screams "sex party" or "cuddle puddle," just in case the invitation gets forwarded or someone takes a screen shot. No need to spell things out, anyway; the guests on the list understand just what kind of party this is. Women too will spread the word among their female friends, and the expectations are hardly hidden. "They might say, 'Do you want to come to this really exclusive hot party? The theme is bondage,'" one female entrepreneur told me. "'It's at this VC or founder's house and he asked me to invite you.'"

Perhaps this culture is just one of the many offshoots of the sexu-ally progressive Bay Area, which gave rise to the desert festival of free expression Burning Man, now frequented by the tech elite. Still, the vast majority of people in Silicon Valley have no idea these kinds of sex parties are happening at all. If you're reading this and shaking your head, saying, "This isn't the Silicon Valley that I know," you may not be a rich and edgy male founder or investor, or a female in tech in her twenties. And you might not understand anyway. "Anyone else who is on the outside would be looking at this and saying, 'Oh my God this is so fucked up,'" one female entrepreneur told me. "But the people in it have a very different perception about what's going on."

This is how the night goes down. Guests arrive before dinner and are checked in by private security guards who will turn you away if you're not on the list. Sometimes the evening is catered. But at the most intimate gatherings, guests will cook dinner together; that way they don't have to kick out the help after dessert. Alcohol lubricates the conversation until, after the final course, the designer drugs roll out. Some form of MDMA, a.k.a. Ecstasy or Molly, known for transforming relative strangers into extremely affectionate friends, is de rigueur, including Molly tablets that have been molded into the logos of some of the hottest tech companies such as Tesla and Snapchat. "People ingest Molly like candy during these events," says a woman who has partaken. Sometimes guests will mix the bitter powder with a fruity drink or stir it into a coconut.

MDMA is a powerful and long-lasting drug whose one-two punch of euphoria and manic energy can keep you rolling for three or four hours. "When you're on it, you feel like you love everybody," says one female entrepreneur. As dopamine fires, connections spark around the room, and normal inhibitions drop away. People start cuddling and making out. These aren't group orgies, per se, but guests will break out into twosomes or threesomes or more. They may disappear into one of the venue's many rooms, or they may simply get down in the open. Night turns to day, and the group reconvenes for breakfast, after which some may have intercourse again. Eat, drugs, sex, repeat.

These sex parties happen so often among the high-end, premier VC and founder crowd that this isn't a scandal or even really a secret, I've been told; it's a lifestyle choice. This isn't Prohibition or the Mc-Carthy era, people remind me; it's Silicon Valley in the twenty-first century. No one has been forced to attend, and they're not hiding anything, not even if they're married or in a committed relationship. They're just being discreet in the real world. Many guests are invited as couples—husbands and wives, boyfriends and girlfriends—because open relationships are the new normal.

While some parties might be devoted primarily to drugs and sexual activity, others may boast just pockets of it, and some guests can be caught unawares. In June 2017, one young woman—let's call her Jane Doe—received a Paperless Post invite for "a party on the edge of the earth." The invite requested "glamazon adventurer, safari chic and jungle tribal attire" for the party, to be hosted at "Casa Jurvey by the Sea"—the home of venture capitalist Steve Jurvetson in the resort beach town of Half Moon Bay, south of San Francisco. It turned out that this was the afterparty for his venture capital firm, DFJ's Big Think "unconference," an exclusive gathering for folks in the tech industry. But two invites went out for the same event, a moody, provocative Paperless Post invite, tiger and all, and then a separate, official email from Jurvetson's firm. This second invite was a straight-forward email from DFJ inviting guests to a daytime retreat that included "expert-led breakout sessions" and "The Afterthought" party at Jurvetson's home. This was just four months before he would leave the firm amid allegations of misconduct.

In photos of the party posted to a private group on Facebook, Tesla CEO Elon Musk—a longtime friend of Jurvetson's—appears, wearing a black armorlike costume adorned with silver spikes and chains. Jurvetson is sporting a feather vest and hat. Google co-founder Sergey Brin was also there, bare-chested in a vest, as was Jonathan Teo, Justin Caldbeck's business partner, who later referred to the party as "Magic" in a Facebook post. Ironically, the gathering was held just a week after sexual harassment allegations against Caldbeck had been reported, but that didn't seem to discourage certain guests from participating in heavy petting in the open.

"It was in the middle of the Binary thing," Jane Doe told me, referring to the scandal at the VC firm. "And it was all so ridiculous." Doe found herself on the floor with two other couples, including a male entrepreneur and his wife. The living room had been blanketed in plush white faux fur and pillows, where, as the evening wore on, several people lay down and started stroking one another, Doe says, in what became a sizeable cuddle puddle. Photos reveal a group of men and women lying close together, kissing and massaging one another. In a later Facebook comment, Jurvetson referred to one snapshot of the scene as "deep cuddle." One venture capitalist, dressed up as a bunny (it's unclear how this fit into the edge-of-the-earth theme), offered Jane Doe some powder in a plastic bag. It was Molly. "They said it will just make you feel relaxed and you're going to like being touched," Doe recounted to me.

Nervous, she dipped her finger into the powder and put it in her mouth. Soon, her guard dropped. Then, the male founder asked if he could kiss her. "It was so weird," she said. "I'm like, 'Your wife is right there, is she okay with this?'" The founder's wife acknowledged that, yes, she was okay with it. Jane Doe, who considers herself fairly adventurous and open-minded, kissed the founder, then became uncomfortable, feeling as if she had been pressured or targeted. "I don't know what I'm doing, I feel really stupid, I'm drugged up because I'd never taken it before and he knew I'd never taken it," she recalled. She tried to escape to a different area of the party. "I felt gross because I had participated in making out with him and then he kept trying to find me and I kept trying to run away and hide. I remember saying to him, 'Aren't people going to wonder?' And he said, 'The people that know me know what is going on and the people that don't, I don't really care.'" Before dawn, she jumped into her car and left. "What's not okay about this scene is that it is so money- and power-dominated. It's a problem because it's an abuse of power. I would never do it again."

While this particular woman felt ambushed, at more private affairs, if it's your first time, a friend might fill you in on what you're signing up for, and you are expected to keep it to yourself. You know that if you do drugs with someone you work with, you shouldn't mention it to anyone, and the same goes with sex. In other words, we're not hiding anything, but, actually, we kind of are. You get invited only if you can be trusted and if you're going to play ball. "You can choose not to hook up with [a specific] someone, but you can't not hook up with *anybody*, because that would be voyeurism. So if you don't participate, don't come in," says one frequent attendee, whom I'll call Founder X, an ambitious, world-traveling entrepreneur. This is the same general spirit at play in the orgy dome at Burning Man, popular among techies. "No spectators" is the slogan out on the playa, and so it is back home.

They don't see themselves as predatory, of course. When they look in the mirror, they see individuals setting a new paradigm of behavior by pushing the boundaries of social mores and values. "What's making this possible is the same progressiveness and openmindedness that allowed us to be creative and disruptive about ideas," Founder X told me. When I asked him about Jane Doe's experience, he said, "This is a private party where powerful people want to get together and there are a lot of women and a lot of people who are fucked up. At any party, there can be a situation where people cross the line. Somebody fucked up, somebody crossed the line, but that's not an indictment on the cuddle puddle, that's an indictment on crossing the line. Doesn't that happen anywhere?" It's worth asking, however, if these sexual adventurers are so progressive, why do these parties seem to lean so heavily toward male heterosexual fantasies? Women are often expected to be involved in threesomes that include other women; male gay and bisexual behavior is conspicuously absent. "Oddly, it's completely unthinkable that guys would be bisexual or curious," says one VC who attends and is married (I'll call him Married VC). "It's a total double standard." In other words, at these parties, men don't make out with other men. And, outside of the new types of drugs, these stories might have come out of the Playboy Mansion circa 1972.

Regardless, a select few at the very top believe it's their *obligation* to tear down traditional sexual expectations. They are just expressing who they are. Founder X summed it up this way: "You build your own team and you get to build your own reality. Why wouldn't that mentally spill over into your sexual life?"

I had a wide-ranging conversation with Twitter co-founder Evan Williams about the peculiar mixture of audacity, eccentricity, and wealth that swirls in Silicon Valley. Williams, who is married with two kids, became an internet celebrity thanks to his first company, Blogger. He pointed out that he was never single, well-known, and rich at the same time and he isn't part of this scene, but recognizes the motivations of his peers. "This is a strange place that has created incredible things in the world and therefore attracts these types of people and enables these types of people. How could it be anything but weird and dramatic and people on the edge testing everything?" On the one hand, he said, "If you thought like everyone else, you can't invent the future," yet also warned that sometimes this is a "recipe for disaster."

Rich men expecting casual sexual access to women is anything but a new paradigm. But many of the A-listers in Silicon Valley have something unique in common: a lonely adolescence devoid of contact with the opposite sex. Married VC described his teenage life as years of playing computer games and not going on a date until he was twenty years old. Now, to his amazement, he finds himself in a circle of trusted and adventurous tech friends with the money and resources to explore their every desire. After years of restriction and longing, he is living a fantasy, and his wife is right there with him. In fact, they've introduced several newbies, including Founder X, to this brave new world.

Married VC's story—that his current voraciousness is explained by his sexual deprivation in adolescence—is one I hear a lot in Silicon Valley. They are finally getting theirs.

FOUNDER HOUNDERS

There is an often-told story that Silicon Valley is filled with women looking to cash in by marrying wealthy tech moguls. Whether there really is a significant number of such women is debatable. The story about them is alive and well, however, at least among the wealthy men who fear they might fall victim. In fact, these guys even have a term for the women who pursue them: founder hounders.

When I asked Founder X whether these men are taking advantage of women by feeding them inhibition-melting drugs at sex parties, he replied that, on the contrary, it's women who are taking advantage of him and his tribe, preying on them for their money.

On their way up to a potential multimillion-dollar payout, younger founders report that more and more women seem to become mysteriously attracted to them no matter how awkward, uncool, or unattractive they may be. Alexis Ohanian, who co-founded Reddit, remembers going to bars with his co-founder, Steve Huffman, in the early days before their company was well known. They'd be proudly wearing T-shirts bearing the Reddit logo, but they had no luck with the ladies. As Reddit became more recognizable, however, the T-shirt attracted more and more attention until eventually Ohanian stopped wearing any Reddit-branded swag. In fact, when he went on dates, he would not mention Reddit at all.

"I would just try to avoid the conversation to see how long I could go before they found out where I worked," Ohanian says. Of course, the internet makes it impossible to hide such information for long. "Fuck you, I can't believe you founded Reddit," one woman texted him after a few dates. Whether she was impressed or felt deceived was a little unclear. Ohanian solved this problem by marrying someone even more famous than he is: the tennis phenomenon Serena Williams.

However many founder hounders exist, the idea of these women lives large in the minds of Silicon Valley founders, who often trade stories about women they've dated. As Founder X puts it, "We'll say whether some girl is a fucking gold digger or not, so we know who to avoid."

When I tell her this, Ava, a young female entrepreneur, rolls her eyes. According to Ava, who asked me to disguise her real identity and has dated several founders, it's the men, not the women, who seem obsessed with displays of wealth and privilege. She tells of being flown to exotic locations, put up in fancy hotels, and other ways rich men have used their money to woo her. Backing up Ava's view are the profiles one finds on dating apps where men routinely brag about their tech jobs or start-ups. In their online profiles, men are all but saying, "Hello, would you like to come up to my loft and see my stock options?"

In Ava's experience, however, once men like this land a woman, they are quick to throw her back. After a few extravagant dates, Ava says, she will initiate a conversation about where the tryst is going. The men have then ended things, several using the same explanation. "They say, 'I'm still catching up. I lost my virginity when I was twenty-five,'" Ava tells me. "And I'll say, 'Well, you're thirty-three now, are we all caught up yet?' In any other context, [these fancy dates] would be romantic, but instead it's charged because no one would fuck them in high school . . . I honestly think what they want is a do over because women wouldn't bone them until now."

Ava's jaundiced view of newly wealthy moguls would be funny if their gold-digger obsession didn't mask something serious. The claim of being stalked by women often becomes an excuse used by some tech stars to justify their own predatory behavior.

What that adds up to is a great deal of ego at play. "It's awesome," says Founder X. At work, he explains, "you're well-funded. You have relative traction." Outside work, "Why do I have to compromise? Why do I have to get married? Why do I have to be exclusive? If you've got a couple girls interested in you, you can set the terms and say this is what I want. You can say, 'I'm happy to date you, but I'm not exclusive.' These are becoming table stakes for guys who couldn't get a girl in high school." His overall plan is this: "I'll sell my company in my thirties, settle down, and have kids in my forties."

Furthermore, these elite founders, CEOs, and VCs see themselves as more influential than most hot-shit bankers, actors, and athletes will ever be.

"We have more cachet than a random rich dude because we make products that touch a lot of people," says Founder X. "You make a movie, and people watch it for a weekend. You make a product, and it touches people's lives for years. If I'm Miranda Kerr [the very successful lingerie model], I'd think Evan Spiegel [the co-founder of Snapchat who is now Kerr's husband] is a much more durable bet than Orlando Bloom [the actor who's now Kerr's ex-husband]." Bloom is only a handsome, highly paid actor, Founder X points out. That can hardly compare with Spiegel: "He's a billionaire, and he's got an empire."

At least on the financial level, Founder X has a point. The payouts of A-list actors and the wolves of Wall Street just aren't that impressive among the Silicon Valley elite. Managing directors at top-tier investment banks may pocket a million a year and be worth tens of millions after a long career. Early employees at tech firms like Uber, Airbnb, and Snapchat can make many times that amount of money in a matter of years. Celebrities such as Ashton Kutcher, Jared Leto, and Leonardo DiCaprio have jumped on that power train and now make personal investments in tech companies. The basketball great Kobe Bryant started his own venture capital firm. LeBron James has rebranded himself as not just an athlete but also an investor and entrepreneur.

With famous actors and athletes wanting to get into the tech game, it's no surprise that some in the Valley have a high opinion of their attractiveness and what they should expect or deserve in terms of their sex lives. In the Valley, this expectation is often passed off as enlightened—a contribution to the evolution of human behavior.

From many women who describe it, however, it's a new immaturity—sexist behavior dressed up with a lot of highfalutin talk—that reinforces traditional power structures, demeans women, and boosts some of the biggest male egos in history; just another manifestation of Brotopia.

One clue that this is far from "evolved" behavior would be the ubiquitous drug use. "When you are on that many drugs it puts you in that mind-set where you're not making good decisions," one female entrepreneur told me. "At the end of the day, there are reasons why drugs are illegal. It makes you fucking crazy and after all the drug stuff is over it feels quite empty. There is a huge morality issue in Silicon Valley and at the very core, it's people with money thinking they can get away with everything. A lot of these guys got lucky, became billionaires on paper, and so they feel they are kings of the universe. This stuff happens everywhere but at least it's kind of shamed in New York and Asia. In Silicon Valley for some reason it's not just okay, it's cool."

When I spoke about Silicon Valley's sex parties—specifically those where women vastly outnumber men—with Elisabeth Sheff, a Chattanooga-based writer and professor who has spent two decades researching open relationships, her reaction was heated: "That's exploitation. That's old-school, fucked-up masculine arrogance and borderline prostitution," she said. "The men don't have to prostitute themselves, because they have the money . . . 'I should be able to have sex with a woman because I'm a rich white guy.' That is not even one particle progressive; that is the same tired bullshit. It's trying to blend the new and keeping the old attitudes, and those old attitudes are based in patriarchy, so they come at the expense of women."

Jennifer Russell, who runs the established Camp Mystic at Burning Man, is more sympathetic. "Men and women are equally drawn to creating a structure that invites their full sexual expression and events like this are a safe place to dabble," she says. "It's way better than a swingers club would feel because this is at a home and you are surrounded by people you know."

Married VC admits, however, that for many men, these parties aren't so much about self-expression than they are about simply sport fucking. "Some guys will whip out their phones and show off the trophy gallery of girls they've hooked up with," he says. "Maybe this is behavior that happened on Wall Street all the time, but in a way they owned it. These founders do this, but try not to own it. They talk about diversity on one side of their mouth, but on the other side they say all of this shit."

THE NEW PARADIGM FOR WOMEN GETTING SCREWED

For successful women in Silicon Valley, the drug and sex party scene is a minefield to navigate. This isn't a matter of Bay Area tech women being more prudish than most; I doubt history has ever seen a cohort of women more adventurous or less restrained in exploring sexual boundaries. The problem is that the culture of sexual adventurism now permeating Silicon Valley tends to be more consequential for women than for men, particularly as it relates to their careers in tech.

Take multi-time entrepreneur Esther Crawford, who is familiar with sex parties (specifically those with an equal gender ratio and strict rules around consent) and talks freely about her sexual experiments and open relationships. For the last four years, she has been in a nonmonogamous (they say "monogamish") relationship with Chris Messina, a former Google and Uber employee best known for inventing the hashtag. At the time we last spoke, Crawford and Messina had decided to start a company together called Molly—perhaps not uncoincidentally the same name as the drug—a "non-judgmental, artificially intelligent friend who will support your path to more self-awareness." They also chose to become monogamous for a while; it was getting too complicated. "The future of relationships is not just with humans but AI characters," Crawford told me. And, as they raise money for their new company, Crawford is acutely aware of the harsh reality that as a female entrepreneur she faces so many more challenges that men don't. What she has found is that for a woman, pushing private sexual boundaries comes with a price.

When Crawford was raising funds for her second company, a social media app called Glmps, she went to dinner with an angel investor at a hip restaurant on San Francisco's Valencia Street. At the end of the meal, he handed her a check for $20,000, then immediately tried to kiss her. "I certainly wasn't coming on to him," she asserts. "I kind of leaned back and he ordered me an Uber and I was like, 'I gotta go home.'" Crawford thinks it's likely that this particular investor knew about her sexual openness and found it difficult to think of her simply as an entrepreneur rather than as a potential hookup. This encounter is an example of a unique penalty women face if they choose to participate in the "we're all cool about sex" scene.

Ava was working as an executive assistant at Google when she ran into her married boss at a bondage club in San Francisco. He was getting a blow job from a woman strapped to a spanking bench, who was being entered by another man from behind. Ava and her boss, an engineer, locked eyes but didn't exchange a word and never spoke of the encounter again. However, a few months later, at a Google off-site event, another married male colleague approached her. "He hits on me and I was like, 'What are you doing, don't touch me. Who are you again?' He was like, 'I know who you are. The other guys said you like all this stuff.'" Someone had outed Ava. She quit working at Google shortly thereafter. "The trust works one way," Ava says. "The stigma for a woman to do it is so much higher. I'm supposed to be in this industry where everyone is open and accepting but as a woman the punishment is so much more unknown."

Crawford can't even count the number of men who've told her how lucky she is to have so many eligible men to date in the male-dominated tech scene. "Of all the privileges in the world, that is not the one I would choose," she says fiercely. "I'd choose equal pay for equal work. I'd choose having better access to capital and power. I'd choose not being passed over for promotions. I'd choose not having to worry about being in the 23.1 percent of undergraduate college women who get sexually assaulted. I'd choose not being slut-shamed if I do opt to explore my sexuality."

While Crawford supports the idea that consenting adults should be able to form the kinds of relationships that work for them, she says, "Those who are in positions of power need to be a lot more thoughtful about how and who they engage with in their free time. It's such a small ecosystem, and the power dynamics between VCs and founders adds a layer of complexity that everyone has to be aware of. It's never okay for a VC to flirt with or proposition a female founder—or a female colleague for that matter!"

Married VC admits he might decline to hire or fund a woman he's come across within his sex-partying tribe. "If it's a friend of a friend or you've seen them half-naked at Burning Man, all these ties come into play," he says. "Those things do happen. It's making San Francisco feel really small and insular because everybody's dated everybody." Men actually get business done at sex parties and strip clubs. But when women put themselves in these situations, they risk losing credibility and respect.

Women can eschew the party scene, of course, but those who do end up running a different risk. That's what Lisa Yu discovered when she started her first company, OfficeBook, with the aim of becoming the Airbnb of office space. Just after she launched, she was invited to a party hosted at the mansion of an angel investor who had made his fortune as an early employee at eBay. There she met a wealthy investor. "He was super friendly and he was listening to my idea and he was like, 'Wow, I want to connect you to my business partner.'" She says he then flashed her a few pictures of his own mansion and his yacht, where, he bragged, he hosted parties of his own. Yu dismissed the yacht photos as unsubtle self-promotion and focused instead on the suggestion that he might provide some value to her company: "I'm thinking, 'Wow, this could actually be a business partnership.'"

The next day, Yu says she received a text from the investor inviting her to dinner on his boat. "I'm like, okay, this is odd," Yu says. "I politely declined and he brushed it off, like 'no worries.'" But the investor apparently wasn't as cool about the rejection as he wanted to seem. A few days later, Yu attended a birthday party for investor Jonathan Teo. For Yu, it was an opportunity to meet new potential backers and hang out with her female founder friends; then she ran into Yacht Guy again. "I was like, 'Oh, crap,'" Yu recalls. She managed to avoid him until the end of the night, when he cornered her and started yelling, claiming that she had missed out on a business opportunity by rejecting his earlier invitation. Yu said she was petrified. "I felt attacked and I was scared. When a drunk man is yelling at you and cornering you, what do you do?"

A girlfriend cut in between them, saying, "Are you interested in Lisa or her business? Because you're making it very confusing." Yacht Guy then unsubtly pivoted, trying to persuade both of them to attend that night's afterparty. "I'm just imagining what's happening at the mansion—drugs and orgies," Yu tells me. "We are like, okay, we are getting out of here."

At home, she says, "I stayed up crying and talking and eating ramen until 3:00 a.m. I just felt so defeated I almost wanted to give up on my business. If this is what it takes to start a business, I don't know if I want to do this." Meeting tech investors requires a certain amount of socializing, but this kind of interaction is not what she signed up for. "If you go to these parties, you're just asking to be objectified. Sometimes you don't even know what you're getting yourself into. You don't know: Is it going to be shady or not?"

Rather than give up, Yu paused her fund-raising conversations and focused on building her business organically. "I went into grind mode. I focused on customers, and within a few months we were profitable," she says proudly. She knows the stronger her business is, the more money she can raise on her own terms, which means no need for shady investor parties. "They invite me to these things . . . but I refuse to go because I know what happens," Yu says.

The party scene is now so pervasive that women entrepreneurs say turning down invitations relegates them to the uncool-kids' table. "It's very hard to create a personal connection with a male investor, and if you succeed, they become attracted to you," one told me. "They think you're part of their inner circle, [and] in San Francisco that means you're invited to some kind of orgy. I couldn't escape it here. Not doing it was a thing." Rather than finding it odd that she would attend a sex party, said this entrepreneur, people would be confused about her *not* attending. "The fact that you *don't* go is weird," the

entrepreneur said, and it means being left out of important conversations. "They talk business at these parties. They do business," she
said. "They decide things." Ultimately, this entrepreneur got so fed up
that she moved herself and her start-up to New York and left Silicon
Valley for good.

The women who do say yes to these parties rarely see a big business payoff. "There is a desire to be included and invited to these
kinds of things and sometimes it felt like it was productive to go and
you could get ahead faster by cultivating relationships in this way,"
one female tech worker told me. "Over time, I realized that it's false
advertising and it's not something women should think is a way to get
ahead. It's very risky—once you're in that circle, once you decide you
want to play the game, you can't back out. If you really believe that's
going to get you to a serious place in your career, that's delusion."

Another female entrepreneur described the unfair power dynamic
that's created. "There is this undercurrent of a feeling like you're pros-
tituting yourself in order to get ahead because, let's be real, if you're
dating someone powerful, it can open doors for you. And that's what
women who make the calculation to play the game want, but they don't
know all the risks associated with it," she said. "If you do participate in
these sex parties, don't ever think about starting a company or having
someone invest in you. Those doors get shut. But if you don't participate, you're shut out. You're damned if you do, damned if you don't."

For women in Silicon Valley, if you aren't at these weekend baccha-
nals, you're missing out on potentially useful connections, not to mention being marginalized as prudish and uncool. If you are there, you're
gossiped about and reduced to a notch on a bedpost. Meanwhile, the
powerful men who claim to be overturning the establishment are instead becoming age-old examples of the worst of it, shaming women
for the very same behavior they give themselves and their buddies a
pass for. They might as well be sad imitations of Don Draper and
Roger Sterling, sniggering over martinis about the secretaries they've

shagged. They're not expanding boundaries, no matter how many times they go to Burning Man or how many drugs they take. Whether they were nerds or not in their teen years, they've now become the worst stereotype of the jock, frat boy, and banker they dismissed.

Great companies don't spring magically to life when a nerd gets laid three times in a row. Great companies are built in the office, with hard work put in by a team. The problem is that weekend views of women as sex pawns and founder hounders can't help but affect weekday views of women as colleagues, entrepreneurs, and peers.

HACKING MONOGAMY

Remember Susan Fowler, the former Uber engineer who blogged that her manager brought up his nonmonogamous relationship as a way to make a pass at her over the internal company chat system? It's worth repeating what she wrote in her viral essay: "He was in an open relationship, he said, and his girlfriend was having an easy time finding new partners but he wasn't." Open and polyamorous relationships—like the one Fowler's manager described—are on the rise among many tech workers in Silicon Valley but not working out to everyone's satisfaction. As Fowler experienced, this new landscape of nonmonogamous dating can infect the workplace with varying results. Uber's response seemed to suggest that the manager's invitation to be part of his open sex life was not a big deal. The company, according to Fowler, told her that it "wouldn't be comfortable punishing [the manager] for what was probably just an innocent mistake."

That tepid response from HR may not be surprising, given that open relationships were being explored at the highest levels of the Uber organization. At the time, then-CEO Travis Kalanick was dating Gabi Holzwarth, a violinist. Holzwarth entered the Silicon Valley scene when Uber investor Shervin Pishevar hired her to play at a fundraiser at his home for soon-to-be senator Cory Booker in 2013. That's where Holzwarth first met Kalanick. Sparks flew—but what she says she didn't realize is that Kalanick didn't want a traditional relationship.

Over a year after the pair broke up, Holzwarth shared with me details of their years together, including moments when Kalanick mixed business with pleasure. She shed light on a story that originally broke in *The Information* of the night when Kalanick joined a group of Uber executives that included the company's head of business, Emil Michael, on a visit to an escort-karaoke bar in Seoul. "The girls were sitting in the center of this ring, shivering in miniskirts," Holzwarth recalled. Each woman had a numbered tag so they could be chosen by the men in the group for a more personal encounter. A female Uber executive who was also in the group at the time later reported it to HR and said the incident made her "feel horrible."

Holzwarth said that Michael called her to ask her not to discuss the night publicly—although Michael has countered that he was only calling "to let her know that reporters may try to contact her directly," as a series of post-Fowler stories about Uber began to break in the news. Feeling he was trying to bully her into silence, she instead became the whistle-blower. It was not the only story she told. In October 2017, she posted on Facebook: "For all the women who are trying to fit in . . . you don't have to hunt for women to bring back for them to fool around with. No, you don't have to rate other women's bodies, call them too ugly or fat to hang around with. No, you don't have to sit around as you hear them compare the number of women they have slept with at one time." When I called Holzwarth to ask what she was referring to, she said that Kalanick regularly encouraged her to find other women to bring into threesomes. She also told me that Kalanick and Michael talked openly in her presence about their sexual adventures. "Travis surrounded himself with men who liked that lifestyle; it was easier for them to get close to him," Holzwarth told me.

A company culture is formed by what people at that company actually say and do together—the norms, standards, and values they collectively uphold. When the two most senior and important leaders of a company are a party to women being treated as objects—as Kalanick and Michael were in that bar in Seoul—it is not hard to imagine how this might poison company culture and lead cases like Susan Fowler's to be overlooked. Again, an external investigation documented forty-seven claims of sexual harassment at Uber.

I reached out to Emil Michael about five months after he had left Uber, on the heels of Holder's investigation. In a statement, he was both defensive and apologetic, clearly affected by the public reaction to Uber's cultural unraveling and his role in it. He told me that he worked hard to build a diverse team, including women, at Uber, and said he deeply regretted "attending and failing to prevent" the visit to the South Korean bar. "My lack of judgment on that evening did not represent [my] values," he told me. "I have learned a lot since those early days about the obligations that I and all leaders have to lead by example in situations like this and the lasting impact that decisions, both good and bad, can have on any organization."

THE SPECTRUM OF OPEN relationships in Silicon Valley is broad. "Polyamory," on one extreme, is defined as the state of being in love with, or romantically involved with, more than one person at the same time. Polyamory shares the same Latin root as "polygamy," the practice of having more than one mate at the same time. But while polygamy is generally rejected in the Western world, polyamory has become a widely accepted social trend, at least in the Bay Area. There are no hard numbers on how many local residents have adopted, often loosely, the tenets of polyamory, but experts I've talked to feel safe to say that a significant majority of those who do are tech workers.

Sociologist Elisabeth Sheff has been studying polyamory since long before it was trendy in Silicon Valley. She says that most polyamorists, nationwide, are highly educated, middle- and upper-middle-class white people who have the freedom to experiment and the means to hire a good lawyer if things end badly. "In the tech industry, specifically, I think people think a lot about what is possible," Sheff says. "If your mind is constantly like, 'Things don't have to be this way' or 'It could be any way at all, let me think of a new way,' then you also start questioning not just binary code but binary relationships, heterosexual relationships, and marriage."

"Polyamory is a hack," says Twitter co-founder Evan Williams (to be clear, not his kind of hack). "It's trying to solve the problem of love and security and excitement and novelty. It's popular here because people see it as a smarter way to live."

Candace Locklear is a partner at the tech public relations firm Mighty, which counts Facebook, Twitter, and Pandora among its clients. When I met her in 2016, she and her husband had been dating another couple for two years. She was sleeping with the other man. Her husband was sleeping with that guy's wife.

"We're all on WhatsApp. There's a lot of coordination. We have date nights where we swap houses," Locklear told me. The rule when they started was "Don't fall in love." "Well, fuck," she said, "everybody fell in love." Locklear asserted that the experience had only made her marriage stronger, because she fell in love with her husband all over again by seeing him through another woman's eyes. Yes, they do have kids, and their kids (six and twelve years old at the time) are in on what's happening, to the extent they can understand. Locklear does worry about how this unconventional love quadrangle may affect her preteen daughter (the younger child belongs to the other couple), but said she is constantly trying to explain and give her as much attention as possible.

To clarify: There is an important distinction between polyamory and everything else that falls under the nonmonogamy umbrella. For example, you and your partner might be "monogamish" (like Crawford and Messina), meaning the two of you agree you can see other people but there are certain rules. For one couple, the rule might be that it's fine to get a little handsy if you stay above the belt. Another couple might countenance one-off hookups or casual side relationships with third parties.

Polyamory is different, in that it involves deep emotional connections, as in Locklear's situation, rather than simply sex with multiple partners. Adherents believe that love is infinite and that you can feel love for multiple people at the same time; they call it "committed nonmonogamy." For these reasons, most polyamorists don't like being compared to 1970s swingers. Advocates describe what they are doing as a brave experiment in human connection. But what happens when the workplace becomes the lab they're experimenting in?

Though the tech community didn't invent polyamory, it has certainly adopted it. There's reportedly even a poly meet-up group at Google. But Susan Fowler's case is just one example of how the "we're so cool about sex" culture can create confusion that can bleed into the workplace and foster an uncomfortable power dynamic.

Chris Messina was still working at Uber when Fowler's blog post hit. "After it happened, I had people ask me about it and I'm like, 'Whoa, whoa, I'm not condoning the rest of this stuff because I've chosen this lifestyle,'" Messina told me. "I see a lot of people looking for excuses for bad behavior—Oh, I can fuck whoever I want whenever I want. No, it's not okay to do this at work; all the same rules apply. What I'm concerned about is the whole trend around nonmonogamy becomes another justification for not being responsible for yourself and that's not the point. It's not a get-out-of-jail-free card. And it creates an environment where, specifically as a woman, you can't get a break."

Elisabeth Sheff says the rise of polyamory and other forms of nonmonogamy can have especially dangerous professional consequences for women if their workplace is already dominated by men. "You can't assume that people will understand that you're off the market because you're married" or in a relationship, she says. "Navigating that, being on the market, even though you're married, can be exhausting, especially for women, who don't have as much power in the workplace.

Now it takes more effort to patrol that boundary. Being on the market never stops."

There is often a social cost to refusing the endless offers or expressing more traditional views that sexual relationships should be monogamous. "It comes across as parochial and prudish in certain settings," says Sheff.

The Uber example, for Sheff, represents how this evolution in various types of relationships can lend cover for a new type of sexual harassment. "That's not polyamory; that's fucked up," she told me when we discussed Fowler's story. "It's just inappropriate to put people in that position in the workplace. You may think you're Steve Jobs, but really you're Roger Ailes or Bill O'Reilly with a Bernie Sanders tattoo."

Even a woman who is nonmonogamous herself could have problems. "If a woman is known to be polyamorous, then there is this assumption, like, of course she'll date," Sheff says. "And if she won't engage, then she's a frigid bitch. Women can be at a double disadvantage around this because they still get the sideways looks from other women and from men who think, 'Well, you're slutty—why don't you fuck *me*?'" One female tech worker who is open-minded told me that her go-to excuse to gently fend off unwanted advances from male colleagues is to tell them she prefers to date women, which is only half true.

Finally, even when all parties consent to some sort of open arrangement, Sheff says, men are more frequently the instigators. "If they are an established couple and one of them says, 'Let's become polyamorous,' very frequently it's the man. Definitely that's a dynamic where the man is like, 'Oh, come on, honey, let's do this,'" she says. "But sometimes it doesn't work out quite the way the man expected. Once couples finally start, it's often easier for the woman to get dates." That appears to have been the situation of the manager who harassed Fowler.

Sheff is no prude. She believes that the modern form of polyamory in fact gives women more power, and that some women are the instigators in their relationships. "Every traditional society that we know of, wealthy men get as many women as they want. I'm talking China,

France, Mongolia, Peru, Canada, everywhere; if you're a rich guy in 300 B.C. or 2075, you get multiple women. The huge difference now is that women can also have multiple partners. Not all polyamorous relationships are empowering for women, but they are certainly not all exploitative."

Finding love and keeping love has puzzled humans through the ages, and one might be a little impressed by the bravery and innovation that this generation of tech workers brings to the challenge. But there is so little separation in tech offices between social life and work life and the power dynamics at play that the romantic confusion created by polyamory and nonmonogamy is seeping into the office, increasing tension and opportunities for misunderstandings.

CONFERENCE ROOM G

San Francisco has long been a place of sexual norm breaking. It was a club in the city's North Beach district that is credited in the 1960s with pioneering topless dancing. That style of entertainment, now with the added titillation of private lap dances, seems somewhat old-fashioned. Still, when I heard there was a downtown strip club that was often packed midday with young men from the tech industry, I threw on a pair of sunglasses and decided to make a visit myself.

My trip to the Gold Club on San Francisco's Howard Street began at 11:45 a.m. on a Friday. The place is already hopping, and by noon there's not a seat left in the joint and the buffet line wraps around the perimeter of the room. One reason is that this may well be the cheapest lunch in San Francisco. Just pay the $5 cover charge and the rest is free—all-you-can-eat mountains of meaty fried chicken, thick juicy ribs, chicken taquitos, and a generous dessert tray. The other reason the Gold Club is packed: unlimited topless entertainment.

I take a seat at a table near the back with a female colleague I have coerced into joining me on this awkward reporting excursion, feeling more than a little naive and dumbstruck. The Gold Club is the lone strip joint in the tech-heavy SoMa district, just a block from the Moscone Center, which hosts the biggest technology conferences in the world (Apple's Worldwide Developers Conference, Salesforce's Dreamforce, and Oracle OpenWorld). Yelp is just blocks away, as is LinkedIn's brand-new twenty-six-story skyscraper.

One step into the Gold Club, and you feel as if you've been transported to a Las Vegas nightclub, LED lights and all. But this isn't your usual late-night casino crowd. Construction workers on their lunch breaks sit next to men in suits and tech engineers in hoodies and T-shirts. In some of these groups, a woman or two has tagged along. At the center of it all, a half-naked dancer shimmies up and down a fifteen-foot pole on the main stage.

Around noon, the hostesses start weaving through the tables, catching the eyes of customers who might want something more intimate than the fried chicken. The Gold Club appears to be staffed so there's a woman for everyone—black, blond, Asian, Latina, tall and short, big- and small-bosomed, tattooed and au naturel.

When a dancer wearing a gleaming-white bra and underwear approaches our table, I introduce myself and confess that I am there to do some reporting. She introduces herself with her stage name, Zorah Rose, and tells me she is a teacher at a public middle school in Berkeley, doing summer day shifts at the club to help pay bills. She says she has met patrons from all of the brand-name tech companies nearby, specifically mentioning Uber, Dropbox, Twitter, and Airbnb. "Salesforce is big here," she adds. "Yelp employees call this place Conference Room G."

I ask Rose what exactly is on the menu, besides the dancing and buffet. She tells me that most of the place clears out after lunch, so "you know that the people who are still here want something more." Besides lunch, nothing's cheap at the Gold Club. (It costs $10 just to withdraw money from the on-premise ATM.) A lap dance costs $20, $60, or $100, depending on how long it runs and how naked the dancer gets. Or you can just go all out and book thirty minutes in a back room for $375.

"Every girl decides how far they want to go back there," one dancer told me. "I'm sure there's all kinds of things going on." Another dancer confirmed that sex is available for those with the cash.

Rose says she definitely attracts a particular type of man. "I get all the mid-forties, white, married tech execs," she explains. Compared with Chicago, where she used to perform for mostly lawyers, doctors, and salesmen, her tech clients in San Francisco are much more interested in having a conversation, in addition to all the other stuff. "Basically, they just want a stripper girlfriend for a few hours," Rose says. "I call it therapy in a sexy outfit."

Another dancer, Nikki Darling, agreed to chat with me later by phone. She too estimates that male tech workers are the predominant clientele. "Sometimes a group will come in, and guys are like, 'Oh yeah, that's my boss that I'm with.'" Business deals happen here all day long, she says. After all, it's much easier to close a sale when everyone's in a really, really good mood.

Darling tells me she has two regulars whom she sees outside the club, including a Google employee who's single and a venture capitalist who's married. While some of her tech clientele are nice guys, she has also encountered her share of Silicon Valley jerks. "They're younger, came into money early, and it makes them act kind of douchey, kind of a bit entitled," Darling says. "They have money or power and know you want their money, and they use that power dynamic in a not-so-nice way."

In case it isn't clear from the description above, going to strip clubs isn't something just a couple of guys in the office are doing once in a while. In certain companies, it rises to the level of a corporate culture that is, in some cases, approved by the men at the very top, with strip club fees being charged back to the company.

Strip clubs are nothing new to business, and they have been part of hard-charging tech culture since at least Trilogy's heyday in the

1990s. The CEO, Joe Liemandt, a.k.a. Hundred-Dollar Joe, led young, impressionable employees on pilgrimages to Las Vegas, where gambling and naked women were the main event.

Christa Quarles, now the CEO of OpenTable, was taken to the Gold Club at the end of an interview—a job interview!—with another tech company. "It was more like, 'Hey, everyone, let's go out and see if this person is a social fit,'" Quarles remembers. She felt it was clearly part of the interview, a sort of test to see if she could, as she puts it, "hang with the bro culture."

Despite feeling uncomfortable, Quarles didn't complain. "I felt like what I needed to be successful was being one of the boys," she says. Quarles ultimately took herself out of the running for that job and kept looking.

Another female founder told me she once shared office space with a male entrepreneur who met friends for the Gold Club buffet weekly. It became such a normal part of his routine that he took new employees to the club for their orientation lunch, including two men and one woman.

What employees do on their own time is, of course, their business. But, without a doubt, attending strip clubs with colleagues during the workday is lethal to company culture. Many of the tech workers who engage in this behavior don't seem to realize it's problematic. One founder and investor told me he's been to the Gold Club at least five times with his friends who also happen to be his co-founders. When I pointed out that outings like this might have influenced the start-up's bro-ey culture, he agreed. "It was hard for us to hire women. We didn't hire women, and we've tried to be very cognizant of not fucking that up anymore. I'm not a saint in this story," the founder admitted.

When I told LinkedIn's co-founder Reid Hoffman about tech employees' regular outings to "Conference Room G," he simply said, "That is not good." Does it matter that they are regularly visiting strip clubs (and attending sex parties) if it's happening outside the workplace? I asked. "Yes, of course it does," he said. "We are the habits that we create . . . You have an extra burden to make sure that's not screw-ing with your workplace."

Visiting strip clubs becomes especially problematic when it be-comes a test for who is on the team. If the woman is on a job inter-view, refusing to go will certainly damage her chances of getting the job. But even for women who are already part of the staff, the strip club invitation is a lose-lose proposition. They can either participate and potentially feel humiliated and awkward in front of their col-leagues or decline and miss the group bonding and business conver-sation that will take place there. Uber engineer Ana Medina says she was issued "an open invite" to accompany her co-workers to the Gold Club, "and I never took it. Other engineers asked me to go to bondage clubs and bars, and it was one of those things that I was like, 'What is this, an SF thing or a tech Valley thing? Or is this company so fucked up that this is what gets talked about?'"

Of course, sometimes women aren't invited to begin with. One fe-male founder told me that every time she went to a conference with her team, a group of men would venture off on their own. "At some point in time, everyone would disappear and I was left. You'll never know how much business happens in those venues," this founder said.

Like the high-end sex parties, the strip club scene is part of the background noise that women in Silicon Valley have to deal with. It's a practice that often leaves women in an untenable position. There is no parallel problem for men. Work and private lives are mixed to-gether in Silicon Valley and the new sexual adventurism inevitably informs how male dominated workforces perceive the few women in their midst. As one Bay Area sex therapist told me, "Women are seen as sexual objects, and their objectification is everywhere."

ONE HACK DOESN'T FIT ALL: HOW TECH DISRUPTS FAMILY

N 2014, FACEBOOK AND Apple simultaneously decided to offer their female employees what appeared to be the ultimate life hack, all expenses paid. The companies would now cover the cost—up to $20,000—for women to freeze their eggs, literally putting their fertility on ice. At the time, Facebook's COO, Sheryl Sandberg, told me the idea for the benefit came about when a young female employee who had recently been diagnosed with cancer confessed she would never be able to have children unless she froze her eggs before starting treatment. "I talked about it with our head of HR and said, 'God, we should cover this,'" Sandberg told me on Bloomberg TV in 2015. "And then we looked at each other and said, 'Why would we only cover this for women with cancer? Why wouldn't we cover this more broadly?'" After Facebook and Apple set the example, Google jumped on board too. It wasn't long before Intel, Spotify, and Salesforce also offered this new perk.

On its face, this was a generous and genuine attempt to give women employees more choice, and an ingenious way to attract and retain female talent in an industry starved of women. Haven't yet met the right partner? Or just not ready to have kids? Or maybe right now you just want to focus on your career? For any woman worried about her biological clock, here was a snooze button.

Egg freezing is just one example of how the tech industry has addressed the thorny issue of work-life balance. In fact, some tech folks are actively pushing back on the idea of "balance" as ideal, because it's nearly impossible to achieve, instead advancing terms like work-life "blend" or "integration." In an era when companies seem to be demanding more of their employees' time than ever, Silicon Valley offers in return not only generous salaries and stock options but incentives and hacks to make work obsession both easier to indulge in and more enjoyable.

At most established tech firms, free food and alcohol are givens, and they are advertised as selling points. "We take care of the details so you can focus on what's really important. You never have to think about what's for breakfast, lunch, and dinner," Dropbox boasts on its website. "We're always looking for ways to take the stress out of each day." Facebook and Google have masseuses, doctors, dentists, even hairdressers on call at their headquarters. Ping-Pong and foosball tables are ubiquitous. Some companies offer fitness classes on-site, discounts on gym memberships, and a laundry service for your dirty gym clothes. Others encourage employees to bring their pets to work and give discounts on dog walking, pet insurance, and pet supplies.

While some of these benefits would appeal to any employee, many skew for the young and single. So many perks, yet day care is not on the list. Few employers offer stipends for child care, and even fewer provide on-site child care. Sure, you can bring your dog to work, but you are (mostly) on your own with your baby.

That's because Silicon Valley companies have largely been created in the image of their mostly young, mostly male, mostly childless founders. They don't call their offices "campuses" for nothing. Facebook employees tell me that although Sandberg has had an immeasurable effect on the company culture (Facebook's website makes a point to emphasize it wants to help employees thrive "at all stages of life"), to a certain extent the campus will always feel a little bit like a nineteen-year-old's dorm room. Google is slightly more mature, a hangout for single PhD candidates. With no kids waiting at home, many young, single employees just out of college are susceptible to making work life their entire life, a tendency the companies are happy to enable. Thanks to the seemingly generous perks they provide, you don't have to leave the Google or Facebook campus except to go home and sleep (at some start-ups, I've heard, employees skip home altogether by keeping cots under their desks). Along with working in a creative environment with brilliant people, you get to play in the Ping-Pong tournament or enjoy a massage at lunch, grab a free beer from the company fridge, and ride the Wi-Fi-enabled company bus home. The last one leaves the Google campus in Mountain View at 10:30 p.m., which lands you in bed in your San Francisco loft by midnight. For the right person, at the right life stage, it can be heaven. But women thirty-five and up are usually not that person, and the usual perks of the job do not address the reasons so many women in that age-group decide to leave.

TECH'S "LEAKY BUCKET"

Women leave tech much faster than men do, and at an alarming rate. One study found women are more than twice as likely to quit tech than men. Women also leave tech jobs much faster than non-tech jobs. In 2013, researchers found that after twelve years 50 percent of women have left STEM jobs to work in other fields. In contrast, only 20 percent of women in other professional fields left over the course of the study, some whose careers spanned thirty years. While 80 percent of women in STEM fields say they love their jobs, 32 percent said they were likely to quit within a year. Many women cite the reasons we've already discussed in this book for leaving (unfairness, lack of advancement, hostile macho culture, feelings of isolation). This "fight or flight" moment also happens to coincide with critical childbearing and child-rearing years. But how much of the "leaky bucket" problem has to do with an unfulfilling balance (or integration!) of work and life?

In a comprehensive report, "What's So Special About STEM?," researchers found that family demands affect women in STEM fields far more dramatically than women in other professions, in fact that staying married and having a second child significantly increase the odds of women exiting the STEM labor force, a trend that's exacerbated the more hours they work. Accounting for various differences in family situations, they found that women in STEM (most of those surveyed were engineers and computer "specialists") were 807 percent more likely to leave their jobs than their peers in other fields. They are not leaving the labor force but are taking jobs in other industries, and once they leave STEM, they rarely come back. What's disturbing, the researchers point out, is that women in STEM often make more money than women in other fields and often have more egalitarian views about gender roles at home—meaning that we might expect to see women staying in STEM jobs longer than in other roles. Instead, the reverse is true, suggesting that there are several features of these jobs that make them difficult to combine with family life and that the difficulty intensifies as women move up in the hierarchy. In a recent survey, women engineers noted work-family imbalance as one of the top reasons for leaving the industry.

Women leave tech at every stage of the game, but the exodus of women in their thirties is particularly unfortunate given that those are prime years in the tech world. You are old enough to have some serious experience but still considered young enough to be connected to the latest industry trends. (Ageism is yet another bias in tech.) This is a period where people in established firms move into positions of real influence. Research by the Founder Institute shows that for an entrepreneur being older correlates to a higher chance of success, up to age forty, after which age has no effect. Though we have romanticized the cult of the young founder, stories like Mark Zuckerberg's are the exception and not the rule.

The stereotype of computer engineers working sixty to eighty hours a week is no myth, and many still believe that for a Silicon Valley tech firm to be successful, programmers must put in superhuman hours. This belief is as baked into Silicon Valley as the stereotype of the boy genius. But now is the time to disrupt that belief, just as tech has disrupted so much of everyone else's life and culture.

The herculean efforts of the Macintosh team prior to the product's January 1984 release are still an industry legend. That team's core group of a few dozen programmers were mostly in their twenties and thirties, and few had families or children. A special garment was made up to commemorate their efforts (perhaps the first appearance of the now-ubiquitous gray hoodie), and on its back was emblazoned "90 Hrs / Wk and Loving It."

Such superhuman performance is not replicated every day in Silicon Valley, but it remains an industry ideal. Take the all-night hackathon, in which developers "hack" together new projects and prototypes. Facebook has held at least fifty since its founding, including one on the night before its 2012 IPO. Day to day, however, employees are expected to show their dedication in more quotidian ways, such as taking meals at the office, being connected to their devices after hours, and responding to messages (via Slack, the hot intra-office messaging app) late into the evening. Not to mention that Silicon Valley history abounds with tales of CEOs counting cars in the parking lot after 6:00 p.m. and yelling at staff for not coming in on Sundays.

These sorts of attitudes and expectations have given rise to the dude army and to campuses that look like college-dorm fantasylands instead of professional and inclusive workplaces for grown-ups.

For many years, Uber served employees a free catered meal, but not until 8:15 p.m. Executives insisted there was no expectation that employees work that late, but even so, whether employees stayed for dinner because they wanted to, had to, felt they should, or simply ended up hanging around, they were still getting out of work well into the evening and long after their kids, if they had found the time to have any, would be asleep.

The fancy perks, of course, are mostly at the big companies. At the thousands of small start-ups just trying to get off the ground, the work hours can be even more brutal, with few extras to speak of except maybe a refrigerator stocked with coconut water, Red Bull, and beer. There's a general nonchalance about retention policies to keep employees engaged over time and a general urgency to get the maximum amount out of every employee now. After all, pulling off that next product launch, or hitting that next milestone, could make the difference between getting the next round of funding or shutting down.

And tech employees may very well leave, no matter how the boss treats them. According to the job search company Indeed, software engineers in San Francisco have the shortest job tenure (just over two years) of software engineers in any metropolitan area, in part because of what Indeed refers to as an "especially ambitious workforce" and a massive supply of opportunity, with new technologies and companies exploding onto the Valley scene every day. Jobs are "gigs," and short stints are common.

Between the tech workforce's penchant for switching jobs and the short life span of many tech businesses, Silicon Valley has not been incentivized to focus on the adult life span of its employees. It makes sense for them to provide the brightest and shiniest perks to help get employees in the door. But why invest in creating work-life balance for the long term if your workers are going to move on soon anyway? It's against that long-standing background that the egg-freezing perk has made its appearance.

AT START-UPS, THE APPROACH to pregnancy and maternity benefits is fairly primitive. You're unlikely to encounter a thoughtfully planned parental leave policy, and your eggs will remain unfrozen unless you shell out the money yourself. Most founders don't realize they even need a parental leave policy until the first employee gets pregnant.

At the biggest tech companies, however, the situation couldn't be more different. Egg freezing isn't the only benefit large tech firms offer their employees. Sperm banking, extensive IVF treatments, and cord-blood banking for newborns are often included, as is support for adoption and surrogacy. Sheryl Sandberg famously asked Sergey Brin to create closer-to-the-door "pregnancy parking" at Google for expectant mothers, then brought the idea with her over to Facebook. (I happily pulled in to one such spot when I interviewed her for this book while eight months pregnant.) Tech companies generally also provide generous vacation and family leave policies. When Google increased its paid maternity leave from twelve to eighteen weeks, Susan Wojcicki told the *Wall Street Journal* that retention of new moms improved by a full 50 percent. Facebook offers four months of parental leave for both moms and dads, and Mark Zuckerberg has signaled that it's okay to use it by famously taking two months of leave for each of his two children. Companies such as Netflix and LinkedIn even offer unlimited vacation time.

Silicon Valley's nature is to look for groundbreaking, innovative solutions, and it all looks great on paper. While high-tech pregnancy perks may make these companies look good, there's substantial evidence that trendy perks like egg and sperm freezing are not solving the problem at hand. Getting pregnant is just the beginning of parenting after all. What workers want, particularly women, is a culture that is friendly to working parenthood over the decades that the commitment demands.

WORKING LONG, HARD, AND SMART

In 1997, in a letter to his shareholders, Jeff Bezos succinctly expressed a core belief about what it takes to succeed in tech when he wrote, "You can work long, hard or smart, but at Amazon.com you can't choose two out of three."

This belief—that for companies to be successful, tech employees must work long, hard, *and* smart every single day—is one reason it's so hard for women who become mothers. While dads are getting better about pitching in on child care, the majority still falls to moms. Added to that, men don't breast-feed (or pump) and are not burdened with the medical condition commonly known as pregnancy.

In 2017, twenty years after Bezos's "long, hard or smart" comment, Blake Robbins, a tech worker turned VC, tweetstormed, "When I first got into tech, I thought it was 'cool' to work on the weekends or holidays. I quickly realized that's a recipe for disaster . . . Not hanging with friends . . . because you're working isn't 'cool.' Burning out isn't 'cool' . . . Your competition isn't beating you because they are working more hours than you, it's because they are working smarter."

Not surprisingly, he encountered resistance. The PayPal Mafia member and venture capitalist Keith Rabois tersely tweeted in response, "Totally false." Then elaborated in his next tweet: "Read a bio of Elon. Or about Amazon. Or about the first 4 years of FB. Or PayPal."

The Twitter tiff resurfaced an essay written by Palantir's director, Shyam Sankar, in 2015 titled "The Case Against Work-Life Balance." Sankar argued that the time to invest those long hours at work is when you're young, because the pace of learning slows as we age, and that having a purpose for the sacrifice makes it acceptable. He urges young engineers to be skeptical of jobs advertising both high stimulation and maximum comfort.

"Provided there's a purpose, sprinting at an unsustainable rate is an act of tremendous optimism," he wrote. "We've been told over and over to choose life over work in order to achieve balance. I'm urging you, especially at the dawn of your career, to instead choose life over balance and make the work so meaningful that you wouldn't want it to exist as a distinct concept. This is how you ensure that your future remains yours."

Sankar makes an eloquent case. I agree that less balance can be worth it, for a while, if you feel you are doing something truly worthwhile (as I have done while juggling three kids and a full-time job in order to write this book). I disagree that this can work over an extended period of time. As much as overnight success makes a great Silicon Valley story, nothing here actually happens overnight (except for those hackathons), and it takes most companies many years to realize their full potential.

WHAT SANKAR ALSO DOESN'T address is that all jobs in Silicon Valley don't have to fall into the same category, because the industry is now mature enough to afford a variety of work options. The twenty-two-year-old recent graduate who wants to create his or her life all around work should put in sixty-plus-hour weeks and be lauded. Certainly that's what many founders and early employees have done, many to great success. But the idea that this is the only way to go, or that this should be the work style across one's entire career, is ridiculous. Silicon Valley doesn't need one more life hack. What it needs is an entirely new operating system.

Family isn't the only thing that gets put on hold in the work-obsessed Silicon culture. Workweeks used to leave hours available that could be devoted not only to children but to community, church, volunteering, and socializing. In return for taking those hours away, companies try to compensate employees by offering money, stock options, and perks. And they seek to replace the traditional social networks on which our communities were built—for example, by encouraging employees to take all of their meals at work or to socialize at the office. So the employee needs to do the economic calculation: Is what Google will compensate me for that hour worth more than the value of keeping that hour for myself or my family? That calculation changes as we age, and as kids enter the picture, it becomes a retention issue.

In a 2012 interview, Sheryl Sandberg rocked Silicon Valley by revealing that she leaves work at 5:30 p.m. every day. Hard to say which left people more incredulous, that such an important female executive could leave work at such an early hour or that she would actually admit it. The press trumpeted the story everywhere, and Sandberg says a friend remarked that she "couldn't have gotten more publicity than if she had murdered someone with an ax." Sandberg told *Bloomberg Businessweek* that the entire legal team at Yahoo sent her flowers, with a card reading, "Thank you, we're all leaving at 5:30 pm now too."

Sandberg has said that she spent years trying to hide her exit time. She'd leave her jacket on her chair so people might think she was still in the office taking a meeting somewhere, or she'd schedule afternoon meetings in other buildings so people wouldn't see her walk to her car. She would send a few emails late at night and early in the morning to show she was still at it. Now she is confident enough in her achievements that she can admit to (gasp) leaving work in time for dinner with her kids. She doesn't pretend that she doesn't pick up work again after they're in bed. "Of course I do. [That's what] gives me the flexibility I need to be home," she told me in a Bloomberg Television interview in 2017. She thinks employers "need to communicate well with our employees. Not everything is an emergency . . . I do send emails late at night. I have a system with people I work with," she explains. "If it's important and I need an answer, I will red flag it. If I don't red flag it, you can wait."

Sandberg's message is that people shouldn't have to choose between being great employees and being great mothers, fathers, husbands, wives, sons, and daughters and that companies need to help make this vision a reality. "Companies have an opportunity and an obligation to step into the gap," she says. "And what's important for companies to understand is this isn't a trade-off between the right thing to do and the smart thing to do. This is both. When companies make a deep commitment to their employees . . . employees make those commitments back."

Sandberg is arguing not just for better corporate and public policy around things like family leave but also for companies and managers to be more attuned to their employees' emotional and personal needs. When it comes to dinner at Facebook, she told me, "We offer dinner, but no one's required to come. I know our people who take their dinner in a box when they go home." Then she reiterated, "I think companies have an obligation to do what they can."

Most companies, unfortunately, don't "step up," as Sandberg advises; they wait to get pushed. It took a report from the former U.S. attorney general Eric Holder for Uber to move its dinner offering from 8:15 to 7:00 p.m. Holder was tasked with critiquing the company's culture after Susan Fowler's accusation of sexual harassment came to light. Holder noted that an earlier dinner would allow a "broader group of employees" to utilize the benefit—including those who "have spouses or families waiting for them at home"—and signal an earlier end to the workday. Uber complied.

In April 2017, as I was writing this book, Apple opened its new spare-no-expense, spaceship-like campus, Apple Park, at a cost of $5 billion. A true marvel, it includes four-story sliding glass doors, rotating elevators, and a 100,000-square-foot wellness center (plus a two-story yoga room), not to mention a carbon-fiber roof and nine thousand drought-resistant trees. One thing it doesn't have is a child-care facility. One blogger quipped, Apple's new campus has "everything an Apple employee could wish for, unless they have children in which case: tough."

Sure, child care might be hard to execute, but Silicon Valley has never claimed to be normal or shied away from hard problems. Large firms have basically reinvented commuting by running fleets of tricked-out buses around the Bay Area. Because child care has proven an effective way to retain female employees, it's curious it hasn't gained more momentum in an industry that prides itself on groundbreaking solutions. But perhaps that's because Silicon Valley doesn't realize just how much this industry is disrupting the families of those who work in it.

PARENTHOOD AND THE PRESSURE TO KEEP UP

Katharine Zaleski had just given birth to her first daughter and had just launched her first start-up, PowerToFly, which aims to find women tech jobs that offer flexible working arrangements, when she publicly apologized to all the moms she had ever worked with. In a *Fortune* article, Zaleski admitted that in her many years running digital products at the *Huffington Post* and the *Washington Post,* she had "silently slandered" women with kids by negatively judging their job performance. She rolled her eyes when they couldn't make post-work drinks, repeatedly questioned their commitment, scheduled last-minute meetings at 4:30 p.m., just when parents might be wrapping up so they could go pick up their kids, and stayed at work late simply to prove she was more dedicated to the job. Some mothers would come in early and leave early, doing more work after dinner, but Zaleski wouldn't value their after-hours contributions. She only realized she'd committed this "long list of infractions" when she had her own child and discovered that "work is so rigged against mothers—and not only mothers, but young women, who are taught, 'You have to outman the men.'"

In tech, however, even men who become parents find it hard to keep up. Bret Taylor, founder of Quip, a workplace collaboration software maker, started working at Facebook in 2009, when he was twenty-eight years old and expecting his first child. Taylor had left Google to start his own company, FriendFeed, which consolidated updates from social-media sites. When Mark Zuckerberg made an offer to buy the company, it was the opportunity of a lifetime for Taylor, who agreed to the sale and was later promoted to chief technology officer. There was only one problem.

Just as he was becoming a father, Taylor recalls, "I was losing control of my own schedule and no longer running my own company and working for someone . . . younger than me [Zuckerberg was twenty-five at the time] who didn't have kids. I was really, really nervous about it."

Taylor says "the culture was younger" at Facebook than at Google and he found it more difficult to feel as if he belonged to the community. "The hardest part for me as a father—which applies infinitely more so to mothers—was the implicit stuff," Taylor says, such as feeling obligated to attend the hackathons that were integral to Facebook's operation. "You face this social trade-off where you say, 'Am I the uncool person who says, "I can't go to this thing that everyone is going to"?' Or, worse, do I tell my boss that I cannot do a meeting at bedtime because I have to be home? Or do you suck it up and . . . tell your spouse, 'Putting the kids down is on you tonight'? I faced that more at Facebook than any other place," Taylor says. "If Mark Zuckerberg asked me to do a dinner meeting, it would be really uncomfortable for me to say no, for obvious reasons."

Taylor believes the women who worked at Facebook faced an even bigger trade-off: "When someone would go on maternity leave, it was like fifty-fifty whether they would come back."

As he struggled to balance work and family, Taylor found both Zuckerberg and Sandberg to be very supportive. Sandberg "had had hard pregnancies too and cared a lot about her kids," he says, while Zuckerberg was always empathetic and, true to his curiosity, asked many questions about Taylor's family. When the CEO eventually had his own first child, he not only served as a role model for other fathers by taking two months' leave; he also posted photos of himself changing diapers. But the reality is most dads don't work for Facebook or Google and often don't take advantage of the leave they're entitled to. According to one 2014 study of new fathers, the vast majority take only a week or two off, feeling that putting family first may stigmatize them among their colleagues and cause resentment.

That leaves women to put in for the parental leave and the risks that come with it. Taking time off from any job has its disadvantages, but perhaps even more so in the tech industry, where the pace of change creates performance pressure for employees. For start-ups, one missed opportunity can be live or die. For the big companies, it can mean a huge missed market. There is little room for error. No surprise, then, that Google keeps meticulous performance data and systematically ushers out the people who aren't measuring up.

That obviously creates issues for parents considering leave. "I look at my friends who've taken breaks, and it has not served them particularly well," one female tech executive told me. "Things in Silicon Valley change ten times faster than anywhere else, so in some respects it's really hard to reengage because there's a lot of catching up to do. The pace of technological change has made it very, very hard for people to successfully take a break and come back."

So, why not push off having kids until later—until you get to a certain level in your career when you can afford child care and your company may be more flexible in order to retain you? The problem is you could wait indefinitely and by then it might be too late.

For entrepreneurs, the work-life calculation is even weightier. Zaleski says she was "like, forty-two weeks pregnant" when she was making her final pitch to investors. Raising a round of funding is never easy for women in Silicon Valley, and being hugely pregnant doesn't help. "There's usually some VC that asks how you're going to [run the business if you] have a family with kids," Zaleski says. "When men pitch a business, it is all about the business. Nobody asks them how they're going to take care of their kids."

Studies show that in all fields working mothers are paid less and perceived as less competent than working fathers. There's every reason to believe the "motherhood penalty" can be especially harsh on female entrepreneurs who are expected to devote their whole selves to making the company a success.

"Women entrepreneurs, especially mothers, are underestimated," Janica Alvarez, CEO of the smart breast pump company Naya Health, tells me. Alvarez says investors frequently ask how she plans to take care of her three sons, while her husband/co-founder never gets that question. When Naya had trouble with fund-raising, the couple moved themselves and their kids into a minivan for a month, to buy themselves extra runway. "If an investor came to me and said, 'Well, we're not sure you can sacrifice enough,' I'd want to punch him in the face," Alvarez says.

Even female investors are racked by these fears. Sarah Tavel, Benchmark's sole female partner, told me she hoped to have a child someday. "I'm so scared of it," she said. "The same thing that female founders face when they think about raising money while pregnant, I'm trying to sell a founder on taking me as a board member. That's scary as a pregnant woman, and then there's taking care of the kid. Of course, it's a fear every woman has who's career oriented, but this is a job where you feel that loss of time more acutely."

There's one kind of employee, of course, whose life is unencumbered by any demand other than work: the unattached young dude. One founder told me the sweet spot for new hires in tech is specifically twenty-five to thirty years old. After age thirty, this founder said, things just get more difficult. They might get married, have kids, slow down, start to leave at 6:00 every night. They might even, God forbid, take their kids to the doctor once in a while.

The Silicon Valley tropes around who becomes successful, and how, are alive and well: the winners will be those groups of young, single guys hacking all night, night after night, in a race to achieve their billion-dollar dreams. No families, no wives, no relationships, no real *anything* except the Product and the Dream. All-night hackathons and creepy Silicon Valley incubator homes are spaces and places habitable only by a very specific type of person, captured in the hit movie *The Social Network* and the popular TV series *Silicon Valley*. Those young men have achieved great things—witness Facebook, Google, and Apple. But just because those companies were successful doesn't mean the model isn't fundamentally flawed or that success can't be achieved in other ways. As in any industry or institution, tech's habits and norms were created by those who were there first. And those habits are hard to change, especially when the companies are bringing in billions upon billions of dollars. It stands to reason that if more types of people were given a shot, the tech industry might boast even more success stories.

BUILDING A NEW OPERATING SYSTEM

Silicon Valley has a tendency to copy itself. "Google had free food, then everyone had free food. Google did brainteasers, then everyone did brainteasers," says the former Facebook CTO Bret Taylor. "You meet these founders who watch *The Social Network,* [which is] not supposed to be positive, and then they are copying it. People copy it all, the good, and the bad, almost blindly, and it creates all of these cultural issues that become self-perpetuating."

When he left Facebook to co-found Quip, Taylor decided to do things his own way. "My co-founder had just had a baby as we were starting the company," Taylor says. "It was their first, and his wife was like, 'You can do a start-up but I need you to have work-life balance.' I said, 'We will leave by 5:30 every day'—and I do that to this day." To encourage others to leave at a reasonable hour, Quip did not serve dinner. "After the kids go to bed, I'll work a little bit, but I do it at home and it's like a secret. I'm not sending a message to the team that that's an expectation of them," says Taylor.

He believes that Quip's family-friendly schedule helped him recruit employees, especially women. "I think it may contribute to [Quip's having] not as stark of a trade-off in terms of gender balance [as other companies] . . . We're 35 percent female engineers, and it's not good enough but it's good."

But don't employees need to work around the clock if the business is going to succeed?

"It's just hard to imagine the return on that is so great as to make a company succeed or fail," Taylor says. In fact, research shows that output starts to decline after workers put in more than fifty hours a week. Some studies go as far as to say that working too long can be counterproductive to both individuals and their companies. The big inflection points at Quip, Taylor notes, had nothing to do with how much sleep was compromised for work. "In general, it's because we made the right decision or the wrong decision about a resources allocation in terms of what are you working on or not working on. I believe that's 100 percent why companies succeed or fail. It's not how fast you're typing." Taylor doesn't believe normal work hours have to come at a cost to the company. In fact, in 2016, Quip was acquired for $750 million by Salesforce, where Taylor later became president and chief product officer. It might not have been the billion-dollar exit start-up founders dream of, but it's still pretty damn good.

So maybe the 5:30 thing works for Sheryl Sandberg, Bret Taylor, and the average tech worker bee. But what if you're a first-time entrepreneur who is trying to make a dent in the universe by taking something from zero to one? We've talked about what start-ups demand of founders and early employees; when your company is on the line, can you really afford to worry about work-life balance?

After working at Twitter and Postmates, Sara Mauskopf gave birth to her first baby and soon after, while managing the demands of motherhood, founded her first company—a start-up named Winnie that aims to make parenting easier. Shortly thereafter, however, her husband was diagnosed with cancer—though at first they had no idea how life threatening it was—and Mauskopf told her co-founder that she needed to go off-line (that is, disconnect from the company) indefinitely. "I couldn't take care of my daughter. I couldn't do anything but get his diagnosis to get him a cure. I felt like I would take a gun and shoot people before I would let him not get a definitive diagnosis," Mauskopf recalls.

Mauskopf's team never bothered her once while she was away and finished Winnie's first product without her. As her husband started getting treatment, however, Mauskopf found herself with more time as she sat through chemotherapy infusions and waited around in doctors' offices. Slowly she got back online and, to her surprise, found that the company was running just fine.

"One thing I didn't mean to do, but I ended up doing, was setting up the culture in a way that I didn't have to be in the office 24/7," Mauskopf observes. "If I was working anywhere else at the time, I would have needed to quit my job." But because Winnie allowed her to work flexibly, she didn't have to. She officially returned to work in time to launch Winnie to the public.

Now Mauskopf's goal is to build a "sustainable" company. Does she believe she has to work long, hard, and smart? Yes, but with a twist. In a response to Keith Rabois and others advancing the idea that less balance is better, Mauskopf blogged that Winnie employees don't work nights and weekends, *because* they know it will take a long time to solve the problem they are focused on and they don't want to burn out. She also pointed out that many start-ups fail expressly due to burnout. "We built Winnie so that we never have to stop working, no matter what comes our way—be it a baby, a deadly disease, or just your run-of-the-mill roadblock," Mauskopf says.

Like Sankar, Mauskopf believes in working with great purpose; she just doesn't think purpose must be combined with ninety-hour weeks. "By building technology to help parents, I'm allowing parents to do less busywork and put in more of their hours actually spending quality time with their children," she says. "That's my motivation. For me, there is no greater incentive or reward."

Imagine an alternate universe where even a start-up focuses on a ten-year time horizon. If more people started companies that operated like Mauskopf's, maybe, just maybe, more women would want to work at them. Silicon Valley is inventing the next generation of products and services, she points out, and if women continue to be underrepresented, the consequences will be dire. "We're not building for them. We're not thinking about them in the solutions," Mauskopf says. "Tech is the future, and an entire industry is getting left behind because they are not represented."

Mauskopf discovered her company could survive without her, but it took her husband's life-threatening illness to make her realize it. Our work is important but rarely is it *the* most important thing in our lives. Companies usually survive just fine without your putting in those twenty extra hours when you could be eating dinner with your family, sleeping, or going for a run. By hiring employees with different lives and different work styles, tech companies could engender new perspectives and creativity. And they would give employees the ability to have a longer-term perspective, not just for their own lives, but for whatever product they're rolling out.

"Tech should be a really great job for women and families," Mauskopf says. "You just need a computer. You don't always have to be in the office. There is nothing inherent about it that should be bad for women. The other day I took Thursday and Friday off. I canceled a trip to Disneyland because Eric got sick. I took the morning off with my daughter, then came in and wrote the best code I've ever written."

8

ESCAPE FROM TROLLTOPIA: WOMEN'S FIGHT TO SAVE THE INTERNET

RIANNA WU HAS BEEN tormented by online trolls for three years. It started in 2014, when Wu spoke up to defend women in the gaming industry, only to find herself plunged into a roiling controversy called Gamergate that turned her life upside down. The threats of rape and murder hurled at her online became so scary that she and her husband fled their home. To this day, they live in a new location under an alias. But sometimes the trolls still manage to track her down, and online harassment becomes an off-line ambush.

"They found our address and smashed a window of my house. Threw a brick right through it," Wu told me in April 2017, when I reached her by phone at a number she instructed me never to share. At the time we spoke, the window was still shattered.

The online attacks, like the one perpetrated on Wu, began and gathered force on sites like 4chan, Twitter, and Reddit, the largely unmonitored town halls of the web. All of these sites allow or encourage anonymity and pseudonymity, as well as a laissez-faire approach to free speech, in keeping with the long-standing libertarian ethos of the internet. All of them have tolerated years of online harassment of women.

It should be of little surprise at this point that the sites that harbor the most vicious trolls—4chan, Twitter, and Reddit included—were all started and led by white men, who aren't usually the targets of the most vicious online harassment. Would these sites be as hostile to women today if they had been built and run by women, or at least included a meaningful number of women leaders early on?

THE MONEY IN MISOGYNY

Few places on the internet are more troubled by misogynistic trolling than the world of online gaming. Gaming is a billion-dollar business—much bigger than movies and rivaling TV—including an exploding generation of mobile and social games, classic PC console games, and rising categories like e-sports and virtual reality. Yet the gaming industry is also saddled with a long-standing history of violence toward and degradation of women, allowing gamers to play out dozens of dark fantasies. One of the earliest rape-simulation games, *Custer's Revenge,* was released in 1982 by the game maker Mystique. The goal was to rape a Native American woman tied to a cactus, with points awarded for every thrust. More than three decades later, our most popular games feature similar scenes. In Take-Two Interactive's monster hit *Grand Theft Auto* (whose fifth iteration is one of the bestselling video games of all time), players can sleep with a prostitute, then murder her. Take-Two's CEO, Strauss Zelnick, has defended the game, saying, "It is art. And I embrace that art, and it's beautiful art, but it is gritty."

Like the broader tech industry, gaming has systematically excluded women for decades. In 2016, the International Game Developers Association (IGDA) reported that women make up just 22 percent of game developers, with men vastly outnumbering them in management and in powerful technical roles such as programming, software engineering, and technical design. Interestingly, the IGDA also found that men were much less likely than women to believe that diversity in the industry, and in the games it produces, was important. Indeed, women have also been poorly represented in the games themselves.

As the report dryly puts it, "Women have long experienced derogatory representations of their gender in videogame content as well as a general invisibility within the wider videogame culture."

It's not surprising, then, that the most notorious case of online trolling sprang out of the gaming industry and that women were the targets. Gamergate was sparked in 2014 by the peevish post of an unhappy former boyfriend of one of the gaming industry's few female developers. "This is written almost entirely in shitty metaphors and bitter snark," wrote Eron Gjoni, a coder in the industry. "It's a post about an ex." Gjoni alleged that his former girlfriend the game developer Zoe Quinn had slept with other people in the gaming industry while she and Gjoni were dating.

For reasons that are still somewhat inexplicable, the missive unleashed a volcanic explosion of hate, all of it directed at Quinn, who was a feminist critic of mainstream video games. Though Gjoni never called for any kind of campaign against Quinn, a certain subset of gamers took his nine-thousand-word, she-done-me-wrong post and turned it into a rallying point from which to defend their sacred, mostly male gaming territory. They derided Quinn's game development as basic, simplistic girl work and claimed she used sexual favors to get good reviews.

Gjoni's post was put up on 4chan (not by him, he would later attest in a note on his original post), an online community founded in 2003 by a then teenager named Christopher Poole. Today 4chan claims some twenty million monthly visitors, including a large population that seems to delight in wreaking havoc online. They were particularly vicious when attacking Quinn and other women in the gaming industry.

With the 4chan members engaged in the fight, accounts sprang up across Twitter and Reddit to attack Quinn and spread the #Gamergate hashtag. The trolling expanded to target other female game developers on the premise that there was a conspiracy of women trying to ruin the industry by promoting more gender equality in the games themselves and in the studios where the products are produced. The

Gamergaters created and shared lists of industry women to target and torment, including Anita Sarkeesian, a media critic who rose to prominence by calling out sexism in the video game industry. The trolls even created a game called *Beat Up Anita Sarkeesian,* which enabled users to punch her virtual face. The game's creators wrote, "There's been a disgusting large imbalance of women who get beaten up in games. Let's add a lady . . . She claims to want equality: Well, here it is."

Once riled, many internet trolls have no shame. They often compete with each other to see who can be the most cruel. And as Quinn and Sarkeesian found out, they don't limit their attacks and threats to a single individual. They will threaten family members, including children. They will also instantly direct their bile toward anyone who comes to the target's defense.

That is where Brianna Wu enters the story. About two months after Gjoni's post, Wu, an established game designer, spoke out against the #Gamergate campaign, sarcastically tweeting a meme suggesting that the trolls were saving everyone from an "apocalyptic future" where women might have slightly more influence in the industry.

That's when all hell broke loose. Shortly after responding to the trolls on Twitter, Wu was inundated with violent, disturbing threats on her life. One series of tweets in particular stands out. "Guess what bitch, I now know where you live"; "Your mutilated corpse will be on the front page of *Jezebel* tomorrow"; and "If you have any kids, they're going to die too." As the threats piled up, Wu and her husband fled their home, crashing on friends' couches and hiding out in extended-stay hotels. They didn't have children to worry about, but they did spend an inordinate amount of money boarding their dog while they were on the run. Wu had a choice to make: speak up for what was right or be silenced. She chose to talk back.

"I was angry. I was scared. I was terrified. But within all of that I was trying to reach inside myself and find that bravery to really change the industry for women," Wu told me. She spent days documenting the dozens of death threats against her so she could provide them to law enforcement officials. At the height of the online vitriol, she hired a full-time staff member to help collect information on her harassers to share with police, but none of that was enough to bring the perpetrators to justice.

Wu wasn't alone. Others who spoke out in support of Quinn or even mildly criticized the trolls or the gaming industry were similarly attacked. Kellee Santiago, a female game developer who now works at Google, likened Gamergate to a witch hunt or public stoning, telling me, "It was really shocking to discover that I live in a time and place in which such animosity toward women existed."

TROLL ARMY ON THE MARCH

Wu would later understand that she had been the victim of the trolling playbook, an extremely effective technique used to silence women that anonymous social-media denizens disagree with. "Find the woman and identify something in her past to distort her with," Wu explains. "If she's gay, attack her on that. Larger than size 12? Attack her on that. Transgender? Attack her on that. Find the spot where the woman feels the most vulnerable and make her feel unsafe until the cost of speaking out is too great."

Use of the troll playbook is not limited to the fans or members of the gaming industry.

Online harassment is now one of the most disturbing problems plaguing the internet at large. Can such widespread cyber hating be chalked up to the dark side of human nature, which is simply finding a new expression on this medium? Or have the internet's most popular sites exacerbated the problem by building their networks in a way that allows, even encourages, bad behavior rather than good? And if the latter, has so little care been given to protecting users because most of these networks have been built and run by men?

To Brianna Wu, the answer is obvious. "If we had more women in positions of authority at Twitter, and in the gaming industry, I don't think our industry would be so complacently terrible."

Evan Williams, the CEO of *Medium* who is most famous for co-founding Twitter, has been building websites to allow people to express themselves on the internet since the late 1990s. "Trolling used to be seen as a fringe activity," he told me. "Many of us that built these systems are surprised there are that many people out there who are that terrible. It's disheartening about humanity. And I don't think anyone would have predicted whatever psychological feedback is encouraging these people."

I asked Del Harvey, the woman in charge of Twitter's Trust and Safety division, whether it mattered that Twitter had been designed primarily by men.

"It may have been a factor," Harvey says. "There are, absolutely, aspects of being male that offer you more privilege and shelter. If you are not a member of a marginalized community in any form, you are less likely to think of those things," she said. Not that Twitter was specifically created to transmit hate, she was quick to point out. "But it was designed by people who tend to be really optimistic—cheerful people who are thinking about really fun, optimistic things to be done with their product. They aren't thinking, 'How can I create a product that will allow people to send death threats really easily?'" (Del Harvey is not her real name, and she won't say much about her own identity—expressly to minimize becoming a target herself.)

Product managers, especially those who design consumer products, will tell you they try to be empathetic and do as much user research as possible, but at the end of the day, building these products requires making choices based on their own opinions. In tech, these choices are made mostly by men.

Early Twitter investor Bijan Sabet believes that the relative cluelessness about the potential of online harassment has a direct connection to the industry's gender imbalance. "These dudes aren't getting it," he says, "because they're not getting harassed."

When I pressed Williams on this, he conceded. "We weren't thinking about it enough," he acknowledges. "Had we had more women on the team, maybe we would have known better."

By the time Dick Costolo was promoted to CEO of Twitter in 2010, Twitter's harassment problem was already out of control. Costolo, who was brought in to make Twitter more attractive to a mainstream audience, saw curbing harassment as one of the main routes to achieving that. But he didn't make much progress.

"I would bang my head against the wall for days and days . . . and then I would move on to other things," he says. "Twitter had lots of reasons why it wouldn't be a good idea to restrict speech to prevent harassment. I was always on the side of 'We should prohibit more things,' and I always got pushback."

The pushback came because attempts to implement specific antiharassment policies bumped up against the principles the company had been founded upon. Twitter's founders had felt it was important that users be allowed to use pseudonyms. This was partly a way of differentiating Twitter from Facebook, where real names are required. Twitter's network is built on mostly public profiles that anyone can follow, while Facebook is built on connections that require mutual consent. More important, Williams told me the founders wanted Twitter to be a safe communication platform for political and human rights activists around the world. This was so embedded in Twitter's DNA that free speech proponents within the company were able to resist executives' attempts to enact policies that would infringe on that freedom.

But while pseudonyms protect free speech, they also liberate users to behave as badly as they like, without consequence. And because tweets are public, Twitter's design can actually amplify harassment. Even if you block someone who's hurling insults at you, others can still see those tweets and pile on, allowing an attack to pick up at breathtaking speed. And Twitter's rules for what it does and does not tolerate—and how it implements those rules—have been consistently inconsistent.

"If I could go back in time, I would go back to a meeting in 2010 and say I don't care what you present me, I want this changed tomorrow. I would totally change the way I did it," Costolo says.

WHAT GAVE RISE TO ONLINE HATE?

Trolling is the modern version of hateful language that has long been directed at prominent or outspoken women. Well-known suffragettes, fighting for women's right to vote, often received vulgar, threatening letters from anonymous men.

Trolling as we know it began in the late 1980s, just as email became a popular business tool. People immediately began to notice that there was something about communicating via computers that seemed to undermine the good manners and social norms that govern most face-to-face encounters. In 1984, a *New York Times* article chronicled the rise of "emotional outbursts" in "electronic mail." "Scientists are documenting and trying to explain the surprising prevalence of rudeness, profanity, exultation and other emotional outbursts by people when they carry on discussions via computer," the *Times* declared. Scientists who were interviewed observed that electronic communications "convey none of the nonverbal cues of personal conversation—the eye contact, facial expressions and voice inflections that provide social feedback and may inhibit extreme behavior."

"It's amazing," Carnegie Mellon professor Sara Kiesler told the *Times*, "we've seen messages sent out by managers—messages that will be seen by thousands of people—that use language normally heard in locker rooms."

Over thirty years later, vulgar discourse and threats of violence now pervade the most prominent sites on the web, including mainstream social networks. Thanks to the anonymity provided by many social-media sites, there are usually zero consequences for the offenders, either reputational or economic.

Perhaps more remarkably still, trolling behavior has been, for many, a path toward fame and power. To take one example, we need look no further than Twitter-happy Donald Trump. In the midst of a petty feud with MSNBC hosts Joe Scarborough and Mika Brzezinski, the president tweeted that he once saw "low I.Q. Crazy Mika . . . bleeding badly from a face-lift." Like many online trolls, Trump directed one of his most offensive verbal assaults yet at a woman, and other trolls parroted his remarks with glee.

To be clear, men do get harassed online, but women experience the more extreme forms, such as rape threats, death threats, and stalking. Studies show that men are far more likely to be called out or belittled because of their sports affiliations, while women are far more likely to be attacked simply because of their gender. Girls are also disproportionately among the victims of cyber bullying. Young women, particularly those aged eighteen to twenty-four, are three times as likely to be sexually harassed online. As one feminist researcher put it, "Rape threats have become a sort of lingua franca—the 'go-to' response for men who disagree with something a woman says." Perhaps that "go-to" aspect is why law enforcement doesn't take such threats very seriously. But women do: 38 percent of women who have been harassed online describe their experience as "extremely upsetting," as opposed to 17 percent of men.

For many women, especially those in the public eye, the hate being thrown around means the internet at large has become a place where they feel unwanted. Marissa Mayer told me she took a monthlong break from Twitter while she was running Yahoo because "it was just so negative." In the summer of 2016, the *Saturday Night Live* star Leslie Jones tweeted, "I feel like I'm in a personal hell," after she was swamped with racist and sexist attacks sparked by her appearance in the all-female *Ghostbusters* remake. She also took a break from Twitter, but before leaving, she wrote, "Twitter I understand you got free speech I get it. But there has to be some guidelines . . . You can see on the profiles that some of these people are crazy sick. It's not enough to freeze Acct. They should be reported."

The message of these negative, upsetting episodes is this: Women, you're not welcome here. And if you choose to show up anyway, be prepared to live with any harassment that comes your way.

I know this from personal experience.

As a journalist, I regularly use social-media sites such as Twitter and Facebook to promote my stories and interviews. They are invaluable platforms for distribution and constructive feedback. However, I often find myself on the receiving end of messages that are obnoxious, dirty, and sometimes downright frightening. One user, who stalked me on Twitter for several months, suggested taking me to a warehouse "for a whipping," eating his "high-quality sperm" and tweeted a hardcore pornographic video at me with the words "Submission Time." He also mentioned my husband by name and suggested they have sex with me together. "Any boy that penises you gets my support," the troll wrote. And when I was pregnant, the user tweeted, "Obeying me is a good thing, looks like you're pregnant with my lil girl in belly." The cherry on top: when the troll responded inappropriately to a tweet in which I had tagged the IBM CEO, Ginni Rometty, after an interview I had conducted with her, Rometty herself was alerted with several cheerful notifications from Twitter.

I've developed the requisite thick skin, and I use a common tactic for dealing with trolls: ignoring them. I quickly scroll past the vitriolic direct replies to my Twitter account, and I never, ever use Reddit. Once an interview I conducted with Apple's co-founder Steve Wozniak ended up on Reddit, and the response was worse than unnerving. (For the same reason, many women in tech avoid using *Hacker News*, the prominent start-up incubator YCombinator's official bulletin board that has since become one of the industry's leading message boards; the trolls are there too.) Most important, I don't respond to the haters.

This is accepted wisdom among many female users: the worst way to deal with a troll is to poke it. Though sometimes the words disturb me, I do my best not to let them make me feel like any less of a journalist, a person, or a woman.

But the internet shouldn't just be for people with thick skin. And being a woman online shouldn't be accompanied by routine threats of sexual assault.

I reported my personal troll to Twitter in March 2017, after the company claimed, yet again, to have improved its harassment controls. Just twelve hours after filing my report, however, I received this message from Twitter: "We reviewed your report carefully and found that there was no violation of Twitter's Rules regarding abusive behavior." Twitter's "rules" state that "you may not incite or engage in the targeted abuse or harassment of others." If telling me to eat his "high-quality sperm" and inviting me to a whipping doesn't count as harassment, what does? Sure, I can mute the account or block it, but all of these tweets are still visible to the public, and this troll can easily set up a new account and start attacking me again. It appears that my troll hasn't tweeted from this particular account for some time. When I asked Twitter for more information about why, the company told me it doesn't comment on individual cases. All of the offensive tweets I have referenced still live online. It feels as if Twitter is telling me, "Just deal with it" or, worse, "You're not worth fixing this." Apparently, I—and so many other women—aren't worth alienating one extremely offensive user.

In a telling example of just how crudely Twitter's rules can be applied, actress Rose McGowan's account was suddenly suspended in October 2017 as she was in the midst of tweeting allegations that Hollywood heavyweight Harvey Weinstein had raped her. In keeping with its policy not to comment on individual accounts, Twitter did not explain why, then faced an epic backlash. Actress Anna Paquin called for women to boycott Twitter, and countless women rallied their accounts behind the cause.

Twitter later broke its own rule and explained that McGowan's account had been temporarily locked because she had tweeted a private phone number. (The number was contained in the signature of an email image McGowan had tweeted as proof that the others at the Weinstein company were aware of his behavior.) While Twitter seems often reluctant to act on behalf of users who have been abused, this is one prominent case in which Twitter was remarkably responsive to censoring someone who was trying to out an abuser. These seemingly inexplicable decisions might be explained in part by a closer look at how offensive content is handled once it is reported. The social networks, including Twitter, outsource most content moderation to contractors around the world. While there's hope that technology, with the help of artificial intelligence, might be able to enforce rules more consistently in the future, for now, the task is up to humans. The contractors faced with the difficult job of filtering and flagging disturbing content on these networks generally don't last long and must constantly be retrained, yet wield an inordinate amount of power when it comes to deciding what stays up and what comes down. Their decisions, informed or not, greatly impact people's lives, whether they be myself, Brianna Wu, Leslie Jones, or Rose McGowan.

McGowan's account was reinstated and Twitter promised to be more transparent about how it makes such decisions in the future. "Today we saw voices silencing themselves and voices speaking out because we're *still* not doing enough," CEO Jack Dorsey tweeted.

THE BUSINESS CASE FOR SCRAPPING THE HATE

Over the years, many social-media executives might have assumed that combating trolls could be bad for the bottom line. To be seen as silencing free speech can be a rallying cry for boycotts and cyber attacks. After all, traffic from trolls is still traffic; who wants to drive users away?

However, we may be at an inflection point. It seems increasingly likely that *not* combating harassment might be even worse for business.

Today, both Reddit and Twitter are fighting to attract not only new users but advertisers, who have become wary of being associated with less-than-mainstream content. The most famous example: When big-name companies including Mercedes-Benz, Johnson & Johnson, Verizon, and JPMorgan discovered, early in 2017, that some of their YouTube ads were running next to neo-Nazi and jihadist videos, they all suspended or pulled advertising from Google. Most returned, but only after the company made changes, including doing a much better job of flagging offensive content by hiring more people and deploying "machine learning tools" (a form of artificial intelligence) to deal with the problem. Ad crisis averted, but the market spoke clearly: hate is bad for business. Google's actions spoke clearly too: they showed that companies can indeed change, when sufficiently motivated.

As Twitter has sought to gain broader adoption, it too has tried to change—not always successfully. In 2015, Costolo stepped down as CEO of Twitter. He was replaced by Twitter co-founder Jack Dorsey, under whose leadership additional steps have been taken to reduce harassment. The network rolled out a new filter that would prevent users from seeing offensive or threatening content, and says it works harder to identify accounts that were obviously spawned to harass others. It's added tools to mute and report hateful speech, tweaked search to hide abusive tweets, and says it is cracking down harder on repeat offenders. In 2017, Twitter said it was taking action against ten times more accounts than it had the year before (although, somehow it seems, my troll is not one of them).

Meanwhile, though Twitter and Reddit still have a fairly large user base, they have been left in the dust by the behemoth that is Facebook. While Facebook was inspired, in part, by the sexist "Hot or Not" ratings site, it has gone on to become a social-networking site that is, by comparison, friendly to a diverse range of users. In the process,

Facebook has attracted over two billion users and, along with them, billions of advertising dollars.

Don't get me wrong: Facebook isn't perfect. The social network has a long way to go to combat online hate, both on the main site and on Instagram, which it owns. But cyber hate is a far bigger, more visible problem on Reddit and Twitter than it is on Facebook and Instagram. Because my Facebook account is private and I have to accept friends before they can interact with me, I almost never see hurtful comments. Even when I do post publicly, the responses are rarely vile. Perhaps that has something to do with the "real names" requirement. But it also has to do with the way the site has been architected to balance product and business concerns.

Facebook insiders say that Sheryl Sandberg, who joined the team in 2008, was critical in transforming the hugely successful start-up into an equally enormous business. Part of that involved developing policies to ensure that Facebook was a safe, hospitable place for both users and advertisers. Sandberg's influence at Facebook goes some way to answering the question of whether major social-media sites might have benefited by having more diverse and inclusive leadership.

"Sheryl is, and I think Mark would agree, probably the most important decision he ever made," the former Facebook mobile director Molly Graham tells me. When Sandberg showed up in 2008, the social network, which then had just 66 million users, was having a dark year amid a storm of privacy issues and a nearly nonexistent business model.

"Facebook's success was not an inevitability," Graham says. Not only did Sandberg help compel immediate changes to company culture; she also took strong stands on the side of user privacy and protections. This was about the same time that Mark Zuckerberg was becoming obsessed with Twitter's growing user base and was considering a series of changes that would have taken Facebook down a very different path.

In the months after Sandberg came aboard, the fledgling Twitter was dominating live conversation on the web and getting international traction. "He was trying to decide why Twitter was so successful," a former Facebook employee tells me. "He got obsessed with openness and how much data they had and why are they owning real-time news? He fixated on this idea that people are actually willing to share more openly than we think they are." Zuckerberg proposed several product tweaks designed to push Facebook users to be even more open in the hopes of driving engagement.

After Facebook introduced location tagging, for example, users could tag others at the same location, but those tagged users couldn't untag themselves. I could have said that Mark Zuckerberg was in Las Vegas, but he wouldn't have been able to say, "Uh, no, I'm actually in Palo Alto." Zuckerberg wanted to extend the same rules to photos, such that if someone tagged another user in a photo, again that second user couldn't then untag himself or herself. Several other Facebook executives including Sandberg and Facebook product head, Chris Cox, were against these changes, feeling they were unfriendly not only to users but to women especially. "The obvious example is you're a woman, someone tags you in something offensive or not related to you, and you can't untag yourself," the former Facebook employee tells me. "It was a *huge* fight inside the company. Massive, teardown walls." Ultimately, Zuckerberg's photo untagging proposal never came to fruition, and the ban on location untagging was removed. "Before, when bad things happened, nobody had anybody to go to when weird decisions were made," the former Facebook employee says. "Sheryl made every voice that was diverse stronger because now they had a place to go."

To his credit, Zuckerberg—though he might have had a few harebrained ideas—was also willing to listen. "More than anyone I've ever met, he has this infinite capacity to learn and change. He has as many flaws as anybody, but I've never met anyone who is so open to change," former Facebook CTO Bret Taylor tells me. The key is Zuckerberg made as much space for Sandberg as she made for him, employees say.

Both Zuckerberg and Sandberg cared very much about making sure Facebook was a free but safe community, but they approached difficult decisions on content differently. Zuckerberg was more likely to consider how issues might affect the broader platform, whereas Sandberg encouraged employees to think about the effect on individuals. "She came at it from more of an individual person's perspective, the empathetic, how might this person feel? These are human beings, in their bedrooms, in their dorm rooms, reacting to something that causes them emotional trauma," a former Facebook executive told me.

Sandberg oversaw the operations team as they refined a detailed set of policies that would guide Facebook's stance on certain kinds of content on a massively complex scale—what gets left up, and what gets taken down—everything from Holocaust deniers to the Arab Spring to offensive satire. "There were a couple of content issues like rape jokes and violence toward women—any sort of content directed at women—it's obviously a topic she cares a lot about," the former Facebook executive said. "And she had a really big impact on helping the company and helping us get to better decisions on that stuff. Sheryl's job was to push on us when she felt we didn't get it right."

Facebook still has an uphill battle to fight offensive and disturbing content that is only getting bigger as the site becomes more influential. In 2017, it added three thousand people to the forty-five hundred already employed to moderate content worldwide. This, as Facebook was roiled by the launch of its video service, Facebook Live, which soon became home to broadcasts of real-time rapes, beatings, suicides, and incidents of police brutality. But the biggest reckoning came later that year when Facebook revealed that the Russians bought thousands of ads on the social network in an attempt to cause political turmoil amid the US elections. Twitter and Google were quickly roped into the scandal. All three companies were called on to testify before Congress about their policies concerning not just political advertising but also fake accounts and fake news. Facebook announced that it was hiring an additional ten thousand people to handle safety and security. In an interview with *Axios*, Sandberg apologized to the

American people, but also reasserted Facebook's commitment to free speech and consideration of itself as a tech company, not a media company.

Facebook, Twitter, and Google, via YouTube, profit off the content that the public provides. This content includes everything from fake news to postings that might be hateful or abusive. But 2017 might well be seen as the turning point, the moment when these internet juggernauts began to take greater responsibility for the substance of the messages, ads, and news they facilitate. No doubt there are heated internal debates happening within Facebook at this very moment, about how to continue to build an online community where people feel both safe and free. The question remains how the company rises to that responsibility.

HOW HARASSERS FIGHT FOR SURVIVAL

Culture change can't be guaranteed by simply putting a woman at the top of the org chart. Changing the moral tone and community standards at a social media company can be particularly tricky because users feel ownership over the site—and rightly so, as they are producing the content. Case in point is the story of Ellen Pao's second epic setback in Silicon Valley. In 2014, just months before she would lose her famous sex discrimination case against Kleiner, Pao was appointed interim CEO of Reddit, where she swiftly tried to crack down on harassment, only to resign, under pressure from users, after just eight months on the job.

Reddit, the so-called front page of the internet, was founded in 2005 by Steve Huffman and Alexis Ohanian, two young male entrepreneurs. They tell me they started the site as a place to have "authentic conversation." If the optimism of that statement reminds you of Twitter's free-speech philosophy, here's something else the two sites share: user pseudonymity. Reddit quickly became a popular destination to discuss everything from puppies to politics, with more than 330 million monthly users to date, who became known as Redditors. But like Twitter, Reddit also became a haven for users spewing misogyny, racism, homophobia, and xenophobia, which made it difficult for the network to develop into a legitimate business. Ellen Pao agreed to take on the challenge of leading Reddit in the hope of making it—and the internet—"a better place for everyone." At the same time, cofounder Alexis Ohanian, who had left the company in 2010, returned to help, with the title executive chairman.

Pao (who got plenty of up close and personal online attacks from trolls during her suit against Kleiner) made it her top priority to clean up the site, first committing to remove revenge porn—explicit photos, usually of ex-girlfriends, that are posted without the subjects' consent. She also shut down several of Reddit's nastiest sub-forums, including antitrans and antiblack communities as well as one called "Fat People Hate," in which users mocked the overweight.

Redditors staged a full-on revolt, attacking Pao and claiming their right to free speech. While that argument might suggest the users were high-minded, their attack tactics showed otherwise. Trolls attempted to post private information about Pao and threatened her life. When one of the site's popular employees—responsible for managing Reddit's famous Ask Me Anything series—was fired, over 200,000 people signed a petition calling for Pao to be fired, and the site's moderators took its most popular sections private—essentially holding Reddit hostage. Days later, Pao resigned.

"The trolls are winning," Pao wrote in an op-ed in the *Washington Post* following her resignation. "The foundations of the Internet were laid on free expression, but the founders just did not understand how effective their creation would be for the coordination and amplification of harassing behavior. Or that the users who were the biggest bullies would be rewarded with attention for their behavior . . . No one has figured out the best place to draw the line between bad and ugly—or whether that line can support a viable business model . . . I'm rooting for the humans over the trolls. I know we can win."

Steve Huffman, Reddit's original co-founder, came back as the company's CEO, while Ohanian remained executive chairman. I sat down with both of them in 2016 in the aftermath of Pao's resignation. Did they believe they took online harassment seriously enough in the company's early days? "Alexis and I grew up in the generation on the leading edge of the internet, as teenagers, as boys going through puberty," Huffman told me. "That comes with a certain desensitization." Translation: they simply got too used to it. After seeing what Pao had endured, however, they insisted they were more committed than ever to cleaning up Reddit for good.

One of Huffman's first efforts was to continue what Pao had started. He strengthened the company's anti-hate policies and shut down a few more nasty sub-forums including "Coontown" (a favorite for racists) and "Raping Women" (a favorite for, well, aspiring rapists). With each ban, users protested; some even turned on him. "I have said many times I thought the way [Pao] was treated on Reddit was despicable," Huffman said. "The changes we made to r/all [shorthand for the Reddit home page] would have mitigated some of the harassment, and I regret we didn't make those changes years ago."

After she left the company, Pao told me, "It is very difficult to change a community, once it has gone in a certain direction. What I hope other internet companies realize is, when you have problems, they scale with your company, and it becomes very hard to revise the approach you have taken once the genie is out of the bottle." However, there is hope.

In a new study, researchers at Georgia Tech found that the changes Pao started on Reddit have made a meaningful difference. After Reddit banned those forums like "Fat People Hate" and "Coontown," more Redditors than expected left the site entirely. Those who stayed were better behaved; their use of hate speech dropped dramatically by at least 80 percent. "Perhaps existing community norms and moderation policies within these other, well-established subreddits prevented the migrating users from repeating the same hateful behavior," the researchers suggest. Some users undoubtedly flocked to other, more permissive sites (you can now find "Fat People Hate" and "Coontown" on a newer Reddit alternative called Voat). But the exercise proves that companies can change, if their leaders understand the problem and are willing to make hard choices.

But what about free speech? That's a red herring, Pao says: "The purpose of free speech is to allow everybody to have a voice, to have these conversations, and if one group is pushing everybody else off you can have this free speech platform, but there are not many voices or opinions being represented."

Pao strongly believes that if more women, especially women of color (she says they get the worst of the online harassment), had been involved at the creation of networks like Reddit and Twitter and Facebook from the start, the internet would be a very different place. "I think people would have invested more in tools, would have invested more in community management, would have had different rules, would have taken down more content faster and banned more people in a more consistent way."

It's an alternative reality we can only imagine.

A COMPANY THAT FOUGHT HARASSMENT AND WON

Could the reforms that helped Reddit have an effect even in the troll haven of online gaming?

Benchmark-backed Riot Games, maker of one of the most popular multiplayer games in the world, *League of Legends,* has attempted to curb online harassment without alienating the game's players.

In *League of Legends*—which boasts 100 million active players monthly—teams of gamers battle in an online arena using magical powers. As with many multiplayer online games, vitriolic, abusive, and misogynistic comments slung at other users have been a long-standing problem. In fact, research shows female gamers receive three times as many negative comments as male gamers. One player, under her gaming pseudonym Jenny Haniver, keeps track of such comments on a blog; entries include "Shut that fucking bitch up" and "Shut your mouth girl before I put my dick in it!" Just another day in the life of a female gamer.

In 2012, however, the game makers behind *League of Legends* noticed that a significant number of players were quitting due to these obnoxious comments. In response, Riot Games put together a "player behavior" team including experts on psychology and neuroscience to examine the issue more closely.

Reporting on what they found, *Wired* reporter Laura Hudson wrote, "If you think most online abuse is hurled by a small group of maladapted trolls, you're wrong. Riot found that persistently negative players were only responsible for roughly 13 percent of the game's bad behavior. The other 87 percent was coming from players whose presence, most of the time, seemed to be generally inoffensive or even positive. These gamers were lashing out only occasionally, in isolated incidents—but their outbursts often snowballed through the community. Banning the worst trolls wouldn't be enough to clean up *League of Legends,* Riot's player behavior team realized. Nothing less than community-wide reforms could succeed."

Riot experimented with several ways to accomplish this, such as turning off the chat function by default but allowing players to turn it on when they wanted to. It saw not only a 30 percent decrease in negative chat but also a nearly 35 percent increase in positive chat. By creating hurdles to bad behavior that were minimal but real, it was able to change that behavior dramatically.

Riot also decided that when it kicked players off the game for negative remarks, it would give those users more details about exactly why they were being penalized. When those players returned, the company found, their incidents of bad behavior dropped significantly. Riot also instituted a system called the Tribunal that enlisted a jury of players to vote on reports of bad behavior. It turns out the Tribunal gave players a greater sense of responsibility to do their part in creating a more positive environment.

Riot Games found that it could decrease negative behavior by enforcing certain consequences, and it could also create more positive norms of behavior. This supports the theory that at least one reason online harassment has proliferated is that there have been no consequences. To put it another way: when you threaten to rape or murder someone in public, you typically experience certain repercussions from the community.

At least one *League of Legends* troll found out that being a model citizen has rewards. A player whose highly negative behavior got him banned from competitive play for an entire year later said, "It took Riot's interjection for me to realize that I could be a positive influence, not just in *League* but with everything. I started to enjoy the game more, this time not at anyone's expense."

If any of the internet's managers need more convincing, there's this: *League of Legends* had 67 million active players per month when Riot unveiled its efforts to reshape online behavior. Two years later, there were 100 million. As Riot waged war on negativity, growth soared.

The Riot example reminds us that the past does not have to be the prologue. The internet has created unparalleled opportunities for human beings to act out their most aggressive, sexually predatory, and emotionally hurtful impulses. Perhaps none of the founders knew that this would happen. But now they do, and it's worth asking whether they are doing enough to reestablish, encourage, or enforce the codes of behavior that people accept in other environments.

They can't control everything—there will always be those who flout social expectations—and we already know that communicating through screens and keyboards creates social distance. However, when these companies fail to do everything they can to create virtual environments that encourage respectful behavior, they should accept at least some responsibility for the impulsive, hostile, and antisocial outcomes.

How these companies decide to proceed really matters, because the internet revolution has only just begun. The future is coming, and there is little doubt we will soon be spending more and more of our lives in sophisticated virtual worlds, for both work and play. Those worlds will be dark and disturbing places—unless cyberspace is fundamentally reshaped.

SAFEGUARDING OUR VIRTUAL FUTURE

In 2016, Jordan Belamire, another female gamer who plays under a pseudonym, was visiting her brother-in-law when she decided to try out a new VR game he owned, *QuiVr*, in which players shoot arrows at zombies and demons in a snowy, medieval world. Belamire put on the headset and played by herself for a while. But soon after she entered multiplayer mode, another gamer, identified as BigBro442, used his avatar to start groping her avatar's chest. Players could hear each other's voices (that was the only way BigBro could have known she was a woman, because all the players' avatars were identical), so she said, "Stop!" He didn't. She moved away, but when she did, BigBro442 started chasing her, then shoved his hand toward her virtual crotch and started rubbing. The virtual groping, Belamire later wrote in a *Medium* post, felt disturbingly real: "You're not physically being touched . . . but it's still scary as hell . . . As VR becomes increasingly real, how do we decide what crosses the line from an annoyance to an actual assault?"

Upon hearing of Belamire's experience, *QuiVr* developers Aaron Stanton and Jonathan Schenker tweaked the game to include a new superpower, one that enables players to surround themselves with a personal bubble that shields them from any kind of virtual assault. But as the industry moves forward, not every developer may act so responsibly. In fact, there's good reason to think that some won't.

Engineers are now working to make virtual reality even more real with the help of new technologies such as haptic feedback, which enables players to physically feel it when they are punched or kicked. Augmented reality promises to further integrate our real and online worlds. Increasingly, these are spaces in which we will live, work, and play that will have dramatic physical and psychological effects. The norms of behavior for these new virtual and augmented worlds are being laid down right now, so right now is the time for the makers of VR and AR technology to build respect and safety into their products.

Let me be clear: Our shared goal shouldn't be to remove all bad behavior, hateful comments, or potentially disturbing imagery from the internet. That is not only impossible, it's undesirable too, because it involves a slippery slope of deciding whose judgment will determine what's objectionable. A more reasonable goal would be to create an online social landscape that roughly mirrors that of a healthy city. In most cities, you can, if you desire, find a dive bar, a strip club, or a rough neighborhood where rude or obnoxious behavior is allowed or even encouraged. But in most public spaces—the parks, restaurants, museums, and theaters—you should be fairly confident that neither you nor your children will be verbally assaulted or followed around by some creep shouting threats. To make the internet a version of that safe and welcoming city, women should be involved in building the next generation of products from the start, from new social networks to the video games of the VR future.

Brianna Wu tells me her heart races when she hears these stories of women being stalked, threatened, and groped in virtual worlds. For her, it feels like déjà vu but on another platform. Running for Congress in Massachusetts in 2018, these are her campaign promises: to help get more women into high-tech fields and to write stronger cyber-security and antiharassment laws. Her goal: to make sure that women on the internet of the future don't fall victim to the mistakes of its past.

9

SILICON VALLEY'S SECOND CHANCE

W RITING THIS BOOK HAS been like going on a trek through a minefield, with fresh mines being laid as I walked. Not a month has gone by without some major revelation about discrimination or harassment in the tech industry exploding in the press (not to mention the deluge of allegations in Hollywood, beginning with Harvey Weinstein, in politics, and in the media). Most followed the same pattern: angry accusations followed first by denials and then by public mea culpas. Several powerful men in Silicon Valley, including the once-untouchable Uber CEO Travis Kalanick and the investors Justin Caldbeck, Dave McClure, Chris Sacca, Steve Jurvetson, and Shervin Pishevar subsequently resigned, were fired, or were publicly disgraced. There were moments when it seemed we had reached a turning point in how Silicon Valley would treat women, and other moments when it felt that if we had not hit rock bottom, it was only because the bottom was lower than we thought.

In response to these scandals, women rose up. At the end of 2017, the Twitter hashtag #MeToo was trending hot, with millions of women sharing their stories of abuse and sexual harassment both through tweets and on Facebook. That wellspring proved not only the size and scale of the problem but also that these social media platforms could be used to create solidarity and seek justice. "I've never seen anything quite like the environment where now women are much freer to speak up than perhaps they were in my professional career," former eBay and Hewlett-Packard CEO Meg Whitman told me. "Every once in a while in history, there's something big that happens that changes the culture and I'm hopeful that this is it."

As we begin 2018, one thing is clear: in tech, people's interest in, anxiety about, and desire for change have become palpable. The exclusion of women didn't have to be the story of how we got here, and it certainly doesn't need to be our future. Let's take advantage of this moment.

In previous chapters, I've asked this question: How different might the world be if women had been included in this transformative industry from the start? In this last chapter, I want to ask a similar set of questions that look ahead: What if the tech industry, starting now, grows up and begins to create a truly diverse workforce? How would the industry make that happen? And what would be the advantages to such a fundamental shift?

Let's imagine a world where women hold half the jobs in Silicon Valley. Where half of entrepreneurs, executives, venture capitalists, board members, and employees—including engineers—are women.

We can't know exactly how that world would look, but some are willing to make educated guesses. "I think there would be two enormous differences," the longtime tech investor Roger McNamee told me. "I think Silicon Valley would be wildly more profitable. I think there would be a significant reduction in the number of absolute failures. And so I think success would go up dramatically."

McNamee's scenario isn't wishful thinking. Research shows that companies with more women represented in their leadership ranks make more money, and their employees, both men and women, are more innovative, diligent, and creative. Higher morale and a more successful company mean lower turnover, higher retention, and higher rates of productivity. Another way to look at this is that gender inequality is expensive, in that it leads to more unhappiness, higher turnover, lower productivity, and more money and time spent on hiring and recruiting. What's good for women is good for men, good for companies, good for their customers, good for the products they produce, good for the economy, and good for our future.

Europe has already begun to mandate gender parity in businesses and is starting to see the value of it. Countries such as Norway and Germany have instituted quotas to get women on corporate boards, and companies in other European countries are responding to pressure to appoint more female directors, even if they are not required to do so by law. In a wide-ranging study of two million public and private companies in Europe, the International Monetary Fund (IMF) found that firms with more women in senior roles realized a "significantly higher return on assets." On average, replacing just one man with one woman in management or on the board led to a 3 to 8 percent increase in profitability. In the tech sector specifically, the benefit was even greater. Tech companies saw a greater boost, the report suggests, because those companies "demand higher creativity and critical thinking that diversity in general may bring."

With those results, one might wonder whether firms would do even better with leadership that was all women. The IMF found that when women occupied over 60 percent of leadership positions, results began to diminish. Having women entirely run our companies would not lead to the best returns, just as having men entirely run them does not. It's the workplaces with balance that appear to have the best results.

SILICON VALLEY 3.0

Silicon Valley has long celebrated failure, encouraging founders to aim big and fail fast, pick themselves up, and try again. In that spirit, there's one big failure to add to the list: Silicon Valley has failed women, period, and it's time for the industry to own it. At the current rate, with

VCs celebrated for hiring their first (first!) female partners and companies ever so slowly achieving single-digit increases in the number of female engineers and managers, it will take us a generation or more to get to anywhere near fifty-fifty. That is unacceptable. Women not only represent half the population but drive 70 to 80 percent of consumer purchases. If only for the sake of profits, women should not be excluded from the process of imagining and creating new products.

There are a few founders who see the opportunity here. Everyone is looking for a competitive advantage, and some tech leaders have realized that there is an abundance of talent and valuable ideas in the populations that, for the last three decades, have been largely untapped. Looking at their new women-inclusive businesses and workplace cultures can give us some idea of the potential payoffs.

I ran into Dick Costolo in April 2016, ten months after he had left Twitter, and he was nearly giddy, having just hired another female engineer at his new personal-fitness start-up, Chorus, the fourth company he has co-founded in two decades. From day one, Costolo focused obsessively on making sure he hired as many women as men, even if it took longer to find them. "Once you fall behind, if just two out of twenty engineers are women, it's impossible to catch up," Costolo told me. "Any one of these companies, the underlying disease is that it's 90 percent men," Costolo says. "Everything, literally everything, is reinforcing the problem."

Jack Dorsey, who returned to Twitter as CEO when Costolo left, is also taking an innovative approach to improving the environment for women at his other company, Square. New female engineers joining the company are placed on teams that include other women rather than alone with a group of men. The hope is to engender camaraderie and networking and mitigate the "imposter syndrome" that women often experience when they are the only female in a room of male engineers. Still, with a limited number of female engineers, there is a trade-off to this strategy: some teams will remain all male. It's an experiment, one that Dorsey believes is worth trying. In the meantime, Square has developed a strong bench of female executives. "It's not just creating a sense of belonging that's important," Dorsey told me, "but also making sure women contribute to decision making."

And then there's the most straightforward strategy, that having women in charge will naturally attract more women. Julia Hartz, co-founder and CEO of Eventbrite, says the company's gender balance is fifty-fifty and that this has happened organically perhaps as a result of simply having strong female role models at the top.

These founders are attempting to create products that will be used by everyone, no computer expertise required. Hiring only the stereo-typical computer nerd that IBM and others were screening for in the late 1960s and early 1970s (those who "don't like people" and "dislike activities involving close personal interaction") would ensure disaster for these sorts of endeavors. Following James Damore's broken logic from his Google memo and hiring mostly men because they suppos-edly systematize rather than empathize would be equally shortsighted. What these companies need is a tech-savvy workforce with a deep empathic understanding of people's behaviors, interactions, and pref-erences. For new technologies like these to reach their potential, they simply must be created by teams with a diverse set of perspectives.

SLACK: A DIVERSITY CASE HISTORY

Stewart Butterfield, another multi-time entrepreneur and founder of Slack, is also proving that building a diverse, family-friendly workforce can be a key to creating a successful start-up. Butterfield had his first success when he co-founded the photo-sharing company Flickr with his then-wife, Caterina Fake. Flickr was meant to be simply a side feature for a video game Butterfield was developing, but the game fi-nancially flopped just as it became clear that photo sharing was about to become the next big thing. Yahoo swooped in, buying Flickr for north of $20 million in 2005, and Butterfield and Fake became dot-com stars. It wouldn't last. Innovation at Flickr died under the Yahoo umbrella and Facebook and Instagram ran away with the mobile photo-sharing market.

Naturally, Butterfield started over. He built another game that failed, then, in 2012, shut the operation down, laying off all but eight people. But again, a side project of his company's showed great promise. Butterfield's employees had built new software to track projects and communicate with each other internally. That accidental, modern take on a chat room—now called Slack—quickly became one of the most highly valued unicorns in Silicon Valley.

Like many tech successes, Slack grew quickly—in four years expanding from twenty to over a thousand employees in five countries. But unlike most tech companies, it grew while hiring a lot of women. In 2017, Slack reported that 43.5 percent of its employees were women, including 48 percent of managers and almost 30 percent of technical employees—far better numbers than almost any tech company in Silicon Valley. The company said of its diversity efforts in a *Medium* post, "We are simultaneously proud of what our people have been able to accomplish so far and determined to improve. This is a work in progress." The real question is this: How did they do it? The answer: Butterfield and his team made a critical decision early to make diversity and inclusion an explicit priority.

I sat down with Butterfield at Slack's SoMa headquarters in December 2016 and asked what he thought it would take to level the Silicon Valley playing field. "It's so funny because I would have had a totally different answer to that on November 7," he said, referring to the day before Donald Trump was elected president. "I just thought that the world was getting better, but then it turns out it's not getting better."

Butterfield is not shy about sharing his political views. He's publicly backed Planned Parenthood, protested President Trump's controversial travel ban targeting Muslims, and sent a companywide memo in 2016 urging his employees to take a pause on Martin Luther King Jr. Day. "Think about how profoundly shameful it is that there even ever had to be a 'civil rights movement,'" Butterfield wrote.

Two years before I sat down with Butterfield, former Google engineer Erica Joy Baker was marching the streets of Ferguson, Missouri, to protest the shooting of a young black man named Michael Brown, when Butterfield tweeted at her, "Be safe." When Baker looked at Butterfield's Twitter page, she realized he cared about diversity almost as much as she did. "He is woke. I want to go work for *him*," Baker said of her discovery. In 2015, she joined the Slack team as a senior engineer fully convinced after reading a powerful *Medium* post by Slack's then-engineering chief of staff, Nolan Caudill, in which he outlined the company's core values. These included diligence, curiosity, and empathy—a stark contrast to Uber's original core tenets: "steppin' on toes," "always be hustlin'," and "meritocracy."

"Our industry has for decades been directed and built by a mostly homogeneous group, and has downplayed the accomplishments of others not in this group," Caudill wrote. "We recognized our own shortcomings in this area and thus wanted to be explicit about what Slack stands for, what we are trying to build, and who we want here to help us build it. By focusing on how we build Slack first, we can hopefully improve the greater industry, in whatever measure."

Butterfield is quick to acknowledge that white male privilege helped land him in the CEO suite in the first place. He recalls his old group of buddies from Yahoo who went on to become great successes in tech, including Jeff Weiner, CEO of LinkedIn, and Andrew Braccia, a venture capitalist at Accel who invested in Slack. "All of them are men," Butterfield says. "It's not a conspiracy, but it's also not a coincidence."

Butterfield admits that his Rolodex gives him a huge, and somewhat unfair, advantage. "It would have been the same experience if you worked at eBay in early days, Google, Facebook, or in this generation Airbnb, Pinterest, Snapchat, Slack," he says. "I have all these amazing contacts that I can call on if I want my company acquired, or I want an investor, or if I want to do a partnership, or I want to hire someone, or whatever. And if you don't have access to that network, it's not impossible to be successful in tech, but it's an order of magnitude more difficult. Not actually insurmountable, but close." There are plenty of women entrepreneurs who deserve funding now, but it is also true that we are in a transition period where men like Butterfield with influence, connections, and access to money can help. Women who gain career momentum at Slack will go on to greater things with their own set of vital connections.

Butterfield grants that Slack's values may sound like "hippie-dippy bullshit," then gets serious: "We have to make money to be a successful business, but the making of the money doesn't determine whether the whole thing was successful and worthwhile and whether I feel like my life was well spent . . . I find it totally plausible that it drives better business outcomes, but I don't think that's the prime reason. The real drivers were, this just seems fairer and better for the world." Butterfield acknowledges that he, personally, is already richer than he ever dreamed of being. Does that make it easier for him to focus on the company's values rather than on its bottom line? To him, they are the same. "For the company to make more money is a good thing because it can reinvest in all kinds of stuff. But having some belief in the mission is going to make us so much more effective in the first place."

Slack can't change who applied to college five years ago, Butterfield points out. "So, how can we have an impact?" he asks. "We can have an impact by making this a good place for people to work. If women are less likely to leave the industry because they worked at Slack, then there will be more people who survived at a higher tenure of experience and therefore a higher role and could go on to be a VP of engineering at Slack or at some other company in the future."

The Slack team is engineering a system that was specifically created to foster teamwork and collaboration. It would simply be bad business not to employ a diverse team that knew something about how people of all types work together to build this product. Though

Butterfield knew the kind of team he wanted, he also knew he couldn't make it happen all by himself: "As an already successful, white, male, straight—fucking go down the list—I'm not going to have the relevant experience to determine what makes this a good workplace, so some of that is just being open but really just making it an explicit focus."

The path to creating the workforce and corporate culture he desired wasn't easy. In 2014, when the company was just fifty employees, almost all of them white and male, Butterfield hired the company's first female executive, Anne Toth, who ultimately ran Slack's people operations and recruiting. "If there was more than one woman in the bathroom, that was kind of an 'Oh my gosh' moment," Toth recalls. "I knew Stewart wanted Slack to be a different kind of workplace . . . He used to say the business fundamentals are solid . . . but we cannot screw up on the people we bring into the company, we can't screw up on the culture, we don't have the same margins for error that we might on the business front. He was very passionate about who we are."

Toth contacted Joelle Emerson, a former lawyer who had started a new business called Paradigm to help tech companies build their diversity and inclusion policies. I first met Emerson in March 2016, at the airy San Francisco headquarters of Airbnb, another company her team was advising. She speaks incredibly fast and with conviction. Right off the bat she said, "None of these companies are winning, and all of them are struggling" when it comes to the representation of women. By September 2017, Emerson was mildly more optimistic: "We've seen a handful of companies (like Pinterest, Intel, and Airbnb, for example) demonstrate progress in some areas, while stalling in others. Sustained progress takes time . . . That companies shouldn't be congratulating themselves doesn't mean there isn't progress; it means we have a long way to go."

One impediment to progress, Emerson says, is that companies have been focused more on raising awareness about unconscious bias rather than educating employees about actions they can take to combat bias. "If you focus on trying to raise awareness, you probably won't see a ton of impact. If you train people on actions they can take, that *can* have an impact," she says.

The research shows that the effects of unconscious-bias training are mixed; there's evidence that it can wear off quickly and even backfire. Emerson says that's reason not to get rid of the training but to improve it, in order to help employees to understand why certain changes are being made and empower them to engage with those changes. That's why Emerson is focused on building her learnings about bias into the everyday structure and operations of companies. First and foremost, she says CEOs and VCs need to buy into the idea that diversity is important and hire a head of HR before the company grows beyond forty to fifty people.

With Emerson's guidance and Toth's execution, Slack started by having employees discuss and articulate the company's values including, most importantly, empathy. And the company started collecting diversity data on its employees.

Restructuring the company's interview process was another key component of Emerson's formula. "When interviews aren't structured, they tend to be about as predictive as a coin toss," Emerson says. "It's only by articulating what you're looking for and assessing for that consistently that we can have any objective evaluation of candidates."

The company also ended "whiteboard coding interviews," a standard practice at many Silicon Valley companies that involves a candidate writing code on a whiteboard in front of a panel of interviewers. "When the candidate is asked to do something they don't normally do and do it in front of someone judging them, it introduces a performance dynamic that can be alienating," Slack's infrastructure engineering head, Julia Grace, wrote in a *Medium* post.

Companies also need to focus on how prospective employees are finding them in the first place. Employee referrals can be one of the most insidious drivers of sameness in company hiring; that is, men are most likely to refer other men. Emerson recommends asking employees explicitly to refer diverse candidates. "Just by thinking harder and being intentional about it," she says, companies can change surprisingly quickly. Pinterest, another client of Emerson's, has seen significant increases in its percentage of women and minority candidates simply by asking employees directly to refer women and underrepresented minorities.

"Stewart has said things I've never heard from a CEO, like 'Can you refer people who look like you to me? I get white guys all the time. You can make a difference.' These are things more people need to say," says former director of engineering Leslie Miley, who is African American.

In fact, whenever Butterfield tweeted about hiring diverse candidates, Toth says the company saw ridiculous spikes in inbound interest.

Slack also diversified its recruiting team. "We have a recruiter who's sixty, we have a Latina woman, two African American women, an African American man, an Asian man, several Caucasian women, and I can't even count the number of LGBT folks," Toth told me. These recruiters were given explicit instructions to source underrepresented candidates from a broader swath of schools (including often overlooked schools such as historically black colleges and those in the South) for every new role at every level of the organization. "We were also looking for candidates who might be older, midcareer, or reentering the workforce from different geographical areas, where typical tech companies weren't looking," Toth said. Recruiting "captains" were designated for various groups, including women, "Earthtones" (referring to people of color), LGBTQ, and veterans, to promote better understanding and support of those specific candidates.

Job postings were reworded. According to Emerson, male-biased terms such as "rock star" and "ninja" are no-no's, along with words such as "brilliant" that convey the belief that intelligence, talents, and abilities are innate, rather than traits that can be developed. Research shows that job descriptions that contain such language get fewer applications overall and fewer from women. Slack also removed explicit requirements like number of years of experience and specific degrees necessary, in the hope that candidates wouldn't opt out prematurely.

Today, Slack's job postings clearly articulate the company's focus on diversity, stating, "We believe everyone deserves to work in a welcoming, respectful, and empathetic culture. We live by our values and hire accordingly . . . Ensuring a diverse and inclusive workplace where we learn from each other is core to Slack's values. We welcome people of different backgrounds, experiences, abilities and perspectives. We are an equal opportunity employer and a fun place to work. Come do the best work of your life here at Slack."

A big bonus of even a little success at diverse hiring is this: once you get more women and underrepresented minorities in the door, more want to join. "The next hire is easier. There's an increasing return dynamic there," Butterfield says. "Now that we have this reputation . . . it feeds on itself."

There is an important myth to dispel. Some people think hiring for diversity is illegal. "They'd be wrong," says Emerson flatly. "Generally, what you can't do . . . is, you can't say, 'Here are two equally qualified candidates, and I'm going to hire you just because you're a woman.' But you can engage in efforts to counterbalance the candidates you're seeing. I would say you have an obligation to do that; not only is it legal, but you should have to."

Which brings me to a point the PayPal Mafia member Keith Rabois raised early in this book: he told me that it's important to hire people who agree with your "first principles"—for example, whether to focus on growth or profitability and, more broadly, the company's mission and how to pursue it. I'd agree. If your mission is to encourage people to share more online, you shouldn't hire someone who believes people don't really want to make their private lives public, or you'll spend a lot of time arguing, time you don't have to waste when you're trying to build a company. But those who believe in your mission and how to execute it aren't limited to people who look and act like you. To combat this tendency, you must first be explicit about what your first principles are. And then, for all of the reasons we discussed, go out of your way to find people who agree with your first principles and who *don't* look like you. Because if you don't build a diverse team when you start, as you scale, it will be incomparably harder to do so.

RETENTION

Of course, it's about not just hiring women but making sure they stay. When it comes to retention, Emerson says it is equally important to build standardized review and feedback structures for employees. Slack reviews its promotion data regularly to make sure (as best it can) there are no differences in how men and women are being promoted.

The next one is a no-brainer: pay equity. Glassdoor, a company that routinely surveys national and Silicon Valley employment data, found that the overall adjusted pay gap between men and women in the United States is 5.4 percent, controlling for factors such as age, location, experience, and job title. For computer programming, however, the pay gap is more than five times bigger, at 28.3 percent. That means women computer programmers make less than seventy-two cents for every dollar a man makes (compared with ninety-five cents on the dollar that women make compared with men nationwide). And remember, tech is an industry that pays in both cash and stock. A tenth of a percentage point in equity can make a multimillion-dollar difference if the company has a big exit later.

In 2015, Slack performed a comprehensive compensation "refresh," and salaries are now routinely monitored by an independent third party. The company is also contributing 1 percent of its equity to support programs to advance women and underrepresented minorities. But Slack admits it still has a lot of work to do, noting that the representation of women and underrepresented minorities drops at more senior levels. And Butterfield worries that as Slack gets bigger, it will become even more difficult to maintain current percentages of women and underrepresented minorities, as has happened at Google and other tech companies. And with Microsoft and Facebook encroaching on Slack's territory as they attempt to build their own workplace collaboration tools, another test will be how the company maintains its focus on diversity and core values as it fends off competition.

This is why it is critical for Slack to retain the diverse workforce it has already created. When I asked Toth if there were any Ping-Pong tables at Slack, she rolled her eyes. "We have an ethos here: 'Work hard and go home,'" she said. That motto is written on posters that can be seen hanging all around the office, which is generally empty by 6:30 p.m. "There is very much a sense here that if you want to play Ping-Pong, you can do that somewhere else," Toth says. The message is that this is a place for grown-ups, and many grown-ups have families. Slack even hosts a daytime Halloween party for the children of employees, with a conference room transformed into a trick-or-treating spot boasting a chocolate fountain.

But no tech company is a diversity Eden. By the time I finished writing this book, Toth, Miley, and Baker had all left Slack. Each situation was different, and Slack points out that its turnover is little less than the average rate for tech companies. But these were marquee hires that boosted the company's reputation as a welcoming place for women and underrepresented minorities. The true measure of Slack's success will be if the company can avoid the fate that befell Google.

A few months after leaving Slack, Baker told me the company still struggles with the stereotypes and misogyny that infect every tech workplace. "They definitely have challenges; there is definitely a James Damore at Slack," Baker says, referring to the ex–Google engineer who said there were fewer women than men in tech and leadership due to biological differences.

Halfway through 2017, Baker posted an industrywide diversity and inclusion "post-mortem" on the social code–hosting site GitHub, which is popular among developers. In the report, Baker wrote, "We are approaching the 10-year anniversary of the first forays into focus on Diversity and Inclusion in the tech industry. The industry has spent over $500M on Diversity and Inclusion efforts with little to no improvements to show for it. Diversity numbers remain stagnant . . . Resolution: This failure is still in progress."

DEBUGGING THE FAILURE

As I approached completion of this book, I was invited to moderate a town hall discussion on solutions to tech's gender problem at *Fortune*'s 2017 Brainstorm Tech Conference in Aspen. The room was filled with entrepreneurs, investors, and executives looking to network and gain new insights, but as the town hall began, I noticed dozens of men sneaking out of what was sure to be an uncomfortable conversation.

The discussion was emotional and electric. In the audience was Niniane Wang, the first woman who went on the record about being sexually harassed by the investor Justin Caldbeck. She took the microphone to propose a third-party organization to oversee the relationship between venture capitalists and entrepreneurs. Right now, she suggested, that third party is the media, which means allegations play out in public without careful arbitration. Nicole Farb, the Goldman Sachs banker turned entrepreneur, said she believes Silicon Valley treats women worse than Wall Street does. Her message: VCs, stop asking women entrepreneurs about their kids!

When one man in attendance said that some women weren't doing enough to support each other, I spotted OpenTable's CEO, Christa Quarles, getting agitated and mouthing the word "Bullshit!" When I handed her the mic, her voice erupted and her body shook. "In Silicon Valley today, there is a sisterhood of women who are supporting each other, telling each other about board opportunities, giving each other business ideas. There is a sisterhood!" Quarles declared. "Talk about sexual harassment . . . You name it, it has happened to me. And I think that what is happening now is that you're all on notice! This stuff can't happen anymore. It has to stop."

Everyone has a role to play: women, men, investors, founders, executives, board directors, parents, teachers. When I asked the audience who needs to change the most, Adam Miller, the CEO of the human resources software company Cornerstone OnDemand, who also happens to be white and male, stood up. "Without a doubt, it's the CEOs . . . We need people that are willing to demand that there's diversity in these organizations, or it's not going to happen," Miller said. "At the end of the day, it has to be a directive from the top."

I agree with Miller. Getting to fifty-fifty is incredibly complex and nuanced, requiring many detailed solutions that will take decades to fully play out. To accelerate the process, change needs to start at the top. Like Stewart Butterfield, CEOs need to make hiring and retaining women an explicit priority. In addition, here is the bare minimum of what we can do at an individual and a systemic level:

- First of all, people, be nice to each other. Treat one another with respect and dignity, including those of the opposite sex. That should be pretty simple.
- Don't enable assholes. Stop making excuses for bad behavior, or ignoring it.
- CEOs must embrace and champion the need to reach a fair representation of gender within their companies, and develop a comprehensive plan to get there. Be long-term focused, not short-term. It may take three weeks to find a white man for the job, but three months to find a woman. Those three months could save three years of playing catch-up in the future. Invest in not just diversity but inclusion. Even if your company is small, everything counts. And take the time to educate your employees about why this is important.
- Companies need to appoint more women to their boards. And boards need to hold company leadership to account to get to fifty-fifty in their employee ranks, starting with company executives.

- Venture capital firms need to hire more women partners, and limited partners should pressure them to do so and at the very least ask them what their plans around diversity are. Investors, both men and women, need to start funding more women and diverse teams, period.
- LPs need to fund more women VCs, who can establish new firms with new cultural norms. Stop funding partnerships that look and act the same.
- Most important, stop blaming everybody else for the problem or pretending that it is too hard for us to solve. It's time to look in the mirror. This is an industry, after all, that prides itself on disruption and revolutionary new ways of thinking. Let's put that spirit of innovation and embrace of radical change to good use. Seeing a more inclusive workforce in Silicon Valley will encourage more girls and women studying computer science now.

"People that just merely point to the pipeline issue, they don't get it," Apple's CEO, Tim Cook, told me at a 2017 fund-raiser for a girls' high school. "The tech companies have a lot to do ourselves. The truth is that in aggregate we all don't do a good job retaining either." Diversity matters at Apple, Cook said, because without that mixture of input it would be impossible to create the most desirable products on the planet. To be clear, Apple's diversity numbers (which include its retail store employees) are also average by Silicon Valley standards, with women representing 32 percent of employees worldwide and 23 percent of tech roles. But the company has accelerated its hiring of women over the last couple of years. Women accounted for 37 percent of new hires at Apple in 2016.

"Our best work comes out of when you have a tremendous level of diversity working on a product. Not only gender, but the artist and musician working with the engineer," Cook said. "When you're like us and you're designing products for the world, don't you want different views?"

TECH'S RISING WORKFORCE

On a Friday afternoon in the summer of 2017, I sat down with a group of teenage girls at Gott's Roadside restaurant on the bustling Embarcadero waterfront in San Francisco. They had come into the city from high schools all over the Bay Area, and now over french fries and chicken tenders they were talking about their experiences learning how to code. All of them had worked with Girls Who Code (GWC), a nonprofit that offers after-school clubs for middle- and high-school-aged girls and immersive summer programs held at tech company offices.

Areeta Wong, sixteen, joined the coding club at San Mateo High School. "When I typed something up and it would magically appear on the screen, that realization that you can create something that works right away is amazing," Wong said. Zaynah Shaikh, a nineteen-year-old computer science major who had recently graduated from the GWC program, added, "Seeing the program work, I think it's pretty empowering. With code you can do so many things." Ria Thakkar, seventeen, taught herself how to code using Khan Academy online tutorials, then helped start the GWC club at her school. "[Learning to code] was a really hard process for me, and I thought, 'How do I make it easier for other girls to do?'"

Ashley Chu, fifteen, joined a GWC club during her sophomore year in high school and attended her first hackathon a few months later. "But the thing is, I was on an all-guys team. They had already taken AP computer science and were really into coding when I was just new, and I felt like I just didn't belong," Chu said.

Still, Chu finished the hackathon. "I was scared, frustrated with my code, and I wanted to quit, but we went through with it," she says. The hackathon has not dampened her aspirations. "I am a really big dreamer, and I've always wanted to be an inventor," Chu said.

Meet the next-gen potential workforce of tech. Shaikh wants to combine her programming skills with her love of sports to make a product that will encourage more young girls to try athletics. Thakkar is obsessed with airplanes and would like to build an aviation app. Chu is a Disney fanatic who would love to join the company's Imagineering research and development arm. Julie Vu, who says she's given up the idea of coding because of what she's read about sexism at Uber, would like to become a recruiter at a tech company so she can help bring in more women and underrepresented minorities (or maybe she'll just go into cosmetics). Saanvi Shreesha wants to start her own business and build all the code for it. Nory Klop-Packel wants to combine her love of spoken language with machine learning. Wong wants to organize hackathons and build education products that bring the opportunity to code to more young girls.

The girls sitting with me that day know all too well that women are grossly underrepresented and sometimes even mistreated in Silicon Valley. "I'm in some 'Women in Tech' Facebook groups," said Zaynah Shaikh. "They talk about being mansplained and all sorts of things. I wish it weren't like this." They all wished for more female role models like Sheryl Sandberg.

Amen to that. But these girls have a very different outlook from women of older generations, and in many respects they are doing pretty well on their own. One day, while Wong was on her way into a coding club meet-up at her local library, a fifth-grade boy asked where she was going. When she replied that she was going to a meeting for Girls Who Code, the boy scoffed, "Why isn't there a Guys Who Code?" Wong exclaimed, "The entire world is Guys Who Code!" Wong is among many young women intent on changing that.

She'll be helped by some cultural shifts happening in the world around her. Yes, some young girls are still getting the message that they got in the 1970s: computers are for boys. But at the same time, more schools are teaching computer science than ever before, and more girls are signing up. According to Code.org, in 2017 almost thirty thousand girls took the 2017 AP computer science exam compared with just over twenty-six hundred in 2007, bringing the percentage of girls taking the test up from 18 percent to 27 percent. For six years starting in 2008, the percentage of girls taking the test remained basically flat, but their share has increased every year for the last four years.

"From kindergarten all the way up through twelfth grade, interest in computer science has been exploding," Code.org's co-founder Hadi Partovi told me. One possible reason: rather than focusing on math, computer science courses are focusing increasingly on the opportunity to be creative, which is attracting a more diverse group of students. (Still, girls' peers in computer science classes are still mostly boys, and their teachers are still mostly men.)

The girls also acknowledge that computer science is becoming more "cool," even for girls. In January 2016, *Seventeen* magazine featured a story titled "We Love Code: Meet the Awesome Girls Who Own It." It was not unlike the *Cosmopolitan* "Computer Girls" article in 1967 that touted the role women could play in this then-new profession. But the 1960s also marked the beginning of a crisis in the teaching of computer science, when students flocked to computer science departments that quickly filled to capacity. By the early 1980s, promising students were being turned away based on their GPA or prior experience in the field, which exacerbated tech's gender imbalance. And something similar is happening now. "In my school, there are a lot of kids and not enough teachers," says Wong, who got waitlisted for a computer science course at San Mateo High School. "Everyone's parents want them to try it out, and we are at the height of demand."

This foreshadows one of the great fears of the longtime Stanford computer science professor Eric Roberts: that once again schools will be unable to meet exploding demand for computer science, and students will be denied the opportunity to participate despite their interest. Roberts reports that the current excitement around computer science mirrors what the industry saw in the early 1980s, around the rise of the Macintosh and the PC. Back then, schools couldn't accommodate the surge in interest, so they started instituting GPA requirements for computer science majors and classes got harder, so that students with prior experience (generally boys who grew up with computers in their bedrooms) might perform better. At about the same time, the number of CS degrees awarded dropped overall, and the percentages of women in the field started to fall. Roberts warns that the young faculty in computer science departments today are not aware of this historical catastrophe. "Our society cannot afford to repeat that mistake," he writes.

"A pattern I've noticed is girls get into the field later in their lives," said Shaikh. "Guys have a much more pre-developed course because they know earlier. There are not a lot of mentors to look up to, so we don't consider it a career option. I've heard so many times the future is female, but how are we going to do that if we are entering so late as women?"

In class one day, Shaikh said, a male classmate made an offhand remark that he doubted the girls in the class had a genuine interest in computers. "I was wearing my Girls Who Code shirt that day, and I was like, 'Bro, that comment is not appreciated here.' There are women like me that want to go into this field and not just for the money. I'm here because I want to make a change in the world," Shaikh explained. "If we want to see change in this industry, we need to inspire the next generation."

It's hard not to be inspired and hopeful listening to these young women's dreams. The girls are already knowledgeable about some of the headwinds that they will face when they open the door to Brotopia. I didn't feel comfortable telling them about the others. They'll find out soon enough. What they made clearer than ever was this: The next generation is coming. They expect to have rewarding careers in tech, and they dream of making a dent in the universe, just as the early founders did. When they open the door, let's welcome them. And change the Valley—and the world—for them and for all.

ACKNOWLEDGMENTS

I AM SO GRATEFUL to the hundreds of people who shared their stories with me. There were far too many to fit in this book, but each story helped shape the narrative and the ideas you've seen here. I am in awe, especially, of the many women in technology I spoke with who've each had careers filled with challenge and triumph. I expect and hope to see them shatter the Silicon Ceiling together.

My deepest thanks go to my writing coach and collaborator in chief, Ethan Watters, who truly embraced the importance of this project and cheered me on every step of the way. Ethan spent many months helping me (an anxious first-time author) navigate the thickets of these very thorny issues, gently guiding, debating, and listening. There is nothing more fulfilling than trudging through difficult writing territory and seeing the ideas crystallize on the other side, and Ethan was there for almost every minute.

There would be no *Brotopia* without my perceptive editor at Portfolio, Stephanie Frerich, who believed in this book from the very beginning. Earlier in her career, Stephanie left publishing for two years to work at a tech company. She's known someone needed to write a book about the difficult issues facing women in technology ever since. I'm so grateful for the dedication she brought to this process. It would never have happened had my agent Pilar Queen not pitched Stephanie the idea in the first place. Pilar was my rock throughout this long journey, a sure and steady hand who was always there to listen, encourage, and remind me to believe in myself.

ACKNOWLEDGMENTS

Of course I'd like to thank the entire team at Portfolio for this opportunity including Adrian Zackheim, Will Weisser, Margot Stamas, Tara Gilbride, Linda Cowen, and Olivia Peluso—who deserves all the credit for the meticulous citations. Judith Coyne brilliantly helped me cut down a five-hundred-page manuscript in what seemed like record time.

Dana Ledyard brought her unparalleled passion for this topic, as a working mom who also spent three years as a managing director at Girls Who Code, to help me hatch the ideas you see brought to life here. Natalie Bonifede, another GWC alum, helped orchestrate the incredible dinner with women engineers at my home in the wake of Susan Fowler's explosive blog post, as well as the meet-up with the young female coders, two high points of this entire journey. Hearing these women, young and old, speak of their challenges and their ambitions was motivation to see this through. And special thanks to Natalie Jones, who made sure that not a fact (hopefully) in this manuscript was out of place!

Brad Stone was my chief confidant who not only encouraged me to write this book (with fair warning of how much of my soul it would consume, of course), and helped me shape the original proposal, but also fielded many of my most panicked moments. He listened and commiserated whenever I hit roadblocks, and inspired me to push forward. Roy Bahat has been a friend, a thoughtful adviser, and one of my biggest—and most brutally honest—advocates along the way.

I especially want to thank the many folks at Bloomberg who have helped build our two television shows into what they are today: *Bloomberg Technology* and *Bloomberg Studio 1.0*. My longtime producer Candy Cheng has always pushed me to be my best and reach for the out of reach. Our managing editor, Danielle Culbertson, was understanding as I juggled the demands of this book with anchoring a daily show. And a huge thanks to Kevin Sheekey, Jason Kelly, Laura Batchelor, Bridgette Webb, Emily Haas-Godsil, Erin Dresch, Jackie Lopez, Cory Johnson, Erin Black, Mallory Abelhouzen, Jose Valenzuela, Jenna Blanchietti, and Meaganne McCandess. My utmost thanks go to the head of Bloomberg Television, Al Mayers, who gave me permission to pursue this passion project alongside my day-to-day responsibilities, and Mike Bloomberg for making everything, literally, possible.

This book, and our show, would not be what they are without the incredibly talented team of *Bloomberg Technology* reporters and editors who are always so generous with their time and their leads, including Olivia Zaleski, Sarah McBride, Sarah Frier, Tom Giles, Ellen Huet, Mark Milian, Dina Bass, Eric Newcomer, Lizette Chapman, and Ashlee Vance.

The idea for this book was conceived over dinner with Sarabeth Berman and Evan Osnos, who championed the topic, and my ability to tackle it, from the start. Writing a book takes time that you would otherwise spend with people you love. I'm so grateful to the many friends who not only forgave me for being preoccupied but offered me such generous support along the way, taking time to hash out ideas over cocktails and at the playground, particularly Darah Roslyn, Marshall Roslyn, Nairi Hourdajian, Nellie Thornton, Alistair Thornton, and Renu Mathias.

I couldn't have done this without the brave souls who came forward across Silicon Valley to share their stories, advice, and support, but a few of them went above and beyond, including Aileen Lee, Niniane Wang, Christina Lee, Ruzwana Bashir, Eric Feng, Selina Tobaccowala, Om Malik, Sukhinder Singh Cassidy, Dick Costolo, Maha Ibrahim, David Kirkpatrick, Katrina Lake, Jennifer Hyman, Chris Messina, Esther Crawford, Gina Bianchini, Nick Bilton, Julia Blystone, Anne Kornblut, Liz Bourgeois, Anda Gansca, Adam Lashinsky, Leena Rao, Ana Medina, Tracy Chou, Laura Holmes, Leah Busque, and Minnie Ingersoll. There are several people who served as sources whom I have not listed here for their own good. Thanks to all of you; you know who you are.

I'd also like to thank all the writers at the Grotto in San Francisco who shared words of encouragement and commiseration in passing, especially Po Bronson, whose veteran expertise I was lucky enough to benefit from during this process. When it came to the cover art, I was fortunate to have the discerning eyes of two incredibly talented designers, Bruno Bergher and Caroline Morchio.

I have an amazing team of representatives, including Scott Wachs and Henry Reisch at William Morris Endeavor Entertainment and my attorney, Nick Dashman, who have always pushed me to aim big. Who knows what is next, but I certainly never thought I'd come this far.

I'd like to give a huge shout-out to the other amazing women and moms in my life: Alison Fisher, Carrie Sponheimer, Joanna Agena, Heather Childs, Allison Lyneham, Colleen Gargan, Renu Mathias, Jo Ling Kent, Fannie Chen, Coble Armstrong, Sara Trucksess, and friends from Hawaii to Bernal Heights.

None of this would have been possible without my "village." First and foremost, I want to thank my mother, Sandy Chang, who has always given me so much love that it's a true miracle she has anything left over for her grandkids. Mom, I love you back for all of that and more. Your drive and dedication to your own work inspires me, and your unwavering support of my life and career pushes me forward every day. My father, Laban Chang, was the artist and the writer in our family. My senior thesis was one of the last things he read before he passed away, and I still remember his incisive comments in the margins. I wish he could have been here to see this, and I hope it lives up to his very high standards. I wouldn't be who I am today without my infinitely wise sister, Sara Chang Scheuerlein, with whom I share a bond that can never be replicated. She and her husband, Eric Scheuerlein, and their children are our second family.

I'd also like to thank my grandmothers, Emilie, my namesake, who is truly the warmest person I know and has watched my show every day since its inception, literally, and Mildred, who taught me the value of hard work and perseverance. My world has always been full of strong women—and incredible extended families from Honolulu to Philadelphia—and for that I am deeply grateful.

We wouldn't have survived the last two years without my acquired family, including Jill and Mark Stull and Whitney and Peter Chiu, who not only pitched in more than their fair share of child care but offered moral support every step of the way. I also want to thank Gabriella Garcia for keeping the village up and running, day in and day out.

Most important, I want to thank my three beautiful little boys, who always gave me the biggest smiles no matter how late I got home or how many weekends I had to take time away to write. They are my air and my heart. I mean it when I say that I believe their lives will be enriched by living in a more inclusive future. On the hardest and most exhausting days, the thought that maybe this book might make their world a better place made it all worthwhile.

Finally, I would like to thank my husband, Jonathan Stull, who lived it all and never once complained. "Superdad" doesn't quite do him justice, but you get the point. Jonathan not only held down the fort over many months but was always my biggest cheerleader, my compass, and my sanity. He picked me up when I was down. He listened when I needed to talk it out. And what makes me most proud is that he truly embraced the importance of these issues and tries to address and improve them every day at his own company. He is my partner and my love for life.

NOTES

This book is the product of more than two hundred interviews across the technology industry. Some interviews were conducted in the course of my reporting for Bloomberg, but the vast majority are original interviews that were conducted for the purposes of this book. These include interviews with Sheryl Sandberg, Marissa Mayer, Susan Fowler, Niniane Wang, Ellen Pao, Katrina Lake, Reid Hoffman, Evan Williams, Dick Costolo, Max Levchin, Stewart Butterfield, John Doerr, and so many more. I also spoke on background to many sources who helped inform and shape what became *Brotopia*.

INTRODUCTION: NOT JUST A PRETTY FACE: TECH'S ORIGINAL SIN

1   **Lena Söderberg started out:** Lenna Sjööblom, "Swedish Accent," *Playboy*, Nov. 1972, 138.

1   **swept up in "America Fever":** Ibid., 135.

2   **ARPA (today known as DARPA):** "Information Sciences Institute," *USC Viterbi Engineer*, Fall 2012, https://issuu.com/uscedu/docs/81696.

3   **The original data set:** "Volume 3: Miscellaneous," Signal and Image Processing Institute Image Database, USC Viterbi, accessed Sept. 13, 2017, http://sipi.usc.edu/database/database.php?volume=misc.

3   **She has served as a test subject:** Corinne Iozzio, "The *Playboy* Centerfold That Helped Create the JPEG," *Atlantic*, Feb. 9, 2016, https://www.theatlantic.com/technology/archive/2016/02/lena-image-processing-playboy/461970.

3   **New research featuring her picture:** Ibid.

3   ***Playboy*, notoriously vigilant:** Team Playboy.com, "How Lenna, Miss November 1972, Became the First Lady of the Internet," *Playboy*, Aug. 9, 2013, http://www.playboy.com/articles/playmate-first-lady-of-the-internet.

3   **In a 2013 article:** Ibid.

3   **Engineers joke that if you want:** Iozzio, "*Playboy* Centerfold That Helped Create the JPEG."

4   **The paper was published:** Deanna Needell and Rachel Ward, "Stable Image Reconstruction Using Total Variation Minimization," *SIAM Journal on Imaging Sciences* 6, no. 2 (Dec. 2013): 1035–1058, https://doi.org/ 10.1137/120868281.

5   **ban Lena's image:** David Munson, "A Note on Lena," *IEEE Transactions on Image Processing* 5, no. 1 (Jan. 1996), https://www.cs .cmu.edu/~chuck/lennapg/editor.html.

5   **history of electronic imaging:** David Zax, "A *Playboy* Model and Nanoscale Printing," *MIT Technology Review*, Aug. 17, 2012, https://www .technologyreview.com/s/428928/a-playboy-model-and-nanoscale-printing.

5   **"When you use a picture":** Iozzio, "*Playboy* Centerfold That Helped Create the JPEG."

6   **women were charging into the field:** Libby Nelson, "In the 1970s, Women Were Making Big Gains in Computer Science. Then They Fell Behind," *Vox*, Oct. 21, 2014, https://www.vox.com/xpress/2014/10/21/ 7028161/computer-science-gender-women-majors.

6   **more women than men:** Nolan Feeney, "Women Are Now More Likely to Have College Degree Than Men," *Time*, Oct. 7, 2015, http://time .com/4064665/women-college-degree.

6   **Today women earn just 22 percent:** "New Data: Are Women Making Gains in Computing and Engineering?," *Change the Equation*, Nov. 22, 2016, http://changetheequation.org/blog/new-data-are-women-making-gains-computing-and-engineering.

7   **women hold a mere quarter:** Catherine Ashcraft, Brad McLain, and Elizabeth Eger, "Women in Tech: The Facts," National Center for Women and Information Technology, 2016, https://www.ncwit.org/sites/default/ files/resources/womenintech_facts_fullreport_05132016.pdf.

7   **women at Google accounted:** "Diversity," Google, last modified Sept. 18, 2017, https://diversity.google.com.

7   **women make up 35 percent:** Maxine Williams, "Facebook Diversity Update: Building a More Diverse, Inclusive Workforce," Facebook Newsroom, Aug. 2, 2017, https://newsroom.fb.com/news/2017/08/ facebook-diversity-update-building-a-more-diverse-inclusive-workforce.

7   **The statistics are downright depressing:** Ashcraft, McLain, and Eger, "Women in Tech."

7   **women are leaving jobs:** Ibid.

7   **In the larger American workforce:** Mark DeWolf, "12 Stats About Working Women," *U.S. Department of Labor Blog*, March 1, 2017, https://blog.dol.gov/2017/03/01/12-stats-about-working-women.

7   **40 percent of businesses:** "The 2016 State of Women-Owned Businesses," American Express OPEN, 2016, http://www.womenable .com/content/userfiles/2016_State_of_Women-Owned_Businesses_ Executive_Report.pdf.

7   **But women-led companies:** Valentina Zarya, "Venture Capital's Funding Gender Gap Is Actually Getting Worse," *Fortune*, March 13, 2017, http://fortune.com/2017/03/13/female-founders-venture-capital.

7   **Women accounted for only:** Gené Teare and Ned Desmond, "The First Comprehensive Study on Women in Venture Capital and Their Impact on Female Founders," *TechCrunch,* April 19, 2016, https://techcrunch.com/2016/04/19/the-first-comprehensive-study-on-women-in-venture-capital.

7   **Of nearly seven thousand:** Candida G. Brush et al., "Diana Report: Women Entrepreneurs 2014: Bridging the Gender Gap in Venture Capital," Arthur M. Blank Center for Entrepreneurship, Babson College, Sept. 2014, http://www.babson.edu/Academics/centers/blank-center/global-research/diana/Documents/diana-project-executive-summary-2014.pdf.

7   **All this despite research:** "Catalyst Study Reveals Financial Performance Is Higher for Companies with More Women at the Top," *Catalyst,* Jan. 15, 2004, http://www.catalyst.org/media/catalyst-study-reveals-financial-performance-higher-companies-more-women-top.

8   **Apple's first version:** Arielle Duhaime-Ross, "Apple Promised an Expansive Health App, So Why Can't I Track Menstruation?," *Verge,* Sept. 25, 2014, https://www.theverge.com/2014/9/25/6844021/apple-promised-an-expansive-health-app-so-why-cant-i-track.

8   **As late as 2016, if you:** Adam S. Miner et al., "Smartphone-Based Conversational Agents and Responses to Questions about Mental Health, Interpersonal Violence, and Physical Health," *JAMA Intern Med* (2016): 619–625, https://doi.org/10.1001/jamainternmed.2016.0400. This oversight has subsequently been remedied.

9   **online harassment and cyber hate:** "Gender Distinctions in Cyber Bullying," soc101group2, *Wikispaces,* Providence College, accessed Nov. 20, 2017, http://soc101group2.providence.wikispaces.net/Gender+Distinctions+in+Cyber+Bullying; Maeve Duggan, "Part 1: Experiencing Online Harassment," Pew Research Center, Oct. 22, 2014, https://doi.org/10.2105/AJPH.2014.302393.

9   **"by the pussy":** "Transcript: Donald Trump's Taped Comments About Women," *New York Times,* Oct. 8, 2016, https://www.nytimes.com/2016/10/08/us/donald-trump-tape-transcript.html.

10   **"I know that so many women":** Sheryl Sandberg, "#metoo. These two simple words . . ." Facebook post, Oct. 16, 2017, https://www.facebook.com/sheryl/posts/10159365581865177.

11   **"Travis can spend eight":** Chris Sacca, "Lowercase Capital Founder Chris Sacca: Studio 1.0," interview by author, *Bloomberg,* June 12, 2015, video, 27:43, https://www.bloomberg.com/news/videos/2015-06-13/lowercase-capital-founder-chris-sacca-studio-1-0-06-12-.

13   **Women account for almost half:** Dan Primack, "Wall Street Outpaces Silicon Valley on Gender Equality," *Axios,* Aug. 8, 2017, https://www.axios.com/wall-street-outpaces-silicon-valley-on-gender-equality-2470698125.html.

14   **"It's bad for shareholder value":** Megan Smith, "Former U.S. CTO on Silicon Valley's Diversity Battle," interview by author, *Bloomberg,* Aug. 7,

2017, video, 7:09, https://www.bloomberg.com/news/videos/2017-08-07/
ex-u-s-cto-on-silicon-valley-s-diversity-battle-video.

14 **"We have a long way to go:** Satya Nadella, "Satya Nadella: Bloomberg
Studio 1.0 (Full Show)," interview by author, *Bloomberg*, Sept. 29, 2017,
video, 23:40, https://www.bloomberg.com/news/videos/2017-09-29/satya-
nadella-bloomberg-studio-1-0-full-show-video.

CHAPTER 1: FROM NERD TO BRO: HOW TECH BYPASSED WOMEN

16 **In his history of the internet:** Walter Isaacson, *The Innovators* (New
York: Simon & Schuster, 2014), 88.

17 **Hopper had an uncanny ability:** Ibid., 90.

17 **She also took a collaborative approach:** Ibid., 117.

17 **many different machines could understand:** Ibid., 93.

17 **machines should be able to work well together:** Ibid., 117.

17 **women to study math:** Ibid., 88.

17 **A woman, Margaret Hamilton:** Robert McMillan, "Her Code Got
Humans on the Moon—and Invented Software Itself," *Wired*, Oct. 13,
2015, https://www.wired.com/2015/10/margaret-hamilton-nasa-apollo.

17 **the term "programmer":** Rose Eveleth, "Computer Programming Used
to Be Women's Work," *Smithsonian*, Oct. 7, 2013, https://www
.smithsonianmag.com/smart-news/computer-programming-used-to-be-
womens-work-718061.

18 **"a girl 'senior systems analyst'":** Lois Mandel, "The Computer Girls,"
Cosmopolitan, April 1967.

18 **But just as *Cosmo*:** Ibid.

18 **"What has sixteen legs":** "What Has Sixteen Legs, Eight Waggly
Tongues and Costs You at Least $40,000 a Year?," Optical Scanning
Corporation, 1968, https://ccs.soic.indiana.edu/files/2017/01/sixteenlegs-
datamation1968.jpg.

19 **personality types that made a great programmer:** Nathan
Ensmenger, *The Computer Boys Take Over: Computers, Programmers, and
the Politics of Technical Expertise* (Cambridge, MA: MIT Press, 2010).

19 **"For many in this period":** Nathan Ensmenger, "Letting the 'Computer
Boys' Take Over: Technology and the Politics of Organizational
Transformation," *IRSH* 48 (2003): 153–80, https://doi.org/10.1017/
S0020859003001305.

19 **Ensmenger estimates that by 1962:** Ensmenger, *Computer Boys Take
Over*, 64.

19 **college fraternities and Elks lodges:** Brenda D. Frink, "Researcher
Reveals How 'Computer Geeks' Replaced 'Computer Girls,'" Clayman
Institute for Gender Research, Stanford University, June 1, 2011, http://
gender.stanford.edu/news/2011/researcher-reveals-how-"computer-
geeks"-replaced-"computergirls".

19 **new mysterious profession:** Thomas J. Misa, ed., *Gender Codes: Why
Women Are Leaving Computing* (New York: Wiley, 2010), 127–28.

19   **profiled 1,378 programmers:** William M. Cannon and Dallis K. Perry, "A Vocational Interest Scale for Computer Programmers," *SIGCPR,* June 27, 1966.

19   **186 of whom were women:** Evelyn Randall Grace, "The Relationship Between Personality Traits and Vocational Interests in the Choice of Field of Study of Selected Junior College Students," North Texas State University, Aug. 1969, https://digital.library.unt.edu/ark:/67531/metadc164347/m2/1/high_res_d/nd_00314.pdf.

19   **therefore success in the field:** Birgitta Böckeler, "Born for It," martinfowler.com, April 20, 2016, https://martinfowler.com/articles/born-for-it.html.

19   **"don't like people":** Cannon and Perry, "Vocational Interest Scale for Computer Programmers."

20   **By one estimate, as many as two-thirds:** Ensmenger, *Computer Boys Take Over,* 35.

20   **such tests were used well into the 1980s:** Ibid., 79.

20   **The prevalence of antisocial personality:** Analucia A. Alegria et al., "Sex Difference in Antisocial Personality Disorder: Results from the National Epidemiological Survey on Alcohol and Related Conditions," *Personality Disorders: Theory, Research, and Treatment* 4, no. 3 (2013): 214–22, https://doi.org/10.1037/a0031681.

20   **And many more boys:** Alycia K. Halladay et al., "Sex and Gender Differences in Autism Spectrum Disorder: Summarizing Evidence Gaps and Identifying Emerging Areas of Priority," *Molecular Autism* 6, no. 36 (2015), https://doi.org/10.1186/s13229-015-0019-y.

21   **"often egocentric, slightly neurotic":** Nathan Ensmenger, "'Beards, Sandals, and Other Signs of Rugged Individualism': Masculine Culture within the Computing Professions," *Osiris* 30, no. 1 (2015): 38–65, https://doi.org/10.1086/682955.

21   **In fact, the word "women":** Cannon and Perry, "Vocational Interest Scale for Computer Programmers."

21   **There is little evidence:** Gerald E. Evans and Mark G. Simkin, "What Best Predicts Computer Proficiency?," *Communications of the ACM* (1989): 1322, https://doi.org/10.1145/68814.68817.

21   **Nor is there evidence:** Sara M. Lindberg, Janet Shibley Hyde, and Jennifer L. Petersen, "New Trends in Gender and Mathematics Performance: A Meta-analysis," *Psychological Bulletin* 136, no. 6 (2010): 1123–35, https://doi.org/10.1037/a0021276.

22   **an electronic mailing list:** "Systers," Anita Borg Institute, accessed Sept. 5, 2017, https://anitaborg.org/systers.

22   **"industry selected for antisocial":** Ensmenger, *Computer Boys Take Over,* 78–79.

22   **"I was afraid to be":** Padmasree Warrior, "NextEV's Padmasree Warrior: Studio 1.0 (Full Show 3/27)," interview by author, *Bloomberg,* March 27, 2016, video, 23:36, https://www.bloomberg.com/news/videos/2016-03-27/nextev-s-padmasree-warrior-studio-1-0-full-show.

23   **A large study of high schoolers:** Lily Shashaani, "Gender-Based Differences in Attitudes Toward Computers," *Computers & Education* 20, no. 2 (1993): 169–81, https://doi.org/10.1016/0360-1315(93)90085-W.

24   **These biases seeped into the curriculum:** Jane Margolis and Allan Fisher, *Unlocking the Clubhouse* (Cambridge, MA: MIT Press, 2001), 4.

24   **Female CS students report being discouraged:** Ibid., 61.

24   **The "geek mythology":** Ibid., 68.

24   **"These stereotypes are incongruent":** Sapna Cheryan et al., "The Stereotypical Computer Scientist: Gendered Media Representations as a Barrier to Inclusion for Women," *Sex Roles* 69 (2013): 58–71, https://doi .org/10.1007/s11199-013-0296-x.

24   **Cheryan referenced a quotation:** Sapna Cheryan, Allison Master, and Andrew N. Meltzoff, "Cultural Stereotypes as Gatekeepers: Increasing Girls' Interest in Computer Science and Engineering by Diversifying Stereotypes," *Frontiers in Psychology* 6, no. 49 (2015), https://doi .org/10.3389/fpsyg.2015.00049.

24   **"I don't dream in code":** Jane Margolis, Allan Fisher, and Faye Miller, "The Anatomy of Interest: Women in Undergraduate Computer Science," *Women's Studies Quarterly* 28, no. 1–2 (2000): 104–27, http://www.jstor .org/stable/40004448.

25   **Demand became so great:** Eric Roberts, "A History of Capacity Challenges in Computer Science," Stanford University, March 7, 2016, http://cs.stanford.edu/people/eroberts/CSCapacity.

25   **electrical engineering and computer science:** Ibid.

25   **In 1977, the MCAT:** William C. McGaghie, "Assessing Readiness for Medical Education: Evolution of the Medical College Admission Test," *JAMA* 288, no. 9 (2002): 1085–90, https://jamanetwork.com/journals/ jama/article-abstract/195259.

26   **"In the 1970s, students":** Roberts, "History of Capacity Challenges in Computer Science."

29   **He majored in economics:** Govind Dandekar, "Trilogy CEO, Stanford Alum Retraces Path to Success," *Stanford Daily,* May 28, 1998, https:// stanforddailyarchive.com/cgi-bin/stanford?a=d&d=stanford19980528- 01.2.26.

30   **"We will, but the price":** Sarah E. Henrickson, "Founder of Trilogy Speaks About His Career," *Harvard Crimson,* Oct. 31, 1997, http://www .thecrimson.com/article/1997/10/31/founder-of-trilogy-speaks-about-his.

30   **IBM, Alcatel, and Boeing:** Ernst & Young, *Net Entrepreneurs Only* (New York: Wiley, 2000), 50.

32   **"The first thing":** Susan Lahey, "Trilogy and the Extraordinary Power of a Great Network," *Silicon Hills News,* March 15, 2015, http://www .siliconhillsnews.com/2015/03/15/trilogy-and-the-extraordinary-power-of- a-great-network.

32   **New hires immediately spent:** Ibid.

32   **"push new recruits":** Noel Tichy, "No Ordinary Boot Camp," *Harvard Business Review,* April 2001, https://hbr.org/2001/04/no-ordinary-boot- camp.

33 **"money, recruiters, beer":** Lahey, "Trilogy and the Extraordinary Power of a Great Network."

34 **In a paper that consolidated:** Emily Grijalva et al., "Narcissism and Leadership: A Meta-analytic Review of Linear and Nonlinear Relationships," *Personnel Psychology* 68, no. 1 (Spring 2015): 1–47, http://dx.doi.org/10.1111/peps.12072.

34 **"Brainteasers are a complete waste":** Adam Bryant, "In Head-Hunting, Big Data May Not Be Such a Big Deal," *New York Times,* June 19, 2013, http://www.nytimes.com/2013/06/20/business/in-head-hunting-big-data-may-not-be-such-a-big-deal.html.

35 **Despite their concrete achievements:** Pauline Rose Clance and Suzanne Imes, "The Imposter Phenomenon in High Achieving Women: Dynamics and Therapeutic Intervention," *Psychotherapy Theory, Research, and Practice* 15, no. 3 (Fall 1978): 241–47, http://dx.doi.org/10.1037/h0086006.

35 **Other researchers have found:** Tara Sophia Mohr, "Why Women Don't Apply for Jobs Unless They're 100% Qualified," *Harvard Business Review,* Aug. 25, 2014, https://hbr.org/2014/08/why-women-dont-apply-for-jobs-unless-theyre-100-qualified.

36 **When the first tech bubble burst:** Marie Thibault, "The Next Bill Gates," *Forbes,* Jan. 19, 2010, https://www.forbes.com/2010/01/19/young-tech-billionaire-gates-google-yahoo-wealth.html#6257bb713333.

36 **Given that entitlement:** Emily Grijalva et al., "Gender Differences in Narcissism: A Meta-analytic Review," *Psychological Bulletin* 141, no. 2 (March 2015): 261–310, https://doi.org/10.1037/a0038231.

37 **prominent role in high finance:** Meredith Lepore, "Analysts Say Having More Female Bankers Could Have Prevented the Financial Crisis," *Grindstone,* Jan. 26, 2012, http://www.thegrindstone.com/2012/01/26/office-politics/analysts-say-having-more-female-bankers-could-have-prevented-the-financial-crisis-181.

37 **"Risk-taking is desirable":** "Women More Than Twice as Likely to Be Cautious About Risk Than Men," *Psychological Consultancy Ltd.,* March 16, 2016, http://www.psychological-consultancy.com/blog/women-twice-likely-cautious-risk-men.

38 **An extensive study:** Jenny Anderson, "Huge Study Finds That Companies with More Women Leaders Are More Profitable," *Quartz,* Feb. 8, 2016, https://qz.com/612086/huge-study-find-that-companies-with-more-women-leaders-are-more-profitable.

38 **According to data compiled:** "Table 349: Degrees in Computer and Information Sciences Conferred by Degree-Granting Institutions, by Level of Degree and Sex of Student: 1970–71 Through 2010–11," National Center for Education Statistics, July 2012, https://nces.ed.gov/programs/digest/d12/tables/dt12_349.asp.

39 **Today, it's estimated:** Jon Swartz, "Businesses Say They Just Can't Find the Right Tech Workers," *USA Today,* March 28, 2017, https://www.usatoday.com/story/tech/talkingtech/2017/03/28/tech-skills-gap-huge-graduates-survey-says/99587888.

NOTES

CHAPTER 2: THE PAYPAL MAFIA AND THE MYTH OF THE MERITOCRACY

41 **"a lucid and profound articulation":** Derek Thompson, "Peter Thiel's *Zero to One* Might Be the Best Business Book I've Read," *Atlantic,* Sept. 25, 2014, https://www.theatlantic.com/business/archive/2014/09/peter-thiel-zero-to-one-review/380738.

42 **"We all have a responsibility":** Peter Thiel, "Peter Thiel: Bloomberg West (Full Show 4/12)," interview by author, *Bloomberg,* April 12, 2016, video, 56:52, https://www.bloomberg.com/news/videos/2016-04-13/peter-thiel-bloomberg-west-full-show-4-12.

43 ***Zero to One:*** Peter Thiel, *Zero to One* (New York: Crown Business, 2014).

44 **Thiel himself told me:** Peter Thiel, "Venture Capitalist Peter Thiel: Studio 1.0 (12/18) *Bloomberg,* Dec. 18, 2014, video, 27:34, https://www.bloomberg.com/news/videos/2014-12-19/venture-capitalist-peter-thiel-studio-10-1218.

44 **Stanford began by instituting:** News release, *Stanford News Service,* April 22, 1991, https://web.stanford.edu/dept/news/pr/91/910422Arc1416.html.

45 **lawsuit against Harvard:** Anemona Hartocollis and Stephanie Saul, "Affirmative Action Battle Has a New Focus: Asian-Americans," *New York Times,* Aug. 2, 2017, https://www.nytimes.com/2017/08/02/us/affirmative-action-battle-has-a-new-focus-asian-americans.html?_r=0.

45 **The *Stanford Review* also targeted feminism:** Lisa Koven and David Sacks, "Rape at Stanford," *Stanford Review,* Jan. 21, 1992.

45 **The word "RAPE":** Ibid., 1.

45 **"If you're male and heterosexual at Stanford":** Ibid., 4.

46 **"Faggot! Hope you die":** "Officials Condemn Homophobic Incident; No Prosecution Planned," Stanford News Service, Feb. 12, 1992, https://news.stanford.edu/pr/92/920212Arc2432.html.

46 **who had reportedly kicked a student out:** David Dirks, "Freshman Loses Housing for Insensitive Conduct," *Stanford Daily,* May 23, 1988, https://stanforddailyarchive.com/cgi-bin/stanford?a=d&d=stanford19880523-01.2.4#.

46 **"The intention was for the speech":** Ibid.

46 **"caused Stanford to resemble":** David O. Sacks and Peter Thiel, *The Diversity Myth* (Oakland, CA: Independent Institute, 1998): 29.

47 **And in 2011, Thiel told:** George Packer, "No Death, No Taxes," *New Yorker,* Nov. 28, 2011, https://www.newyorker.com/magazine/2011/11/28/no-death-no-taxes.

47 **"seductions that are later regretted":** Sacks and Thiel, *Diversity Myth,* 144.

47 **"More than two decades ago":** Ryan Mac and Matt Drange, "Donald Trump Supporter Peter Thiel Apologizes for Past Book Comments on Rape," *Forbes,* Oct. 25, 2016, https://www.forbes.com/sites/ryanmac/2016/10/25/peter-thiel-apologizes-for-past-book-comments-on-rape-and-race/#7c635d0e4e48.

47   **In late 2017, however:** Andrew Granato, "How Peter Thiel Built a Silicon Valley Empire," *Stanford Politics*, Nov. 27, 2017, https://stanfordpolitics.org/2017/11/27/peter-thiel-cover-story.

47   **"This is college journalism written over 20 years ago":** Kara Swisher, "Zenefits CEO David Sacks Apologizes for Parts of a 1996 Book He Co-wrote with Peter Thiel That Called Date Rape 'Belated Regret,'" *Recode*, Oct. 24, 2016, https://www.recode.net/2016/10/24/13395798/zenefits-ceo-david-sacks-apologizes-1996-book-co-wrote-peter-thiel-date-rape-belated-regret.

47   **"I do believe in diversity":** David Sacks, "Zenefits CEO on Closing the Chapter on Compliance Issues," interview by author, *Bloomberg*, Oct. 18, 2016, video, 12:23, https://www.bloomberg.com/news/videos/2016-10-18/zenefits-ceo-on-closing-the-chapter-on-compliance-issues.

48   **"sleep and get some air-conditioning":** Max Levchin, "PayPal Co-Founder Max Levchin: Studio 1.0 (02/05)," interview by author, *Bloomberg*, Feb. 6, 2015, video, 27:34, https://www.bloomberg.com/news/videos/2015-02-06/paypal-co-founder-max-levchin-studio-1-0-02-05-.

49   **"they must work quickly":** Thiel, *Zero to One*, 122–23.

49   **Except for the office manager, who was female:** Jodi Kantor, "A Brand New World in Which Men Ruled," *New York Times*, Dec. 23, 2014, https://www.nytimes.com/interactive/2014/12/23/us/gender-gaps-stanford-94.html.

50   **"I think there is this way":** Thiel, interview by author, *Bloomberg*, Dec. 18, 2014.

51   **"of the six people":** Thiel, *Zero to One*, 173.

51   **"I ended up recruiting":** Ibid.

54   **"sex in the stairwells":** Rolfe Winkler, "Zenefits Once Told Employees: No Sex in Stairwells," *Wall Street Journal*, Feb. 22, 2016, https://www.wsj.com/articles/zenefits-once-told-employees-no-sex-in-stairwells-1456183097.

54   **Mafia's "dynastic privilege":** Adam Pisoni, "In Defense of Diverse Founding Teams," *Medium*, Jan. 12, 2017, https://medium.com/@adampisoni/in-defense-of-diverse-founding-teams-e9f0b5b81f25.

56   **He left Square in the midst:** Evelyn M. Rusli, "Square Executive Resigns Amid Sexual-Harassment Claims," *Wall Street Journal*, Jan. 25, 2013, https://www.wsj.com/articles/SB10001424127887324539304578264153187663828.

60   **"If meritocracy exists":** Kantor, "A Brand New World in Which Men Ruled."

61   **"would have died":** Roger Parloff, "Peter Thiel Disagrees with You," *Fortune*, Sept. 4, 2014, http://fortune.com/2014/09/04/peter-thiels-contrarian-strategy.

61   **"It is good sense":** Michael Young, "Down with Meritocracy," *Guardian*, June 28, 2001, https://www.theguardian.com/politics/2001/jun/29/comment.

62 **But is it just a coincidence:** "Economic Diversity and Student Outcomes at Stanford University," *New York Times,* 2017, https://www .nytimes.com/interactive/projects/college-mobility/stanford-university? mcubz=3.

63 **while the national median:** "Income, Poverty, and Health Insurance Coverage in the United States: 2016," U.S. Census Bureau, Sept. 12, 2017, https://www.census.gov/newsroom/press-releases/2017/income-poverty.html.

63 **Research shows when companies:** Emilio J. Castilla and Stephen Benard, "The Paradox of Meritocracy in Organizations," *Administrative Science Quarterly,* Dec. 1, 2010, http://hdl.handle.net/1721.1/65884.

63 **When you are convinced:** Leah Eichler, "The Problem with Working for a Supposed Meritocracy," *Globe and Mail,* March 4, 2016, https:// www.theglobeandmail.com/report-on-business/careers/career-advice/life-at-work/the-problem-with-working-for-a-supposed-meritocracy/ article29033411.

63 **"'Meritocracy' takes as its core":** Megan Garber, "The Perils of Meritocracy," *Atlantic,* June 30, 2017, https://www.theatlantic.com/ entertainment/archive/2017/06/the-perils-of-meritocracy/532215.

64 **"I no longer believe":** Peter Thiel, "The Education of a Libertarian," Cato Unbound, April 13, 2009, https://www.cato-unbound.org/ 2009/04/13/peter-thiel/education-libertarian.

65 **revealed that he was gay:** Owen Thomas, "Peter Thiel Is Totally Gay, People," *Gawker,* Dec. 19, 2007, http://gawker.com/335894/peter-thiel-is-totally-gay-people.

65 **"When I was a kid":** Will Drabold, "Read Peter Thiel's Speech at the Republican National Convention," *Time,* July 21, 2016, http://time .com/4417679/republican-convention-peter-thiel-transcript.

65 **"We care deeply about diversity":** Jeff John Roberts, "Mark Zuckerberg Says Trump Supporter Peter Thiel Still Has a Place on Facebook's Board," *Fortune,* Oct. 19, 2016, http://fortune.com/ 2016/10/19/zuckerberg-thiel.

66 **"I think you need":** Melanie Ehrenkranz, "Mark Zuckerberg's Defense of Peter Thiel Reveals a Flawed Understanding of Diversity," *Mic,* March 14, 2017, http://www.businessinsider.com/mark-zuckerbergs-defense-of-peter-thiel-reveals-a-flawed-understanding-of-diversity-2017-3.

66 **"whole, you know, age of computer":** Jeremy Diamond, "Trump, the Computer and Email Skeptic-in-Chief," CNN, Dec. 30, 2016, http:// www.cnn.com/2016/12/29/politics/donald-trump-computers-internet-email/index.html.

CHAPTER 3: GOOGLE: WHEN GOOD INTENTIONS AREN'T ENOUGH

67 **"I wish I could say":** Susan Wojcicki, "Studio 1.0: Susan Wojcicki Opens Up About Being a Working Mother in the Tech Industry," interview by author, *Bloomberg,* Nov. 14, 2016, https://www.bloomberg

.com/news/articles/2016-11-14/studio-1-0-susan-wojcicki-opens-up-about-being-a-working-mother-in-the-tech-industry.

68 **And it's worth examining:** Erik Larson, "Google Sued for Allegedly Paying Women Less Than Male Peers," *Bloomberg,* Sept. 14, 2017, https://www.bloomberg.com/news/articles/2017-09-14/google-sued-by-women-workers-claiming-gender-discrimination.

70 **Google had no marketing budget:** Adam Levy, "Susan Wojcicki: From Google Doodles to YouTube CEO," Motley Fool, July 5, 2015, https://www.fool.com/investing/general/2015/07/05/susan-wojcicki-from-google-doodles-to-youtube-ceo.aspx.

70 **"You do the content":** Steven Levy, *In the Plex* (New York: Simon & Schuster, 2011), 84.

71 **In this particular column:** Rachel Hutton, "Meeting Our Campus Celebrities," *Stanford Daily,* Nov. 9, 1998, https://stanforddailyarchive.com/cgi-bin/stanford?a=d&d=stanford19981109-01.1.4&e=-------en-20--1--txt-txIN-------.

71 **"outstandingly attractive woman":** Hutton, "Meeting Our Campus Celebrities."

72 **Research backs this up:** "Stereotype Threat Widens Achievement Gap," *American Psychological Association,* July 15, 2006, http://www.apa.org/research/action/stereotype.aspx.

73 **One of her first jobs:** Laura M. Holson, "Putting a Bolder Face on Google," *New York Times,* Feb. 28, 2009, http://www.nytimes.com/2009/03/01/business/01marissa.html.

73 **By 2004, the year after AdSense:** U.S. Securities and Exchange Commission, Google Inc. Form 10-K for the Fiscal Year Ended Dec. 31, 2014, Feb. 6, 2015, https://www.sec.gov/Archives/edgar/data/1288776/000128877615000008/goog2014123110-k.htm.

74 **Sandberg's first assignment:** Kashmir Hill, "Sheryl Sandberg to Harvard Biz Grads: 'Find a Rocket Ship,'" *Forbes,* May 24, 2012, https://www.forbes.com/sites/kashmirhill/2012/05/24/sheryl-sandberg-to-harvard-biz-grads-find-a-rocket-ship.

74 **She went on to create:** "Facebook Names Sheryl Sandberg Chief Operating Officer," Facebook Newsroom, March 4, 2008, https://newsroom.fb.com/news/2008/03/facebook-names-sheryl-sandberg-chief-operating-officer.

76 **"I think the thing":** Wojcicki, interview by author, *Bloomberg,* Nov. 14, 2016.

80 **"something out of a rebooted soap opera":** Reed Albergotti, "Google Reckoning with History of Interoffice Romance by Top Execs," *The Information,* Nov. 29, 2017, https://www.theinformation.com/google-reckoning-with-history-of-interoffice-romance-by-top-execs.

80 **In the long, hot summer:** Caroline Graham, "The £5.4 Billion Google Love Rat: How Boss, 58, of Internet Giant Resisting Online Porn Crackdown Has a String of Exotic Lovers in His 'Open Marriage' . . . but DOESN'T Want You to Know About It," *Daily Mail,* July 20, 2013, http://

www.dailymail.co.uk/news/article-2371719/Googles-Eric-Schmidts-open-marriage-string-exotic-lovers.html.

81   **Schmidt's New York apartment:** Sam Biddle, "Google Boss Enjoys $15 Mil Manhattan Sex Penthouse," *Valleywag,* July 25, 2013, http://valleywag.gawker.com/google-boss-enjoys-15-mil-manhattan-sex-penthouse-909299764.

81   **"the most daring CEO":** Ryan Chittum, *"Fast Company's* Daring 23andMe Cover," *Columbia Journalism Review,* Nov. 23, 2013, http://archives.cjr.org/the_audit/fast_companys_daring_23andme_c.php.

81   **Longtime chief legal counsel:** Albergotti, "Google Reckoning with History of Interoffice Romance by Top Execs."

82   **Executives, she tweeted:** Shawn Paul Wood, "Google Engineer Accused of Sexual Harassment Allegedly Does Nothing," *Adweek,* March 9, 2015, http://www.adweek.com/digital/google-engineer-accused-of-sexual-harassment-allegedly-does-nothing.

83   **Andy Rubin, the mastermind:** Reed Albergotti, "Android's Andy Rubin Left Google After Inquiry Found Inappropriate Relationship," *The Information,* Nov. 28, 2017, https://www.theinformation.com/androids-andy-rubin-left-google-after-inquiry-found-inappropriate-relationship.

83   **In 2016, longtime Google executive:** Barry Schwartz, "Amit Singhal, The Head of Google Search, to Leave the Company for Philanthropic Purposes," *Search Engine Land,* Feb. 3, 2016, https://searchengineland.com/amit-singhal-the-head-of-google-search-to-leave-the-company-for-philanthropic-purposes-241707.

83   **Google reported numbers:** "Google Diversity," Google, 2017.

84   **"The department has received":** Sam Levin, "Google Accused of 'Extreme' Gender Pay Discrimination by US Labor Department," *Guardian,* April 7, 2017, https://www.theguardian.com/technology/2017/apr/07/google-pay-disparities-women-labor-department-lawsuit.

84   **The following September:** Larson, "Google Sued for Allegedly Paying Women Less Than Male Peers."

84   **"Job levels and promotions":** Ibid.

88   **In it, Damore argued:** Mike Cernovich, "Full James Damore Memo—Uncensored Memo with Charts and Cites," *Medium,* Aug. 8, 2017, https://medium.com/@Cernovich/full-james-damore-memo-uncensored-memo-with-charts-and-cites-339f3d2d05f.

88   **though Damore's citations, some from Wikipedia:** Megan Molteni and Adam Rogers, "The Actual Science of James Damore's Google Memo," *Wired,* Aug. 15, 2017, https://www.wired.com/story/the-pernicious-science-of-james-damores-google-memo.

89   **Another site that came:** Toni Airaksinen, "Libertarian Site Suffers DDoS Attack After Supporting Google Worker," *PJ Media,* Aug. 9, 2017, https://pjmedia.com/trending/2017/08/09/libertarian-site-suffers-ddos-attack-after-supporting-google-worker.

89   **The mainstream media quickly picked up:** Jack Nicas and Yoree Koh, "At Google, Memo on Gender and Diversity Sparks Firestorm," *Wall*

Street Journal, Aug. 9, 2017, https://www.wsj.com/articles/memo-sparks-firestorm-at-google-1502246996.

89   **Pichai issued a harshly worded rebuke:** Sundar Pichai, "Note to Employees from CEO Sundar Pichai," *Google,* Aug. 8, 2017, https://www.blog.google/topics/diversity/note-employees-ceo-sundar-pichai.

90   **calling for Pichai's resignation:** David Brooks, "Sundar Pichai Should Resign as Google's C.E.O.," *New York Times,* Aug. 11, 2017, https://www.nytimes.com/2017/08/11/opinion/sundar-pichai-google-memo-diversity.html.

90   **"It's really a shame":** James Damore, "Fired Google Engineer Says Company Executives Smeared Him," interview by author, *Bloomberg,* Aug. 9, 2017, video, 3:51, https://www.bloomberg.com/news/videos/2017-08-10/fired-google-engineer-says-company-smeared-him-video.

91   **there is a vast body of research:** Brian A. Nosek et al., "National Differences in Gender-Science Stereotypes Predict National Sex Differences in Science and Math Achievement," *PNAS* 106, no. 26 (2009): 10593–97, https://doi.org/10.1073/pnas.0809921106.

91   **One of the most insightful:** Yonatan Zunger, "So, About This Googler's Manifesto," *Medium,* Aug. 5, 2017, https://medium.com/@yonatanzunger/so-about-this-googlers-manifesto-1e3773ed1788.

92   **"What *is* news is that this employee":** Erica Joy Baker, "I Am Disappointed but Unsurprised . . ." *Medium,* Aug. 5, 2017, https://medium.com/projectinclude/i-am-disappointed-but-unsurprised-by-the-news-that-an-anti-diversity-sexist-racist-manifesto-is-5fdafbe19352.

92   **"almost class action":** Megan Smith, "Former U.S. CTO on Silicon Valley's Diversity Battle," interview by author, *Bloomberg,* Aug. 7, 2017, video, 7:09, https://www.bloomberg.com/news/videos/2017-08-07/ex-u-s-cto-on-silicon-valley-s-diversity-battle-video.

92   **"We know when we work with dudes":** Cate Huston, "We Know Who He Is," *Medium,* Aug. 6, 2017, https://medium.com/@catehstn/we-know-who-he-is-596fdd93d7c2.

93   **"I've had my abilities":** Susan Wojcicki, "Read YouTube CEO Susan Wojcicki's Response to the Controversial Google Anti-diversity Memo," *Fortune,* Aug. 9, 2017, http://fortune.com/2017/08/09/google-diversity-memo-wojcicki.

93   **_Forbes_ recently ranked her:** "The World's Most Powerful Women In 2016," *Forbes,* Jun. 6, 2016, https://www.forbes.com/sites/alixmcnamara/2016/06/06/the-worlds-most-powerful-women-in-2016/#54f8fb971c83.

94   **"the cold weather":** Susan Wojcicki (@SusanWojcicki), "Super cold weather @Davos2016 is it's easy to store breast milk. No freezer required. #moms." Twitter post, Jan. 22, 2016, https://twitter.com/susanwojcicki/status/690467560396029952.

94   **"When I'm in the office":** Susan Wojcicki, interview by author, *Bloomberg,* Nov. 14, 2016, video, 23:36, https://www.bloomberg.com/

news/videos/2016-11-14/susan-wojcicki-bloomberg-studio-1-0-11-13.

95 **she flourished at Google:** Claire Cain Miller, "In Google's Inner Circle, a Falling Number of Women," *New York Times,* Aug. 22, 2012, http://www.nytimes.com/2012/08/23/technology/in-googles-inner-circle-a-falling-number-of-women.html.

96 **"New Yahoo CEO Marissa":** Jenna Goudreau, "New Yahoo CEO Marissa Mayer Is Pregnant. Does It Matter?," *Forbes,* July 17, 2012, https://www.forbes.com/sites/jennagoudreau/2012/07/17/new-yahoo-ceo-marissa-mayer-is-pregnant-does-it-matter/#7fd59ae9fa00.

96 **"The Pregnant CEO":** LearnVest, "The Pregnant CEO: Should You Hate Marissa Mayer?," *Forbes,* July 19, 2012, https://www.forbes.com/sites/learnvest/2012/07/19/the-pregnant-ceo-should-you-hate-marissa-mayer/#5df5db293d14.

96 **"Marissa Mayer's Brief Maternity Leave":** Katherine Reynolds Lewis, "Marissa Mayer's Brief Maternity Leave: Progress or Workaholism?," *Fortune,* Oct. 2, 2012, http://fortune.com/2012/10/02/marissa-mayers-brief-maternity-leave-progress-or-workaholism.

97 **One blogger quipped:** Penelope Trunk, "Marissa Mayer Becomes CEO of Yahoo and Proves Women Cannot Have It All," blog.penelopetrunk.com, July 17, 2012, http://blog.penelopetrunk.com/2012/07/17/marissa-mayer-becomes-ceo-of-yahoo-and-proves-women-cannot-have-it-all.

97 **By that point, Mayer had been leading:** Marissa Mayer, "Marissa's Tumblr," https://marissamayr.tumblr.com.

98 **on the wrong side of history:** Richard Branson and Sheryl Sandberg, "Sheryl Sandberg and Richard Branson: Balancing Act (04/24)," interview by author, *Bloomberg,* April 23, 2015, video, 20:53, https://www.bloomberg.com/news/videos/2015-04-25/sheryl-sandberg-richard-branson-balancing-act-04-24-.

100 **Under her direction, Facebook's revenues:** Matt Rosoff, "Look at How Much Sheryl Sandberg Has Done for Facebook," *Business Insider,* Mar. 23, 2016, http://www.businessinsider.com/sheryl-sandberg-8-years-at-facebook-2016-3.

100 **not to "lean back":** Sheryl Sandberg, "Why We Have Too Few Women Leaders," TED talk, Dec. 21, 2010, video, 14:58, https://www.ted.com/talks/sheryl_sandberg_why_we_have_too_few_women_leaders.

100 **"Although couched in terms":** Anne-Marie Slaughter, "Why Women Still Can't Have It All," *Atlantic,* July/Aug. 2012, https://www.theatlantic.com/magazine/archive/2012/07/why-women-still-cant-have-it-all/309020.

101 **"Why I hate Sheryl":** Rosa Brooks, "Recline, Don't 'Lean In' (Why I Hate Sheryl Sandberg)," *Washington Post,* Feb. 25, 2014, https://www.washingtonpost.com/blogs/she-the-people/wp/2014/02/25/recline-dont-lean-in-why-i-hate-sheryl-sandberg/?utm_term=.d6cbcc2012c1.

101 **"The False Promise":** Bryce Covert, "Lean In, Trickle Down: The False Promise of Sheryl Sandberg's Theory of Change," *Forbes,* Feb. 25, 2013, https://www.forbes.com/sites/brycecovert/2013/02/25/lean-in-trickle-

down-the-false-promise-of-sheryl-sandbergs-theory-of-change/
#469c7d5c4256.

101 **"Why I Won't Lean In"**: Vanessa Garcia, "Why I Won't Lean In,"
Huffington Post, July 19, 2013, https://www.huffingtonpost.com/vanessa-
garcia/why-i-wont-lean-in_b_3586527.html.

102 **"Mayer and Sandberg"**: Joanne Bamberger, "The New Mommy Wars,"
USA Today, Feb. 5, 2013, https://www.usatoday.com/story/opinion/
2013/02/25/the-new-mommy-wars-column/1947589.

102 **"blaming other women"**: Maureen Dowd, "Pompom Girl for
Feminism," *New York Times,* Feb. 23, 2013, http://www.nytimes
.com/2013/02/24/opinion/sunday/dowd-pompom-girl-for-feminism.html.

102 **The *Lean In* backlash:** Anna Holmes, "Maybe You Should Read the
Book: The Sheryl Sandberg Backlash," *New Yorker,* March 4, 2013,
https://www.newyorker.com/books/page-turner/maybe-you-should-read-
the-book-the-sheryl-sandberg-backlash.

CHAPTER 4: DINNER WITH WOMEN ENGINEERS

105 **Fowler joined Uber:** Susan J. Fowler, "Reflecting on One Very, Very
Strange Year at Uber," www.susanjfowler.com, Feb. 19, 2017, https://
www.susanjfowler.com/blog/2017/2/19/reflecting-on-one-very-strange-
year-at-uber.

105 **Fowler did not have the typical:** Susan J. Fowler, "Twenty Books That
Shaped My Unconventional Life," www.susanjfowler.com, Aug. 17, 2016,
https://www.susanjfowler.com/blog/2016/8/15/20-unconventional-books-
that-changed-my-life.

106 **"He was trying to stay":** Fowler, "Reflecting on One Very, Very Strange
Year at Uber."

109 **claimed that a "smear campaign":** Susan Fowler, "Research for the
smear campaign has begun. If you are contacted by anyone asking for
personal and intimate info about me, please report asap," Twitter post,
Feb. 24, 2017, https://twitter.com/susanthesquark/status/
835193441814392833.

109 **Uber denied being behind:** Sarah Buhr, "Uber Says It's 'Absolutely
Not' Behind a Smear Campaign Against Ex-employee Susan Fowler
Rigetti," *TechCrunch,* Feb. 24, 2017, https://techcrunch.com/2017/02/24/
uber-says-its-absolutely-not-behind-a-smear-campaign-against-ex-
employee-susan-fowler-rigetti.

110 **"Yeah, we call that Boob-er":** Mickey Rapkin, "Uber Cab
Confessions," *GQ,* Feb. 27, 2014, https://www.gq.com/story/uber-cab-
confessions.

110 **video of Kalanick:** Eric Newcomer, "In Video, Uber CEO Argues with
Driver over Falling Fares," *Bloomberg,* Feb. 28, 2017, https://www
.bloomberg.com/news/articles/2017-02-28/in-video-uber-ceo-argues-with-
driver-over-falling-fares.

110 **Uber's new head of engineering:** Kara Swisher, "Uber's SVP of Engineering Is Out After He Did Not Disclose He Left Google in a Dispute over a Sexual Harassment Allegation," *Recode,* Feb. 27, 2017, https://www.recode.net/2017/2/27/14745360/amit-singhal-google-uber.

110 **A story broke:** Amir Efrati, "Uber Group's Visit to Seoul Escort Bar Sparked HR Complaint," *The Information,* March 24, 2017, https://www.theinformation.com/uber-groups-visit-to-seoul-escort-bar-sparked-hr-complaint.

110 **"Why Is Silicon Valley So Awful to Women?":** Liza Mundy, "Why Is Silicon Valley So Awful to Women?," *Atlantic,* April 2017, https://www.theatlantic.com/magazine/archive/2017/04/why-is-silicon-valley-so-awful-to-women/517788.

115 **she attended the Grace Hopper Celebration of Women:** Sheryl Sandberg et al., "GHC 2013 Keynote Sheryl Sandberg, Maria Klawe, Telle Whitney," Grace Hopper Celebration of Women in Computing, Nov. 9, 2013, https://www.youtube.com/watch?v=362AygQGMGk.

115 **Chou wrote a *Medium* essay:** Tracy Chou, "Where Are the Numbers?," *Medium,* Oct. 11, 2013, https://medium.com/@triketora/where-are-the-numbers-cb997a57252.

117 **The "Elephant in the Valley" study:** Trae Vassallo et al., "The Elephant in the Valley," www.elephantinthevalley.com, 2017, https://www.elephantinthevalley.com.

118 **"If I was 20 years younger":** Ibid.

119 **According to the stories:** Ibid.

121 **Lydia Fernandez has seen the tech industry:** Fernandez, interview by Helena Price, www.techiesproject.com, Feb. 11, 2016, http://www.techiesproject.com/lydia-fernandez.

122 **software community GitHub:** Josh Terrell et al., "Gender Differences and Bias in Open Source: Pull Request Acceptance of Women Versus Men," *Peer J,* July 26, 2016, https://doi.org/10.7717/peerj-cs.111.

122 **One former engineer at Facebook:** Deepa Seetharaman, "Facebook's Female Engineers Claim Gender Bias," *Wall Street Journal,* May 2, 2017, https://www.wsj.com/articles/facebooks-female-engineers-claim-gender-bias-1493737116.

125 **That reminded her of:** Cedric L. Alexander, "Three Days in July: Where Do We Go from Here?," CNN, July 11, 2016, http://www.cnn.com/2016/07/11/opinions/three-days-in-july-cedric-alexander/index.html.

127 **"It's not as 'good' as being":** Tracy Chou, "The Uncomfortable State of Being Asian in Tech," *Medium,* Oct. 19, 2015, https://medium.com/little-thoughts/the-uncomfortable-state-of-being-asian-in-tech-ab7db446c55b.

128 **"abhorrent and against everything":** Eric Newcomer, "Uber Investigating Sexual Discrimination Claims by Ex-engineer," *Bloomberg,* Feb. 20, 2017, https://www.bloomberg.com/news/articles/2017-02-20/uber-investigating-sexual-discrimination-claims-by-ex-engineer.

128 **video was leaked:** Newcomer, "In Video, Uber CEO Argues with Driver over Falling Fares."

128 **the company would stop hiring "brilliant jerks":** Mike Isaac, "Inside Uber's Aggressive, Unrestrained Workplace Culture," *New York Times,* Feb. 22, 2017, https://www.nytimes.com/2017/02/22/technology/uber-workplace-culture.html.

128 **"What has driven Uber":** Mike Isaac, "Uber Releases Diversity Report and Repudiates Its 'Hard-Charging Attitude,'" *New York Times,* March 28, 2017, https://www.nytimes.com/2017/03/28/technology/uber-scandal-diversity-report.html.

131 **"You better read this":** Kara Swisher and Johana Bhuiyan, "Uber CEO Kalanick Advised Employees on Sex Rules for a Company Celebration in 2013 'Miami Letter,'" *Recode,* June 8, 2017, https://www.recode.net/2017/6/8/15765514/2013-miami-letter-uber-ceo-kalanick-employees-sex-rules-company-celebration.

131 **sexually assaulting his passenger:** Eric Newcomer, "Uber Workplace Probe Extends to Handling of India Rape Case," *Bloomberg,* June 7, 2017, https://www.bloomberg.com/news/articles/2017-06-07/uber-workplace-probe-extends-to-handling-of-india-rape-case.

131 **An Uber employee who oversaw operations:** Kara Swisher and Johana Bhuiyan, "How Being 'Coin-Operated' at Uber Led to a Top Exec Obtaining the Medical Records of a Rape Victim in India," *Recode,* June 11, 2017., https://www.recode.net/2017/6/11/15758818/uber-travis-kalanick-eric-alexander-india-rape-medical-records.

131 **Uber finally revealed the results:** Mike Isaac, "Uber Fires 20 Amid Investigation into Workplace Culture," *New York Times,* June 6, 2017, https://www.nytimes.com/2017/06/06/technology/uber-fired.html.

131 **Uber's board adopted:** "Uber Report: Eric Holder's Recommendations for Change," *New York Times,* June 13, 2017, https://www.nytimes.com/2017/06/13/technology/uber-report-eric-holders-recommendations-for-change.html.

132 **his own "selfish ends":** Mike Isaac, "Uber Investor Sues Travis Kalanick for Fraud," *New York Times,* Aug. 10, 2017, https://www.nytimes.com/2017/08/10/technology/travis-kalanick-uber-lawsuit-benchmark-capital.html.

132 **A Kalanick spokesperson:** Ibid.

133 **sued Uber (while she was still employed):** Heather Somerville, "Three Women Sue Uber in San Francisco Claiming Unequal Pay, Benefits," *Reuters,* Oct. 25, 2017, https://www.reuters.com/article/us-uber-lawsuit/three-women-sue-uber-in-san-francisco-claiming-unequal-pay-benefits-idUSKBN1CU2Z1.

CHAPTER 5: SUPERHEROES AND SUPERJERKS:
THE ROLE OF THE VENTURE CAPITALISTS

136 **Moritz stepped back:** D. D. Gutenplan, "Behind Oxford Donation, a Personal Story," *New York Times,* July 15, 2012, http://www.nytimes.com/2012/07/16/world/europe/16iht-educside16.html.

136 **"We think about it a lot":** Michael Moritz, "Sir Michael Moritz: Studio 1.0 (Full Show 12/02)," interview by author, *Bloomberg,* Dec. 2, 2015, video, 30:08, https://www.bloomberg.com/news/videos/2015-12-03/sir-michael-moritz-studio-1-0-full-show-12-02-.

137 **"Here's some news":** Emily Jane Fox, "Silicon Valley V.C. Firm Can't Find Any Women," *Vanity Fair,* Dec. 3, 2015, https://www.vanityfair.com/news/2015/12/michael-moritz-sequoia-women-partners-tech.

137 **"I'm a history major":** Moritz, interview by author, *Bloomberg,* Dec. 2, 2015.

137 **On the heels of my interview:** "The Midas List," *Forbes,* 2015, https://www.forbes.com/data/midas-interactive-2015.

138 **61 percent of the top:** Sukhinder Singh Cassidy, "Do You Need a STEM Degree to Be a Successful VC? The Answer Is No," *Medium,* Dec. 4, 2015, https://medium.com/@sukhindersinghcassidy/do-you-need-a-stem-degree-to-be-a-successful-vc-the-answer-is-no-fe974145e6a8.

138 **"We need to do better":** Sequoia Capital, "We need to do better," Twitter post, Dec. 3, 2015, https://twitter.com/sequoia/status/672502717131034624.

138 **"We're not going to run":** Michael Moritz speaks at the Exploratorium, March 16, 2016.

139 **"It makes zero sense":** Michael Moritz, "The Next Billion-Dollar Idea," Interview by Andrew Ross Sorkin, Vanity Fair New Establishment Summit, Oct. 14, 2016, video, 30:08, https://video.vanityfair.com/watch/the-new-establishment-summit-the-next-billion-dollar-idea.

139 **"Diversity fuels innovation":** Beth Comstock, "How Diversity Fuels Innovation," interview by Andrew Ross Sorkin, Vanity Fair New Establishment Summit, Oct. 14, 2016, video, 1:17, https://video.vanityfair.com/watch/the-new-establishment-summit-how-diversity-fuels-innovation.

139 **kept her as a sex slave:** Connie Loizos, "Longtime VC Michael Goguen Was Just Hit with an Explosive Lawsuit," *TechCrunch,* March 11, 2016, https://techcrunch.com/2016/03/11/longtime-vc-michael-goguen-was-just-hit-with-an-explosive-lawsuit/.

139 **Although Goguen denied:** Connie Loizos, "Michael Goguen's Counter-complaint Calls Accuser an 'Exotic Dancer' Who Was 'Looking for a Payday,'" *TechCrunch,* March 14, 2016, https://techcrunch.com/2016/03/14/michael-goguens-counter-complaint-calls-accuser-an-exotic-dancer-who-was-looking-for-a-payday.

140 **By 1999, women accounted:** Brush et al., "Diana Report: Women's Entrepreneurs 2014: Bridging the Gender Gap in Venture Capital," dianaproject.org, http://www.babson.edu/Academics/centers/blank-center/global-research/diana/Documents/diana-project-executive-summary-2014.pdf

142 **"Please, please, really take":** *Ellen Pao v. Kleiner Perkins Caufield & Byers,* 1 (Cal. 2012), http://s3.documentcloud.org/documents/358553/pao-complaint.pdf.

142   **Pao had a romantic:** Heather Somerville, "Timeline: Ellen Pao's Career,
      Key Moments at Kleiner Perkins," *Mercury News,* March 27, 2015, http://
      www.mercurynews.com/2015/03/27/timeline-ellen-paos-career-key-
      moments-at-kleiner-perkins.

142   **Pao's case piled up:** *Ellen Pao v. Kleiner Perkins Caufield & Byers.*

143   **her memoir,** *Reset:* Ellen Pao, *Reset* (New York: Spiegel & Grau, 2017).

143   **"white girls—Eastern European":** Ibid.

143   **"kill the buzz":** *Ellen Pao v. Kleiner Perkins Caufield & Byers.*

143   **Chien denied saying this:** Nellie Bowles and Liz Gannes, "All-Male
      Ski Trip and No Women at Al Gore Dinner: Kleiner's Chien Takes the
      Stand in Pao Lawsuit," *Recode,* Feb. 25, 2015, https://www.recode
      .net/2015/2/25/11559418/all-male-ski-trip-and-no-women-at-al-gore-
      dinner-kleiners-chien-takes.

143   **Chien also testified:** Beth Winegarner, "Kleiner Partner Held All-Male
      Al Gore Dinner, Jury Told," *Law360,* Feb. 25, 2015, https://www.law360
      .com/articles/625265/kleiner-partner-held-all-male-al-gore-dinner-jury-
      told.

144   **"The two people who":** Sam Colt, "Ellen Pao Complained She Had
      Gotten a 'Demotion' When Kleiner Perkins Downsized in 2012," *Business
      Insider,* March 3, 2015, http://www.businessinsider.com/ellen-pao-trial-
      demotion-2015-3.

145   **Pao's story appeared:** David Streitfeld, "Ellen Pao Suit Against Kleiner
      Perkins Heads to Trial, with Big Potential Implications," *New York Times,*
      Feb. 22, 2015, https://www.nytimes.com/2015/02/23/technology/ellen-
      pao-suit-against-kleiner-perkins-heads-to-trial-with-big-potential-
      implications.html.

145   **tech blogs had a field day:** David Streitfeld, "Ellen Pao Loses Silicon
      Valley Bias Case Against Kleiner Perkins," *New York Times,* March 27,
      2015, https://www.nytimes.com/2015/03/28/technology/ellen-pao-kleiner-
      perkins-case-decision.html.

150   **only 5 out of 78:** Rolfe Winkler, "Secretive, Sprawling Network of
      'Scouts' Spreads Money Through Silicon Valley," *Wall Street Journal,* Nov.
      12, 2015, https://www.wsj.com/articles/secretive-sprawling-network-of-
      scouts-spreads-money-through-silicon-valley-1447381377.

151   **In fact, men run 92 percent:** Jonathan Sherry, "A Data-Driven Look at
      Diversity in Venture Capital and Startups," CB Insights, June 15, 2015,
      https://www.cbinsights.com/research/team-blog/venture-capital-diversity-
      data.

152   **What may be more surprising:** Sarah McBride, "At Top VC Firms,
      More Women Partners Doesn't Mean More Women Funded," *Bloomberg,*
      May 31, 2017, https://www.bloomberg.com/news/articles/2017-05-31/at-
      top-vc-firms-more-women-partners-doesn-t-mean-more-women-funded.

152   **a little over $58 billion:** Valentina Zarya, "Venture Capital's Funding
      Gender Gap Is Actually Getting Worse," *Fortune,* March 13, 2017, http://
      fortune.com/2017/03/13/female-founders-venture-capital.

154 *Forbes* **reports there was:** Ryan Mac, "Stitch Fix: The $250 Million Startup Playing Fashionista Moneyball," *Forbes,* June 1, 2016, https://www.forbes.com/sites/ryanmac/2016/06/01/fashionista-moneyball-stitch-fix-katrina-lake/#5445e8fd59a2.

154 **"Women: Stop making startups":** Jolie O'Dell (@jolieodell), "Women: Stop making startups about fashion, shopping, & babies. At least for the next few years. You're embarrassing me," Twitter post, Sept. 13, 2011, https://twitter.com/jolieodell/status/113681946487422976.

154 **In a comprehensive survey:** Gené Teare, "In 2017, Only 17% of Startups Have a Female Founder," *TechCrunch,* April 19, 2017, https://techcrunch.com/2017/04/19/in-2017-only-17-of-startups-have-a-female-founder.

154 **But the vast majority of venture capital:** Cory Cox et al., "Global Innovation Report: 2016 Year in Review," Crunchbase, 2016, https://static.crunchbase.com/reports/annual_2016_yf42a/crunchbase_annual_2016.pdf.

155 **"First, you have women's own self-limiting views":** Sharon G. Hadary, "Why Are Women-Owned Firms Smaller Than Men-Owned Ones?," *Wall Street Journal,* May 17, 2010, https://www.wsj.com/articles/SB10001424052748704688604575125543191609632.

155 **"young and promising":** Malin Malmstrom et al., "We Recorded VCs' Conversations and Analyzed How Differently They Talk About Female Entrepreneurs," *Harvard Business Review,* May 17, 2017, https://hbr.org/2017/05/we-recorded-vcs-conversations-and-analyzed-how-differently-they-talk-about-female-entrepreneurs.

155 **In one study in which women:** Alison Wood Brooks et al., "Investors Prefer Entrepreneurial Ventures Pitched by Attractive Men," *Proceedings of the National Academy of Sciences of the United States of America,* Feb. 20, 2014, https://doi.org/10.1073/pnas.1321202111.

156 **investors tend to have lower expectations:** Sarah Thébaud, "Status Beliefs and the Spirit of Capitalism: Accounting for Gender Biases in Entrepreneurship and Innovation," *Social Forces* 94, no. 1 (2015), https://doi.org/10.1093/sf/sov042.

156 **"This finding suggests that when a man":** Ibid.

158 **$977 million in annual:** Stitch Fix Form S-1, U.S. Securities and Exchange Commission, Oct. 19, 2017, https://www.sec.gov/Archives/edgar/data/1576942/000119312517313629/d400510ds1.htm.

161 **Wang told her story:** Reed Albergotti, "Silicon Valley Women Tell of VC's Unwanted Advances," *The Information,* June 22, 2017, https://www.theinformation.com/silicon-valley-women-tell-of-vcs-unwanted-advances.

162 **"I strongly deny":** Ibid.

162 **"found a few examples":** Ibid.

162 **"Where's the outrage?":** Sarah Lacy, "Binary Capital's Justin Caldbeck Accused of Unwanted Sexual Advances Towards Female Founders. Where's the Outrage?," *Pando,* June 22, 2017, https://pando.com/

2017/06/22/binary-capitals-justin-caldbeck-accused-unwanted-sexual-advances-towards-female-founders-wheres-outrage.

162 **"We drive women":** Ellen K. Pao (@ekp), "Here are VCs who called out Justin Caldbeck's behavior. We drive women out of tech if we don't speak up. Ty @niniane @susan_ho @leitihsu," Twitter post, June 22, 2017, https://twitter.com/ekp/status/878061184666058752.

163 **"The Human Rights of Women":** Reid Hoffman, "The Human Rights of Women Entrepreneurs," LinkedIn, June 23, 2017, https://www.linkedin.com/pulse/human-rights-women-entrepreneurs-reid-hoffman.

163 **"significant lapse of judgment":** Lizette Chapman, "Greylock COO Frangione Leaves VC Firm After 'Lapse of Judgment,'" *Bloomberg,* Aug. 2, 2017.

164 **A week after the Caldbeck revelations:** Katie Benner, "Women in Tech Speak Frankly on Culture of Harassment," *New York Times,* June 30, 2017, https://www.nytimes.com/2017/06/30/technology/women-entrepreneurs-speak-out-sexual-harassment.html.

164 **"There is no doubt":** Chris Sacca, "I Have More Work to Do," *Medium,* June 30, 2017, https://medium.com/@sacca/i-have-more-work-to-do-c775c5d56ca1.

164 **Another entrepreneur, Sarah Kunst:** Benner, "Women in Tech Speak Frankly on Culture of Harassment."

164 **"I'm a Creep":** Dave McClure, "I'm a Creep. I'm Sorry," *Medium,* July 1, 2017, https://medium.com/@davemcclure/im-a-creep-i-m-sorry-d2c13e996ea0.

165 **"Dave kept pouring scotch":** Cheryl Yeoh, "Shedding Light on the 'Black Box of Inappropriateness,'" cherylyeoh.com, July 3, 2017, https://cherylyeoh.com/2017/07/03/shedding-light-on-the-black-box-of-inappropriateness/.

166 **yet another prominent investor, Shervin Pishevar:** https://www.bloomberg.com/news/articles/2017-12-01/uber-investor-shervin-pishevar-accused-of-sexual-misconduct-by-multiple-women.

168 **called his claims "delusional":** Twitter post, Nov. 6, 2017, https://twitter.com/Timodc/status/927748124684075008.

168 **"Obviously, I am deeply disturbed":** Albergotti, "Silicon Valley Women Tell of VC's Unwanted Advances."

168 **At the height of the scandal:** *Ann Lai vs. Binary Capital Management, LLC* (Cal. 2017), https://assets.documentcloud.org/documents/3881456/Complaint-against-Binary-Capital-by-Ann-Lai.pdf.

169 **"They wanted their office":** Miranda Agee, "Go Inside Incredibly Chic Office Spaces," *Architectural Digest,* Jan. 21, 2016, https://www.architecturaldigest.com/gallery/inside-chic-office-spaces.

170 *Recode* **added Katrina Lake's name:** Kara Swisher and Jason Del Rey, "Stitch Fix's CEO Complained About the Behavior of Investor Justin Caldbeck Years Ago," *Recode,* June 27, 2017, https://www.recode.net/2017/6/27/15880434/stitch-fix-ceo-justin-caldbeck-complaint-katrina-lake-sexual-harassment.

170 **"In light of what we have learned"**: Lightspeed, "4/ In light of what we have learned since, we regret we did not take stronger action. It is clear now that we should have done more," Twitter post, June 27, 2017, https://twitter.com/lightspeedvp/status/879731401242705920.

172 **"we have never had reference checks"**: Sarah McBride and Lizette Chapman, "Venture Capital's Secret Code Is Being Tested by Harassment Scandals," *Bloomberg*, July 27, 2017, https://www.bloomberg.com/news/articles/2017-07-27/venture-capital-s-secret-code-tested-by-harassment-scandals.

172 **From 2014 to 2017, venture investors:** Kyle Stanford, "These 16 Charts Illustrate Current Trends in the US VC Industry," *PitchBook*, July 27, 2017, https://pitchbook.com/news/articles/these-16-charts-illustrate-current-trends-in-the-us-vc-industry.

174 **widely used term "unicorn"**: Aileen Lee, "Welcome to the Unicorn Club: Learning from Billion-Dollar Startups," *TechCrunch*, Nov. 2, 2013, https://techcrunch.com/2013/11/02/welcome-to-the-unicorn-club.

175 **"complete with sunset cruises":** Rosewood Hotel: Venture Social Club email message, March 2017.

CHAPTER 6: SEX AND THE VALLEY: MEN PLAY, WOMEN PAY

195 **"He was in an open relationship"**: Fowler, "Reflecting on One Very, Very Strange Year at Uber."

196 **incident made her "feel horrible"**: Efrati, "Uber Group's Visit to Seoul Escort Bar Sparked an HR Complaint."

199 **poly meet-up group at Google:** Julian Sanction, "The Ins and Outs of Silicon Valley's New Sexual Revolution," *Wired*, April 4, 2017.

CHAPTER 7: HOW TECH DISRUPTS FAMILY

206 **"I talked about it"**: Branson and Sandberg, interview by author, *Bloomberg*, April 23, 2015.

206 **It wasn't long before:** Alison DeNisco, "How Egg-Freezing Is Keeping More Women in the Tech Industry," *TechRepublic*, Aug. 15, 2017, https://www.techrepublic.com/article/how-egg-freezing-is-keeping-more-women-in-the-tech-industry-the-inside-story/.

207 **"We take care of the details":** "Benefits and Perks," Dropbox, 2017, https://www.dropbox.com/jobs/perks.

207 **"at all stages of life":** "Benefits," Facebook, 2017, https://www.facebook.com/careers/benefits.

208 **One study found:** Quora, "Why Women Leave the Tech Industry at a 45% Higher Rate Than Men," *Forbes*, Feb. 28, 2017, https://www.forbes.com/sites/quora/2017/02/28/why-women-leave-the-tech-industry-at-a-45-higher-rate-than-men/#2a6603db4216.

208   **In 2013, researchers found:** Jennifer L. Glass et al., "What's So Special About STEM? A Comparison of Women's Retention in STEM and Professional Occupations," *PMC*, Aug. 21, 2013, https://doi .org/10.1093/sf/sot092.

208   **While 80 percent of women:** Sylvia Ann Hewlett and Laura Sherbin, "Athena Factor 2.0: Accelerating Female Talent in Science, Engineering, and Technology," *Center for Talent Innovation*, 2014, http://www .talentinnovation.org/assets/Athena-2-ExecSummFINAL-CTI.pdf.

209   **In a comprehensive report:** Glass et al., "What's So Special About STEM?"

209   **In a recent survey:** Nadya A. Fouad, "Women's Reasons for Leaving the Engineering Field," *Frontiers in Psychology*, June 30, 2017, https://doi .org/10.3389/fpsyg.2017.00875.

209   **Research by the Founder Institute:** Adeo Ressi, "Is There a Peak Age for Entrepreneurship?," *TechCrunch*, May 28, 2011, https://techcrunch .com/2011/05/28/peak-age-entrepreneurship.

210   **"90 Hrs / Wk and Loving It":** Andy Hertzfeld, "90 Hours a Week and Loving It!," *Folklore*, Oct. 1983, https://www.folklore.org/StoryView .py?story=90_Hours_A_Week_And_Loving_It.txt.

211   **"especially ambitious workforce":** "Is Silicon Valley at Risk of a Brain Drain?," *Indeed* blog, April 3, 2017, http://blog.indeed.com/2017/04/03/ silicon-valley-tech-job-migration.

212   **When Google increased its paid maternity:** Susan Wojcicki, "Paid Maternity Leave Is Good for Business," *Wall Street Journal*, Dec. 16, 2014, https://www.wsj.com/articles/susan-wojcicki-paid-maternity-leave- is-good-for-business-1418773756.

212   **Facebook offers four months:** Mark Zuckerberg, "When Max was born, I took two months of paternity leave . . ." Facebook post, Aug. 18, 2017, https://www.facebook.com/photo.php?fdib=10103974023786271 &set=a.612287952871.2204760.4&type=3&theater.

212   **"You can work long":** Jeff Bezos, "Amazon.com Exhibit 99.1," *U.S. Securities and Exchange Commission Archives*, 1998, https://www.sec.gov/ Archives/edgar/data/1018724/0001193125117120198/d373368dex991.htm.

213   **"When I first got into tech":** Blake Robbins (@blakeir), "When I first got into tech. I thought it was 'cool' to work on the weekends or holidays. I quickly realized that's a recipe for disaster," Twitter post, May 29, 2017, https://twitter.com/blakeir/status/869273958478118913.

213   **"Not hanging with friends":** Robbins, "Not hanging with friends and family because you're working isn't 'cool.' Burning out isn't 'cool,'" Twitter post, May 29, 2017, https://twitter.com/blakeir/status/ 869274892298063873.

213   **"Your competition isn't beating you":** Robbins, "I promise you . . . your competition isn't beating you because they are working more hours than you. It's because they are working smarter," Twitter post, May 29, 2017, https://twitter.com/blakeir/status/869275129712443393.

213 **The PayPal Mafia member:** Keith Rabois (@rabois), "Totally false," Twitter post, May 29, 2017, https://twitter.com/rabois/status/ 869292464120541184.

213 **"Read a bio of Elon":** Rabois, "Read a bio of Elon. Or about Amazon. Or about the first 4 years of FB. Or PayPal. Or Bill Bellichick," Twitter post, May 29, 2017, https://twitter.com/rabois/status/ 869293322581401600.

213 **The Twitter tiff resurfaced:** Shyam Sankar, "The Case Against Work-Life Balance: Owning Your Future," shyamsankar.com, Nov. 16, 2015, http://shyamsankar.com/the-case-against-work-life-balance-owning-your-future.

214 **In a 2012 interview:** Sheryl Sandberg, "I Am Leaving Work at 5:30p," *Makers,* 2012, https://www.makers.com/moments/leaving-work-530pm.

215 **"couldn't have gotten more publicity":** Sarah Frier, "How Sheryl Sandberg's Manifesto Drives Facebook," *Bloomberg,* April 27, 2017, https://www.bloomberg.com/news/features/2017-04-27/how-sheryl-sandberg-s-sharing-manifesto-drives-facebook.

215 **"Thank you, we're all leaving":** Ibid.

215 **hide her exit time:** Ibid.

215 **"Of course I do":** Sheryl Sandberg, "Sheryl Sandberg: Bloomberg Studio 1.0 (Full Show)," interview by author, *Bloomberg,* Aug. 9, 2017, video, 24:16, https://www.bloomberg.com/news/videos/2017-08-10/sheryl-sandberg-bloomberg-studio-1-0-full-show-video.

216 **"broader group of employees":** "Uber Report: Eric Holder's Recommendations for Change."

216 **A true marvel:** Steven Levy, "One More Thing: Inside Apple's Insanely Great (or Just Insane) New Mothership," *Wired,* May 16, 2017, https:// www.wired.com/2017/05/apple-park-new-silicon-valley-campus.

216 **"everything an Apple employee":** Beth Spotswood, "Apple's Campus Has Everything—Oh, Except Daycare," *SFist,* May 19, 2017, http://sfist .com/2017/05/19/apples_campus_has_everything_-_oh_e.php.

216 **Because child care has proven:** Rose Marcario, "Patagonia's CEO Explains How to Make On-Site Child Care Pay for Itself," *Fast Company,* Aug. 15, 2016, https://www.fastcompany.com/3062792/patagonias-ceo-explains-how-to-make-onsite-child-care-pay-for-itself.

217 **"silently slandered" women:** Katharine Zaleski, "Female Company President: 'I'm Sorry to All the Mothers I Worked With,'" *Fortune,* March 3, 2015, http://fortune.com/2015/03/03/female-company-president-im-sorry-to-all-the-mothers-i-used-to-work-with.

218 **According to one 2014 study:** Brad Harrington et al., "The New Dad: Take Your Leave," *Boston College Center for Work and Family,* 2014, http://www.thenewdad.org/yahoo_site_admin/assets/docs/BCCWF_The_ New_Dad_2014_FINAL.157170735.pdf.

219 **Studies show that in all fields:** Claire Cain Miller, "The Motherhood Penalty vs. the Fatherhood Bonus," *New York Times,* Sept. 6, 2014,

https://www.nytimes.com/2014/09/07/upshot/a-child-helps-your-career-if-youre-a-man.html.

221 **research shows that output:** John Pencavel, "The Productivity of Working Hours," *IZA*, April 2014, http://ftp.iza.org/dp8129.pdf.

222 **working too long can be counterproductive:** Sarah Green Carmichael, "The Research is Clear: Long Hours Backfire for People and for Companies," *Harvard Business Review*, Aug. 19 2015, https://hbr.org/2015/08/the-research-is-clear-long-hours-backfire-for-people-and-for-companies.

223 **In a response to Keith Rabois:** Sara Mauskopf, "I Actually Agree with Keith Rabois," LinkedIn, May 31, 2017, https://www.linkedin.com/pulse/i-actually-agree-keith-rabois-sara-mauskopf.

223 **She also pointed out:** "The Top 20 Reasons Startups Fail," *CB Insights,* Oct. 8, 2014, https://www.cbinsights.com/research/startup-failure-reasons-top.

CHAPTER 8: ESCAPE FROM TROLLTOPIA: WOMEN'S FIGHT TO SAVE THE INTERNET

225 **Brianna Wu has been tormented:** David Whitford, "Brianna Wu vs. the Gamergate Troll Army," *Inc.*, April 2015, https://www.inc.com/magazine/201504/david-whitford/gamergate-why-would-anyone-want-to-kill-brianna-wu.html.

226 **Gaming is a billion-dollar business:** "Market Brief: Global Games 2017: The Year to Date," *Superdata*, 2017, https://www.superdataresearch.com/market-data/market-brief-year-in-review.

226 **One of the earliest rape-simulation:** Marcel Klum, "Top Ten Shameful Games," *Neowin*, Dec. 29, 2002, https://www.neowin.net/news/top-ten-shameful-games.

226 **In Take-Two Interactive's monster hit:** Paul Tassi, "Here Are the Five Best-Selling Video Games of All Time," *Forbes*, July 8, 2016, https://www.forbes.com/sites/insertcoin/2016/07/08/here-are-the-five-best-selling-video-games-of-all-time/#28654775926c.

226 **"It is art":** Strauss Zelnick, "'Grand Theft Auto' Hits Next Gen Platforms," interview by Stephanie Ruhle, *Bloomberg*, Nov. 18, 2014, video, 9:47, https://www.bloomberg.com/news/videos/2014-11-18/grand-theft-auto-hits-next-gen-platforms.

226 **In 2016, the International Game Developers Association:** Joanna Weststar et al., "Developer Satisfaction Survey 2014 & 2015," International Game Developers Association, June 12, 2016, https://c.ymcdn.com/sites/www.igda.org/resource/collection/CB31CE86-F8EE-4AE3-B46A-148490336605/IGDA_DSS14-15_DiversityReport_Aug2016_Final.pdf.

227 **"This is written almost entirely":** Eron Gjoni, "Why Does This Exist?," *Zoe Post*, Aug. 16, 2014, https://thezoepost.wordpress.com.

227 **They derided Quinn's game:** "What Is Gamergate?," Reddit, 2014, https://www.reddit.com/r/OutOfTheLoop/comments/2f7g5l/what_is_ gamergate/.

228 **"There's been a disgusting large imbalance":** Bendilin Spurr, "Beat Up Anita Sarkeesian," *New Grounds,* July 5, 2012, https://www .newgrounds.com/portal/view/598591.

232 **"emotional outbursts" in "electronic mail":** Erik Eckholm, "Emotional Outbursts Punctuate Conversations by Computer," *New York Times,* Oct. 2, 1984, http://www.nytimes.com/1984/10/02/science/ emotional-outbursts-punctuate-conversations-by-computer.html.

233 **"low I.Q. Crazy Mika":** Donald Trump (@realDonaldTrump), "I heard poorly rated @Morning_Joe speaks badly of me (don't watch anymore). Then how come low I.Q. Crazy Mika, along with Psycho Joe, came," Twitter post, June 29, 2017, https://twitter.com/realDonaldTrump/ status/880408582310776832.

233 **"bleeding badly from a face-lift":** Donald Trump (@realDonaldTrump), ". . . to Mar-a-Lago 3 nights in a row around New Year's Eve, and insisted on joining me. She was bleeding badly from a face-lift. I said no!" Twitter post, June 29, 2017, https://twitter.com/realDonaldTrump/ status/880410114456465411.

233 **Studies show that men:** Nadia Kovacs, "Online Harassment: Halting a Disturbing 'New Normal,'" W. W. Norton, Oct. 10, 2016, https:// community.norton.com/en/blogs/norton-protection-blog/online- harassment-halting-disturbing-new-normal.

233 **Girls are also disproportionately:** Eric Rice et al., "Cyberbullying Perpetration and Victimization Among Middle-School Students," *PMC,* March 2015, https://doi.org/10.2105/AJPH.2014.302393.

233 **Young women, particularly those aged:** Maeve Duggan, "Online Harassment," Pew Research Center, Oct. 22, 2014, http://www .pewinternet.org/2014/10/22/online-harassment.

233 **"Rape threats have become":** Gillian McNally, "All Feminists Should Be Gang-Raped: Inside the Disturbing World of Online Misogyny," *Daily Telegraph,* July 30, 2015, http://www.dailytelegraph.com.au/news/nsw/ why-do-men-threaten-women-with-rape-to-shut-them-up-on-the-web/ news-story/0abd8403e59747a51717f54b81a21b46.

233 **38 percent of women:** Asibo, "Gender, Trolls, and Cyber-harassment," Storify, 2014, https://storify.com/asibo/gender-trolls-and-cyber- harassment.

233 **"I feel like I'm in a personal hell":** Leslie Jones (@lesdoggg), Twitter post, July 18, 2016, https://twitter.com/lesdoggg/status/ 755261962674696192.

234 **"Twitter I understand":** Anna Silman, "A Timeline of Leslie Jones's Horrific Online Abuse," *Cut,* Aug. 24, 2016, https://www.thecut .com/2016/08/a-timeline-of-leslie-joness-horrific-online-abuse.html.

235 **"you may not incite":** "The Twitter Rules," *Twitter,* 2017, https:// support.twitter.com/articles/18311.

237 **When big-name companies:** Mark Bergen, "Google Updates Ads Policies Again, Ramps Up AI to Curtail YouTube Crisis," *Bloomberg,* April 3, 2017, https://www.bloomberg.com/news/articles/2017-04-03/google-updates-ads-polices-again-ramps-up-ai-to-curtail-youtube-crisis.

237 **"machine learning tools":** "Introducing Expanded YouTube Partner Program Safeguards to Protect Creators," *YouTube Creator Blog,* April 6, 2017, https://youtube-creators.googleblog.com/2017/04/introducing-expanded-youtube-partner.html.

237 **says it works harder:** Deepa Seetharaman, "Twitter Takes More Proactive Approach to Finding Trolls," *Wall Street Journal,* March 1, 2017, https://www.wsj.com/articles/twitter-takes-more-proactive-approach-to-finding-trolls-1488394514.

238 **66 million users:** Brad Stone and Miguel Helft, "Facebook Hires Google Executive as No. 2," *New York Times,* March 4, 2008, http://www.nytimes.com/2008/03/04/technology/04cnd-facebook.html.

240 **In 2017, it added:** Olivia Solon, "Facebook Is Hiring Moderators. But Is the Job Too Gruesome to Handle?," *Guardian,* May 4, 2017, https://www.theguardian.com/technology/2017/may/04/facebook-content-moderators-ptsd-psychological-dangers.

240 **In an interview with *Axios*:** Mike Allen, "Exclusive Interview with Facebook's Sheryl Sandberg," *Axios,* Oct. 12, 2017, https://www.axios.com/exclusive-interview-facebook-sheryl-sandberg-2495538841.html.

242 **"a better place for everyone":** Pao, *Reset,* 166.

242 **When one of the site's:** Mike Isaac, "Details Emerge About Victoria Taylor's Dismissal at Reddit," *New York Times,* July 13, 2015, https://bits.blogs.nytimes.com/2015/07/13/details-emerge-about-victoria-taylors-dismissal-at-reddit.

242 **"The trolls are winning":** Ellen Pao, "Former Reddit CEO Ellen Pao: The Trolls Are Winning the Battle for the Internet," *Washington Post,* July 16, 2015, https://www.washingtonpost.com/opinions/we-cannot-let-the-internet-trolls-win/2015/07/16/91b1a2d2-2b17-11e5-bd33-395c05608059_story.html?utm_term=.9c3c31e3f4ca.

243 **"I have said many times":** Spez, "With So Much Going On in the World, I Thought I'd Share Some Reddit Updates to Distract You All," Reddit, Aug. 2017, https://www.reddit.com/r/announcements/comments/6qptzw/with_so_much_going_on_in_the_world_i_thought_id.

243 **In a new study, researchers:** Eshwar Chandrasekharan et al., "You Can't Stay Here: The Efficacy of Reddit's 2015 Ban Examined Through Hate Speech," *Proceedings* of the *ACM on Human Computer Interaction* 1, no. 2 (Nov. 2017), http://comp.social.gatech.edu/papers/cscw18-chand-hate.pdf.

244 **In *League of Legends*:** Phil Kollar, "The Past, Present, and Future League of Legends Studio Riot Games," Polygon, Sept. 13, 2016, https://

www.polygon.com/2016/9/13/12891656/the-past-present-and-future-of-league-of-legends-studio-riot-games.

245 **In fact, research shows:** Jeffrey H. Kuznekoff and Lindsey M. Rose, "Communication in Multiplayer Gaming: Examining Player Responses to Gender Cues," *New Media & Society* 15, no. 4 (2013), https://doi .org/10.1177/1461444812458271.

245 **"Shut that fucking bitch up":** Jenny Haniver, "Quiet Time," *Not in the Kitchen Anymore*, Sept. 13, 2017, http://www.notinthekitchenanymore .com.

245 **"If you think most online abuse":** Laura Hudson, "Curbing Online Abuse Isn't Impossible. Here's Where We Start," *Wired*, May 15, 2014, https://www.wired.com/2014/05/fighting-online-harassment.

245 **It saw not only a 30 percent:** Ibid.

246 **"It took Riot's interjection":** Ibid.

246 **there were 100 million:** Kollar, "Past, Present, and Future League of Legends Studio Riot Games."

246 **They can't control everything:** John Suler, "The Online Disinhibition Effect," *CyberPsychology & Behavior* 7, no. 3 (July 2004): 321–26, http:// truecenterpublishing.com/psycyber/disinhibit.html.

247 **"You're not physically being":** Jordan Belamire, "My First Reality Groping," *Medium*, Oct. 20, 2016, https://mic.com/articles/157415/my-first-virtual-reality-groping-sexual-assault-in-vr-harassment-in-tech-jordan-belamire#.SBtg4xhEG.

247 *QuiVr* **developers:** Julia Carrie Wong, "Sexual Harassment in Virtual Reality Feels All Too Real—'It's Creepy Beyond Creepy,'" *Guardian*, Oct. 26, 2016, https://www.theguardian.com/technology/2016/oct/26/virtual-reality-sexual-harassment-online-groping-quivr.

248 **Running for Congress:** Brianna Wu, "Bold Leadership for Massachusetts," Brianna Wu for Congress, 2017, https://briannawu2018.com/platform.

CHAPTER 9: SILICON VALLEY'S SECOND CHANCE

250 **"I've never seen anything quite":** Meg Whitman, "Meg Whitman Says Sexual Harassment Cases May Change Workplace," interview by author, *Bloomberg*, Nov. 28, 2017, https://www.bloomberg.com/news/articles/ 2017-11-28/hpe-s-whitman-says-sexual-harassment-cases-may-change-workplace.

250 **Research shows that companies:** Susan Sorenson, "How Employee Engagement Drives Growth," Gallup, June 20, 2013, http://news.gallup .com/businessjournal/163130/employee-engagement-drives-growth.aspx.

250 **Higher morale and a more:** Eric G. Lambert, Nancy Lynne Hogan, and Shannon M. Barton, "The Impact of Job Satisfaction on Turnover Intent: A Test of a Structural Measurement Model Using a National Sample of Workers," *Social Science Journal* 38, no. 2 (Summer 2001): 233–50, https://doi.org/10.1016/S0362-3319(01)00110-0.

250 **Another way to look at this:** Michael Kimmel, "Why Gender Equality Is Good for Everyone—Men Included," TED talk, May 2015, https:// www.ted.com/talks/michael_kimmel_why_gender_equality_is_good_for_ everyone_men_included.

251 **In a wide-ranging study:** Lone Christiansen et al., "Gender Diversity in Senior Positions and Firm Performance: Evidence from Europe," *IMF*, March 2016, https://www.imf.org/external/pubs/ft/wp/2016/wp1650.pdf.

252 **Women not only represent:** "Statistics About Women," *Female Factor*, 2016, http://www.thefemalefactor.com/statistics/statistics_about_women .html.

253 **It's not just creating":** Jack Dorsey, "Square's Dorsey on Earnings, New Growth, Outlook," interview by author, *Bloomberg*, Aug. 2, 2017, video, 14:00, https://www.youtube.com/watch?v=Po9XQcAyvTE.

254 **"We are simultaneously proud":** "Diversity at Slack," *Slack*, April 26, 2017, https://slackhq.com/diversity-at-slack-d44aba51d4b6.

255 **Butterfield tweeted at her:** Stewart Butterfield (@stewart), "@EricaJoy Be safe," Twitter post, Nov. 25, 2014, https://twitter.com/stewart/ status/537433607174770689.

255 **"He is woke":** Melody Hahm, "How a Single Tweet Landed Erica Baker a Top Engineering Job at Slack," *Yahoo*, May 11, 2016, https://finance .yahoo.com/news/slack-senior-engineer-erica-baker-stewart-butterfield- diversity-in-tech-silicon-valley-154010403.html.

255 **she joined the Slack team:** Erica Joy Baker, "Seeking Happy," *Medium*, May 11, 2015, https://medium.com/this-is-hard/seeking-happy- 58a2a375340a.

255 **These included diligence:** Nolan Caudill, "Building the Workplace We Want," Slack, Jan. 12, 2015, https://slackhq.com/building-the-workplace- we-want-31fff8d6ffe0.

258 **The research shows that the effects:** Iris Bohnet, *What Works* (Cambridge, MA: Belknap Press, 2016).

258 **Emerson says that's reason:** Joelle Emerson, "Don't Give Up on Unconscious Bias Training—Make It Better," *Harvard Business Review*, April 28, 2017, https://hbr.org/2017/04/dont-give-up-on-unconscious- bias-training-make-it-better.

258 **"When the candidate is asked":** Julia Grace, "A Walkthrough Guide to Finding an Engineering Job at Slack," Slack, May 4, 2016, https:// slack.engineering/a-walkthrough-guide-to-finding-an-engineering- job-at-slack-dc07dd7b0144.

259 **Pinterest, another client:** Abby Maldonado, "Diversifying Engineering Referrals at Pinterest," *Medium*, Jan. 15, 2016, https://medium.com/ pinclusion-posts/diversifying-engineering-referrals-at-pinterest- de3978556990.

259 **Research shows that job:** Emily Peck, "Here Are the Words That May Keep Women from Applying for Jobs," *Huffington Post*, June 2, 2015, https://www.huffingtonpost.com/2015/06/02/textio-unitive-bias- software_n_7493624.html.

260 **"We believe everyone deserves":** "Career Opportunities," Slack, accessed Nov. 20, 2017, https://slack.com/careers#openings.

261 **Glassdoor, a company:** Andrew Chamberlain, "Demystifying the Gender Pay Gap," Glassdoor, March 23, 2016, https://www.glassdoor.com/research/studies/gender-pay-gap/.

261 **For computer programming:** Andrew Chamberlain, "The Widest Gender Pay Gaps in Tech," Glassdoor, Nov. 15, 2016, https://www.glassdoor.com/research/studies/gender-pay-gap/.

261 **In 2015, Slack performed:** "Inclusion and Diversity at Slack," Slack, Sept. 9, 2015, https://slackhq.com/inclusion-and-diversity-at-slack-e42f93845732.

261 **The company is also contributing:** "Diversity at Slack," Slack, April 26, 2017, https://slackhq.com/diversity-at-slack-d44aba51d4b6.

262 **Halfway through 2017:** Erica Joy Baker, "Tech Diversity and Inclusion Post-mortem," GitHub, June 22, 2017, https://gist.github.com/EricaJoy/f13441a2ec9a014ae00e5e9c1704ea4a.

263 **She took the microphone:** Niniane Wang, "Brainstorm Tech: Fixing Inequality in Silicon Valley," interview by author, Fortune Brainstorm Tech Town Hall, July 18, 2017, video, 39:08, https://www.youtube.com/watch?v=cWXw_bclArI.

263 **VCs, stop asking women entrepreneurs:** Nicole Farb, at "Brainstorm Tech: Fixing Inequality in Silicon Valley."

263 **"In Silicon Valley today":** Christa Quarles, at "Brainstorm Tech: Fixing Inequality in Silicon Valley."

264 **"Without a doubt":** Adam Miller, at "Brainstorm Tech: Fixing Inequality in Silicon Valley."

265 **Apple's diversity numbers:** "Inclusion and Diversity," Apple, accessed Nov. 20, 2017, https://www.apple.com/diversity.

267 **According to Code.org:** Code.org, "Girls Set AP Computer Science Record . . . Skyrocketing Growth Outpaces Boys," *Medium,* July 18, 2017, https://medium.com/@codeorg/girls-set-ap-computer-science-record-skyrocketing-growth-outpaces-boys-41b7c01373a5.

268 **Still, girls' peers in computer science:** Ibid.

268 **their teachers are still mostly men:** Samuel F. Way et al., "Gender, Productivity, and Prestige in Computer Science Faculty Hiring Networks," Proceedings 2016 World Wide Web Conference (2016): 1169–79, https://doi.org/10.1145/2872427.2883073.

268 **"We Love Code":** "We Love Code: Meet the Awesome Girls Who Own It," *Seventeen,* Dec./Jan. 2016.

268 **But the 1960s also marked:** Roberts, "A History of Capacity Challenges in Computer Science."

268 **that once again schools will be:** Ibid.

31192021436108